DISCOVER THE EXTREME WORLD

Contributors:
Camilla de la Bedoyere
Clive Gifford
John Farndon
Steve Parker
Stewart Ross
Philip Steele

Discovery CHANNEL™

Miles Kelly

This edition first published in 2013
by Miles Kelly Publishing Ltd
Harding's Barn, Bardfield End Green,
Thaxted, Essex, CM6 3PX, UK

10 9 8 7 6 5 4 3 2 1

Publishing Director Belinda Gallagher
Creative Director Jo Cowan

Managing Editors Rosie McGuire, Amanda Askew
Proofreaders Carly Blake, Claire Philip
Editorial Assistant Lauren White

Managing Designer Simon Lee
Design Simon Lee, Rocket Design (East Anglia) Ltd
Additional Design Joe Jones, Kayleigh Allen
Cover Designer Simon Lee

Production Manager Elizabeth Collins
Image Manager Liberty Newton
Reprographics Stephan Davis, Thom Allaway

ISBN 978-1-84810-908-7

Printed in China

British Library Cataloguing-in-Publication Data
A catalogue record for this book is available from the British Library

Made with paper from a sustainable forest

www.mileskelly.net
info@mileskelly.net

www.factsforprojects.com

CONTENTS

Active EARTH

Our planet is at the mercy of awesome natural forces. Even beneath its rocky surface, Earth is constantly on the move.

◀ The pattern of lines in this rock face in the Paria Canyon-Vermilion Cliffs Wilderness, on the border of Utah and Arizona, U.S., is caused by layers of compressed sandstone worn smooth by glacier erosion.

Visitors from SPACE

Our planet is a boiling, heaving, freezing, dynamic place to live. Mud bubbles, winds whip the air into spinning spirals, and vast cracks open in the ground. Our extreme Earth formed 4.6 billion years ago, but visitors from space constantly remind us of our place in a bigger, even more extreme, Universe.

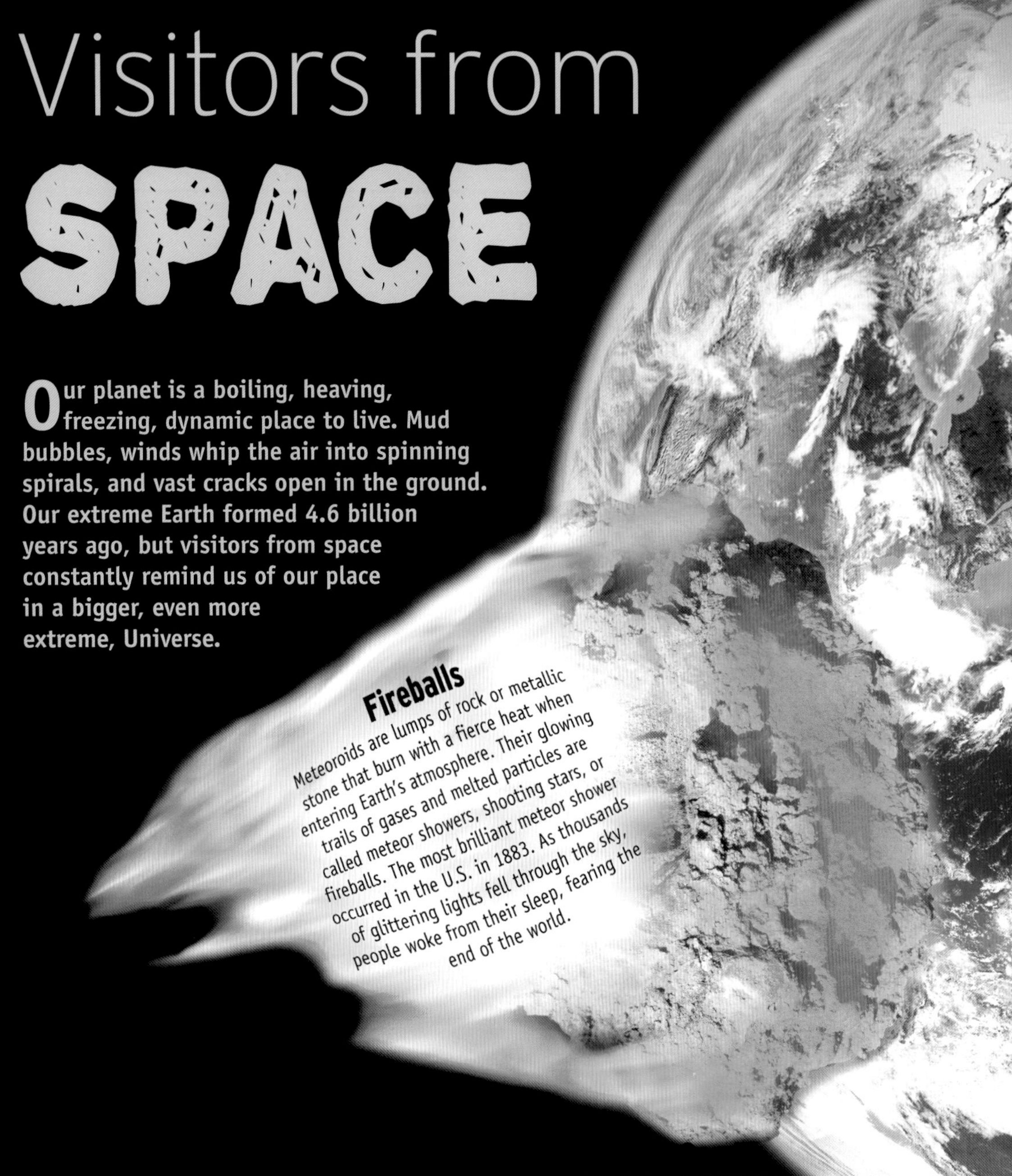

Fireballs

Meteoroids are lumps of rock or metallic stone that burn with a fierce heat when entering Earth's atmosphere. Their glowing trails of gases and melted particles are called meteor showers, shooting stars, or fireballs. The most brilliant meteor shower occurred in the U.S. in 1883. As thousands of glittering lights fell through the sky, people woke from their sleep, fearing the end of the world.

Total wipeout!

The cataclysmic K-P Event occurred 65.5 million years ago. The impact of a meteorite crash near Chicxulub, Mexico, threw dust and rock into the air, blocking sunlight and affecting the climate for 10,000 years. Scientists believe this caused the extinction of about 80 percent of animal species, including dinosaurs.

If another giant meteorite heads toward Earth, it could raise the temperature of the air beneath it to 100,000°F (about 60,000°C)—ten times hotter than the Sun's surface. The impact could blast 250 cu mi (about 1,000 cu km) of rock and gas into the air, and produce shock waves that trigger earthquakes.

Polar light show

Some of Earth's most staggering sights are the aurorae, when night skies around the North and South poles are lit up by ghostly curtains of light that sweep across the darkness. This extreme effect is caused by the action of Earth's magnetic field on streams of particles that have been carried from the Sun on a solar wind.

▲ *Aurora australis* (Southern Lights), seen from the International Space Station (ISS).

THE LARGEST METEORITE CRATER IS AT VREDEFORT IN SOUTH AFRICA. IT HAS A DIAMETER OF 180 MI (ABOUT 300 KM).

Burning ice

Comets are chunks of ice, rock, and frozen gases that become superheated as they near the Sun, and produce flares of bright light. In 1996 the path of the comet Hyakutake took it close to Earth—a mere 9 million mi (15 million km) away—and it became one of the brightest celestial events for 200 years. The comet is now heading toward the edges of the Solar System and won't be seen again for 72,000 years.

▼ Comet Hyakutake, seen on March 21, 1996.

▲ U.S. astronaut James Irwin described Earth from space as "a sparkling blue-and-white jewel."

CRACKING Up

At Earth's center, temperatures reach a staggering 9,800°F (about 5,400°C). Like a mighty engine room, this hot core powers vast movements of rock and causes the planet's outer crust to break into sections and move. The result is an array of awesome seismic events, from the creation of mountains to earthquakes in all their destructive power.

TECTONIC PLATES

North American Plate

Eurasian Plate

Philippine Plate

Australian Plate

The Pacific Ring of Fire

Thanks to its fearsome history, the world's most violent area of seismic activity is known as the Pacific Ring of Fire. With more than 75 percent of the world's volcanoes and active plate movements, this region is responsible for much of the planet's geology, including the Andes, Mount St. Helens, the islands of Japan, and Krakatau, one of the planet's most explosive volcanoes.

Solid inner core made from iron and nickel

Liquid outer core

Heat from the core passes through the almost-solid lower mantle

Material in the upper mantle can flow slightly

Pressure from the mantle can cause the rocky crust to crack

▲ Inside Earth, there are layers of different material, heated by the core.

◀ Volcanic steam escapes from a vent in Antarctica.

A growing ocean

The Atlantic Ocean conceals the world's longest mountain chain—the Mid-Atlantic Ridge. These massive underwater peaks create a ridge 10,000 mi (about 16,000 km) in length, where plates meet over a hot region of mantle. Lava adds to the crust, building up the plates and forcing them further apart.

▶ Cracks and tears appear in Iceland, following the line of the Mid-Atlantic Ridge.

◀ In 2010, Iceland's Eyjafjallajökull volcano wreaked travel havoc when it spewed plumes of dust across the North Atlantic Ocean and Europe. The highest plume was almost 7 mi (11 km) high and pumped out thousands of tons of ash, grounding planes for a week.

Island of fire and ice

Iceland is an island of extremes. Largely covered in glaciers, it was formed from active volcanoes on the Mid-Atlantic Ridge. About one third of all Earth's lava flows in the last 2,000 years have occurred there.

Mightiest MOUNTAIN

The Himalayas are not just the biggest mountain range on land, they are also one of the youngest at just 50 million years old. Mount Everest, the highest peak of the Himalayas and in the world, is known as *Chomolungma* in Tibet, and *Sagarmatha* in Nepal.

THE SOUTHEAST RIDGE IS THE MOST CLIMBED ROUTE. IT IS REACHED FROM NEPAL.

MOUNT EVEREST SUMMIT
29,035 ft (8,850 m)

DEATH ZONE
Surviving at altitudes above 26,000 ft is tough, due to low oxygen and freezing temperatures. Climbers who die are often left on the mountain. Eventually, sometimes years later, their frozen bodies are removed for proper burial.

CAMP 4
26,000 ft (8,000 m)

CAMP 1
20,000 ft (6,000 m)

KHUMBU ICEFALL
The Khumbu Icefall must be crossed with the aid of ladders and ropes—it is one of the most dangerous parts of the route.

BASE CAMP
On the Khumbu Glacier at 17,700 ft (5,400 m), climbers get used to the altitude before ascending.

Climbers use a ladder to traverse the crevasse at Khumbu Icefall.

TIMELINE

1841
The location of peak "b" (as Everest was then known) is recorded by Sir George Everest, Surveyor General of India.

1856
Height of peak "b" is calculated as 29,002 ft (8,840 m).

1865
Peak "b" is renamed Mount Everest.

1924
First attempt at climbing Everest fails, though one climber reaches 28,126 ft (8,570 m).

1953
Edmund Hillary (from New Zealand) and Tenzing Norgay (from Nepal) are the first people to reach Everest's summit on May 29.

2007
Retired Japanese teacher Katsusuke Yanagisawa scales Everest at age 71.

TOP 5 PEAKS

EVEREST 29,035 ft (8,850 m)
K2 28,251 ft (8,611 m)
KANGCHENJUNGA 28,169 ft (8,586 m)
LHOTSE 27,940 ft (8,516 m)
MAKALU 27,838 ft (8,485 m)

AFTER YEARS OF DISAGREEMENTS ABOUT **EVEREST'S HEIGHT**, CHINA AND NEPAL AGREE IT IS **29,029** FT (8,848 M) HIGH, INCLUDING 13 FT (4 M) OF SNOW, BUT THE NATIONAL GEOGRAPHIC SOCIETY CLAIMS IT IS **29,035** FT (8,850 M) TALL.

NUPTSE (peak) 25,790 ft (7,860 m)

LHOTSE (peak) 27,940 ft (8,516 m)

CAMP 3 24,500 ft (7,500 m)

GENEVA SPUR Climbers use ropes to scramble over this raised black rock.

CAMP 2 21,300 ft (6,500 m)

WHAT RUBBISH!

Everest can now claim fame as the world's highest garbage heap. Tourists and climbers are responsible for leaving plastic bottles, food packaging, tents, and even oxygen tanks on the mountain.

Climbers use iceaxes and crampons—metal spikes attached to boots—to scale vertical sheets of ice.

Ultimate VOLCANO

Earth's crust breaks open and molten rock, ash, and toxic gases spew out of the vent. The awesome force of a volcanic eruption like this hints at the incredible temperatures and pressures that exist far beneath the surface. But what exactly happens to create the ultimate volcano?

▶ In 1980, Mount St. Helens erupted. The top 4,600 ft (1,400 m) of the volcano was destroyed.

VOLCANIC ERUPTIONS ARE MEASURED ON THE VOLCANIC EXPLOSIVITY INDEX (VEI), WHICH RANGES FROM "GENTLE" TO "MEGA-COLOSSAL."

Lava

Rock that has literally melted to a semiliquid state is known as lava. The speed of its flow depends on temperature, and the minerals it contains. One of the fastest lava flows ever measured was from the Nyiragongo volcano in the Democratic Republic of the Congo. It poured out at over 35 mph (60 km/h).

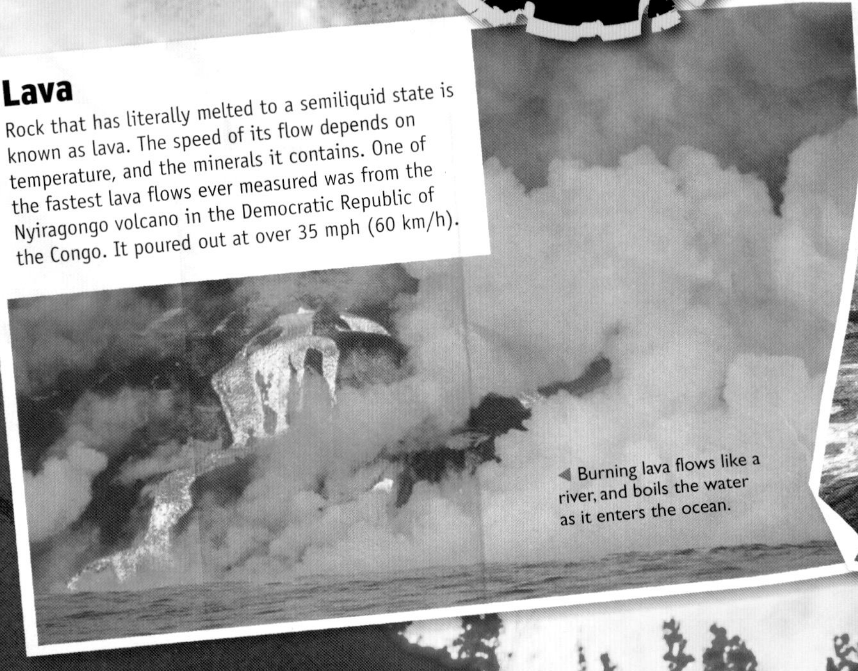

◀ Burning lava flows like a river, and boils the water as it enters the ocean.

Ash

Vast plumes of ash often erupt from a volcano, and can remain airborne for days—and travel great distances—before settling. When Mount Vesuvius erupted in AD 79, a huge column of pumice ash was ejected from the crater at a rate of 1.7 million tons per second. The column reached a height of 2 mi (3.3 km) before collapsing and covering the ground with a suffocating layer of ash.

Eruption

Volcanoes erupt when heat and pressure become too great for the crust to bear, and the huge amounts of energy below the surface are released. In the last of many eruptions in AD 186, a New Zealand volcano ejected an incredible 25 cubic mi (110 cubic km) of rock in one of the most violent eruptions ever recorded. Its crater is now Lake Taupo.

◀ Clouds of ash are carried upward by the force of exploding gas.

BENEATH THE SURFACE

Molten rock inside the Earth (magma) collects in chambers just below the surface. Heat and pressure force the magma upward, through weak areas in the crust, sometimes until it reaches the surface.

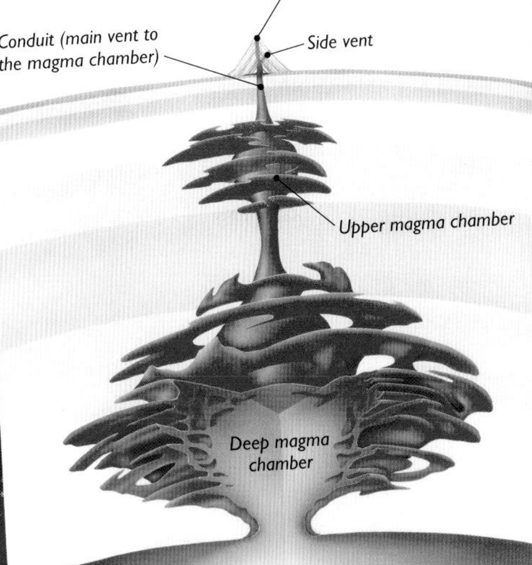

Crater

A crater marks the opening of the vent. Lava builds up around it, creating the familiar cone shape. If the cone walls collapse, the crater will get bigger. The volcanoes of Hawaii are among the most active on Earth. Steam and volcanic gases pour out of their craters.

HOT Spots

In some places, evidence of Earth's extraordinary inner heat comes to the surface. Soaring temperatures bake the rock underfoot, and boil water that lurks within it, causing jets of superheated steam to spurt into the air. Even mud can start to bubble!

Yellowstone

One third of the world's hydrothermal features are in Yellowstone Park in the U.S., which also has more geysers than anywhere else on Earth—150 of them in just one square mile (2.6 sq km). The whole area sits astride a supervolcano, and while normal volcanoes make mountains, supervolcanoes explode them to smithereens. The most recent eruption was 640,000 years ago, and 1,000 times more powerful than the eruption of Mount St. Helens in 1980. The land continues to reach temperatures of 400°F (around 200°C), and new geysers, mud pools, and fumaroles are constantly created.

Old Faithful

The world's most famous geyser, Old Faithful of Yellowstone Park, U.S., shoots hot water and steam up to 180 ft (about 55 m) into the air. It erupts, on average, every 85–95 minutes because it takes this long for the chamber beneath to refill with water.

The greatest geyser

The tallest geyser ever witnessed existed for only four years, after a volcanic eruption in New Zealand in 1900. Waimangu's jets of black water, rocks, and steam were 1,500 ft (460 m) high—taller than the Empire State Building. Four tourists died in 1903 after being swept away by a sudden, and violent, eruption.

▶ Old Faithful is probably the world's most studied, and best-known, geyser.

▶ Macaques enjoy a hot soak so much they sometimes doze off in the pool.

Monkey baths

Warm water pools created by hot springs in Nagano, Japan, have been adopted by macaque monkeys. They bathe in these natural hot tubs during the freezing winter months.

Cotton Castle

At Pamukkale in Turkey, cascading pools create one of the world's most breathtaking natural wonders. The hot springs, which are rich in minerals, pour down the hillside, filling the pools with warm, blue water. The name Pamukkale means "Cotton Castle."

▶ Pamukkale's hot water pools are created by minerals in the hot water, which turn to stone.

THE GROUND IN SOME VOLCANIC REGIONS IS SO HOT IT CAN TURN MUD INTO BOILING POOLS, AS GASES RISE TO THE SURFACE AND BREAK THROUGH.

CRUNCH Time

Rock is tough but brittle, so it's no wonder that the active Earth, with all of its subterranean stirrings, puts the rocky landscape under more pressure than it can bear. When crunch time comes, giant sections of rock buckle and slip, creating monumental movements that cause Earth's surface to quake and shatter.

WHAT'S AT FAULT?

A fault is an enormous crack in Earth's crust, either side of which giant slabs of rock, called tectonic plates, move in different directions. As the slabs slide slowly past each other they may get stuck, causing a buildup of pressure that, when released, results in sudden jolts.

Direction of plate movement
Plate 1
Plate 2
Epicenter
Seismic waves
Focus, or hypocenter

▲ Massive movements along faults release energy around the focus. Seismic waves radiate outward, wreaking destruction in built-up areas.

IN 2010 A QUAKE IN CHILE WAS SO POWERFUL THAT IT LITERALLY MOVED THE ENTIRE CITY OF CONCEPCION 10 FT (3 M) TO THE WEST.

Extreme damage

Locals walk along damaged roads as they are evacuated from the earthquake-hit Beichuan County, southwest China, in 2008.

Major disaster

The 1906 San Francisco earthquake was caused by movement along the San Andreas fault.

Safety measures

A controlled explosion collapses a disused building, simulating an earthquake, and allowing scientists to test a "cage" (red) that would protect people inside.

Predicting quakes

Earthquakes are one of the most catastrophic of all extreme events, yet predicting them remains virtually impossible. Earthquake-proof construction, however, can save lives. Buildings in Japan and California, U.S., are constructed with elastic building materials and shock-absorbing foundations to withstand tremors.

Mega-tsunami

The Indian Ocean mega-tsunami of 2004 devastated the Phi Phi Islands.

Seafloor shake-up

Tsunamis are caused by sudden, massive movements along fault lines on the seafloor. When faults are close to land, the chance of a mega-tsunami—a high wave of devastating proportions—is greatly increased.

Water from the glaciers and mountains of the Andes pours into the Amazon River at its source.

This waterfall on the Jari River brings water from Guyana's Highlands to the Amazon.

The Urubamba River is an Amazon headwater—a tributary forming part of the Amazon's source.

Rivers have the power to demolish walls of rock and grind them to dust. They have the strength to carry millions of tons of soil and sand, and enough energy to provide electricity for entire cities. There are long rivers, wide rivers, and deep rivers, but by almost any measure the Amazon is the greatest of them all.

A tributary is a river or stream that flows into a larger river. About 200 tributaries flow into the Amazon—more than any other river in the world.

TOP 5 RIVERS

The Nile is generally agreed to be slightly longer than the Amazon, but in terms of volume it's just a trickle by comparison. Every second, the Nile empties 6,600 yd^3 (about 5,100 m^3) of water into the sea, but the Amazon empties 290,000 yd^3 (about 220,000 m^3)—43 times as much. That is enough, in one day, to supply a city with fresh water for ten years!

PARANA
23,000 yd^3 (about 17,700 m^3) of water into the sea per second

YENISEI
25,000 yd^3 (about 19,000 m^3) of water into the sea per second

CONGO
55,000 yd^3 (about 42,000 m^3) of water into the sea per second

During the wet season, the Amazon basin covers 135,000 sq mi (around 350,000 sq km)—an area similar to that of Germany. In the dry season it shrinks by two thirds.

River dolphins live in the Amazon's slow-moving, muddy water. They feed on fish and crabs, but little is known about their behavior.

WATER FROM THE AMAZON SUPPORTS THE AMAZON RAIN FOREST, WHICH COVERS 2 MILLION SQ MI (5 MILLION SQ KM). THAT'S TWO THIRDS OF THE AREA OF AUSTRALIA.

THE AMAZON DELIVERS 106 MILLION CU FT (3 MILLION CU M) OF SEDIMENT INTO THE OCEAN EVERY DAY.

The area of land that is regularly covered by water following seasonal rains is called a floodplain.

As it meets the ocean, extreme surfers take advantage of the unusually long waves (tidal bores) that occur here. It's possible to ride a single wave for 6 mi (10 km)!

The Amazon becomes the widest river on Earth near its mouth—up to 25 mi (40 km) wide in the wet season.

THE AMAZON HOLDS ABOUT 20 PERCENT OF THE WORLD'S TOTAL FRESH WATER.

Extreme EROSION

On our dynamic planet, nothing remains the same for long. The landscape is continually being molded, eroded, and changed by forces we are scarcely aware of. Human lives are too short for individuals to bear witness to these extraordinary processes, but the remarkable results are all around us.

▲ Hoodoos are tall columns of rock. The rock on the top of a column is harder than the rock beneath it.

A slot canyon is formed by rushing water passing through rock, and eroding a tall, narrow channel.

Sandblasting

In dry places, wind picks up grains of sand and whips them through the air like a sandblaster. The effects can be spectacular. In the Arches National Park of Utah, lofty monoliths, huge arches of rock, balancing rocks, and tablelike mesas stand as monuments in the desert.

▶ The Devil's Marbles, or balancing rocks, of Australia have been shaped by sandblasting.

WATER EROSION

The Colorado River in the U.S. has proved itself the ultimate abrader of rock. Its erosive course began 17 million years ago—the blink of an eye in geological time. Since then it has created a canyon 277 mi (446 km) long, up to 18 mi (29 km) wide, and, in some places, more than one mile (1.6 km) deep, reaching rocks that are 2.5 billion years old.

The Colorado's enormous power of erosion is due to the river's great speed and volume, and the large amount of mud, sand, and gravel it carries. Also, the rocks through which it passes are relatively soft.

▼ The eroding power of the Colorado River is responsible for the Grand Canyon, one of the world's greatest natural wonders.

▶ The Painted Cliffs in Tasmania are carved by wave erosion, and stained with orange-red minerals.

Breaking waves

In coastal areas, big waves crash against rocks and gradually wear them away in a process known as erosion. The ocean water not only has power and energy to do its work, it also carries grains of sand and mud, which rub away at the rock surfaces. Over time, cliffs are undercut, eventually collapsing into the ocean.

FREEZING Flow

In the world's coldest places snow falls but rarely melts. Layer upon layer of it collects, and the fluffy stuff is eventually compressed into dense packs of ice. Huge rivers of ice—glaciers—creep slowly downhill under the force of gravity. As they move, these heavyweight scourers carve a spectacular path through the landscape.

Ice cycles

Glacial ice is constantly melting and freezing, depending on the time of day, the season, and changing temperatures. When more ice freezes than melts, a glacier grows bigger and is said to be advancing. When ice is melting, a glacier shrinks and is described as retreating.

▲ Giant chunks of ice fall from the Perito Moreno glacier into Argentina's largest lake—Lago Argentino.

AGES OF ICE

The global climate is continually changing, and extreme climate changes that lead to ice ages are not unusual. In fact, we are probably experiencing a warm spell during a big ice age even now. During the last ice age so much water was trapped as ice that the world's sea levels fell by 300 ft (about 100 m).

▲ An artist's impression of the landscape and animals of the last Ice Age, about 10,000 years ago. Animals grew thick fur coats as protection against the cold. Many creatures, such as woolly mammoths, survived on plants such as mosses. Others, such as cave lions, were fierce hunters.

MOST GLACIERS MOVE SLOWLY, BUT THE JAKOBSHAVN GLACIER IN GREENLAND IS REPUTED TO BE ONE OF THE FASTEST FLOWING, MOVING AT A RATE OF AROUND 65 FT (20 M) PER DAY.

◄ The enormous Hubbard glacier reaches into the Gulf of Alaska. It has been slowly advancing for more than 100 years.

Icebergs

When ice sheets and glaciers meet the sea large sections may break off. These enormous frozen chunks float with ten percent of their mass above water because solid water is less dense than liquid water. Drifting icebergs are a hazard to shipping—it was an enormous iceberg that sank the liner *Titanic* in 1912, in which 1,517 people lost their lives.

THE ICECAP ON THE TOP OF MOUNT KILIMANJARO IN AFRICA IS MELTING SO FAST THAT IT MAY DISAPPEAR WITHIN THE NEXT 25 YEARS.

A cruise ship is dwarfed by the massive Hubbard glacier

▼ A colony of penguins hitches a ride onboard an iceberg. They will dive back into the water and hunt for fish when they want to eat again.

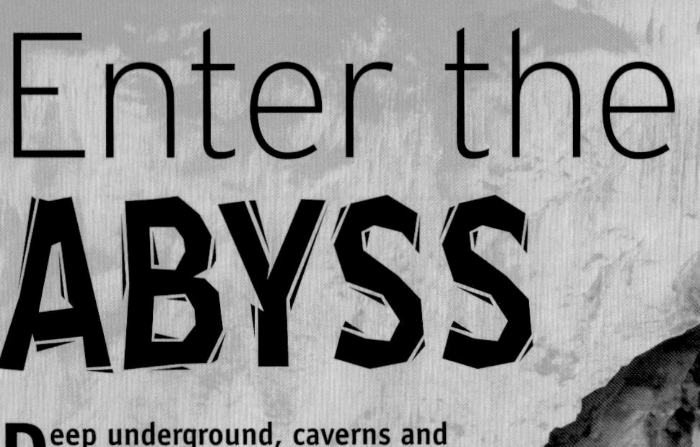

Enter the ABYSS

A long-term drip of dissolved limestone can build up to create icicle-shaped stalactites

Deep underground, caverns and caves create dark and eerie natural theaters. Dramatic features adorn their walls, and tunnels extend far into Earth's hidden depths. Brave explorers who make the journey underground are often rewarded with awesome sights.

A sinking feeling

Acidic water can create a hole that descends vertically and creates an underwater waterfall. These sinkholes, as they are known, can form suddenly when large areas of weakened rock fall into caverns below. The result can be catastrophic when houses or roads collapse with them.

▼ This 30-story-deep sinkhole was caused by heavy rain during a hurricane in Guatemala.

▲ Drips of water fall to the cave floor and evaporate, and the solid minerals that are left behind build up over thousands of years, creating stalagmites.

Leaky limestone

Most underground caves form in karst landscapes—places where limestone is the dominant rock. As rain and river water seep through limestone it becomes acidic, and dissolves solid rock. The liquid it creates can turn back into limestone, creating stalactites, stalagmites, and other strange features.

Spelunkers

Caves are some of the least explored places on Earth, so there is a special thrill to be had from finding new caves and tunnels to navigate. People who undertake these often dangerous treks are known as spelunkers and pot-holers. The risks they have to be prepared for include cave collapse, hypothermia, falling, flooding, and getting lost.

AT OVER 390 MI (630 KM), MAMMOTH CAVE IN KENTUCKY, U.S., IS THE LONGEST CAVE SYSTEM IN THE WORLD.

▲ When exploring a cave system, spelunkers may be faced with long stretches of tiny tunnels as well as vast, impressive caverns.

▼ Giant crystals of aragonite, a form of calcium carbonate, may develop in some limestone cave systems.

Sizing it up

Cave experts have been mapping a cave network in Sarawak, Borneo, for more than 30 years. By taking measurements using lasers, they have gathered data on over 200 mi (320 km) of the Gunung Mulu network. It contains the world's largest cave—Sarawak Chamber is 2,300 ft (700 m) long and 330 ft (100 m) high.

▼ The gigantic Gunung Mulu caves were only discovered in 1976, beneath a rain forest.

Ancient history

The major mineral in limestone is calcium carbonate, which comes from the shells and skeletons of sea creatures. Over millions of years, the shells and skeletons collected on the seafloor and were, under great pressure, eventually turned into rock.

BURIED Treasure

Earth's crust contains a treasure trove of minerals that civilization depends upon. Many substances that we take for granted—iron, oil, gold, even talcum powder and the "lead" (graphite) in pencils—are formed in Earth's crust. Extracting them can demand feats of human endurance and technological wizardry.

MARBLE *This smooth, strong stone is used in sculpture and buildings.*

STEEL *A tough metal made by mixing iron with other minerals.*

ALUMINUM *Strong but lightweight, this metal has many uses.*

DEADLY COLTAN
Coltan is a mineral used in the manufacture of cell phones, but extracting it is a life-threatening activity for people in the Democratic Republic of the Congo. Miners use their bare hands to dig, and risk facing collapsing mine shafts, radioactive minerals, and other deadly toxins.

FLUORITE *This pretty mineral is fluorescent (emits light) under ultraviolet light.*

HEMATITE *Ground up, this mineral makes a red paint used since prehistory.*

MERCURY *This liquid metal is used in thermometers to measure temperature.*

GRAPHITE *Its flexible network of carbon atoms makes graphite very soft.*

COAL *Burning this fossil fuel releases heat and light energy.*

IN DEEP WATER

When the *Deepwater Horizon* rig exploded in 2010 it killed ten men, sparked the world's largest accidental oil spill, and caused environmental catastrophes. The rig was built to research a reservoir of oil on an area of the seafloor beneath 5,000 ft (about 1,520 m) of water, a challenge that has been described as being more technically difficult than exploring the Moon.

▲ The explosion of the oil rig *Deepwater Horizon* on April 20, 2010 caused an estimated 5 million barrels—210 million gal (800 million l)—of oil to spill into the Gulf of Mexico.

Deep-sea DIVE

The deep ocean is the world's least explored and most mysterious environment. It is a high-pressure, dark wilderness, so hostile to life that few creatures can survive there. Those that can are bizarre, ranging from colossal squid with eyes bigger than a human head, to glow-in-the-dark fish, and giant worms.

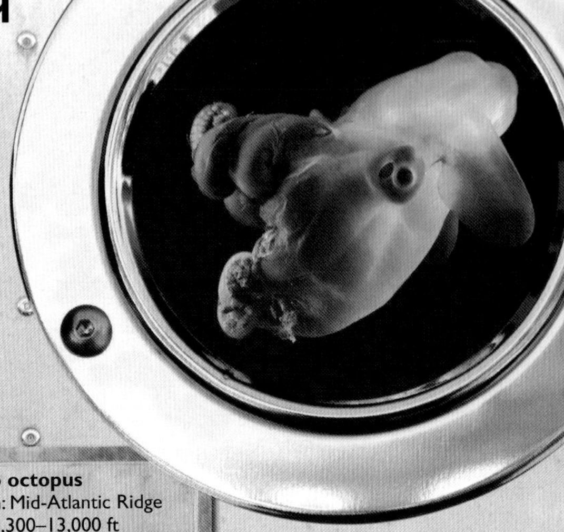

Dumbo octopus
Location: Mid-Atlantic Ridge
Depth: 1,300–13,000 ft (400–4,000 m)

Journey to the bottom of the sea

In 1960 two explorers, Jacques Piccard and Don Walsh, embarked on one of the most treacherous journeys ever undertaken. Their submersible, the *Trieste*, took them 35,800 ft (10,900 m) into the Mariana Trench, the deepest point of any ocean. To this day they remain the only two people to have made the journey. By contrast, 12 people have traveled to the Moon, which is 238,600 mi (384,000 km) away.

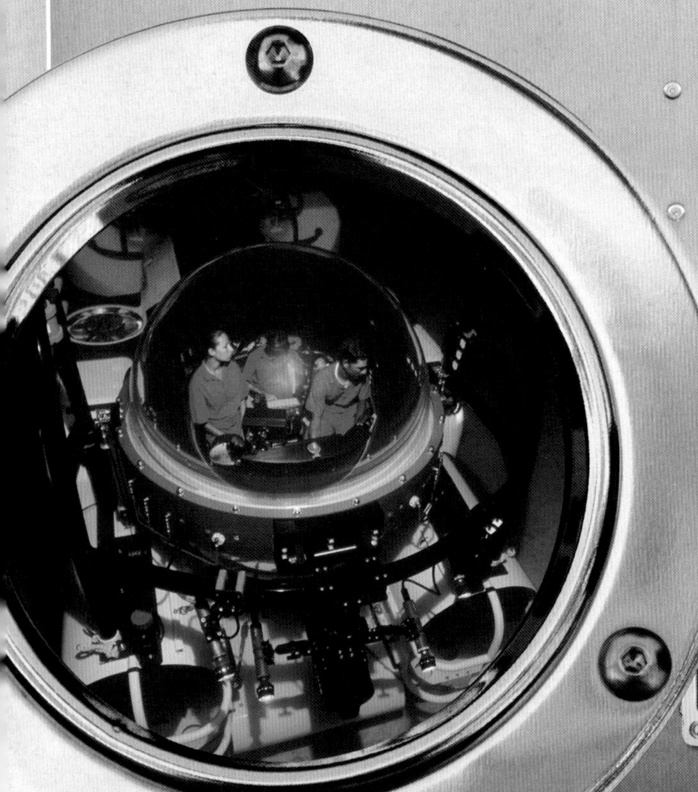

Snow and ooze

Bits of detritus from dead animals and plants are known as marine snow. They drift down to the deep seabed and, over time, build up to create enormous sediments of fine mud and ooze. Some of them are 1,480 ft (450 m) thick.

DeepSee submersible
Carries up to three people to depths of 1,500 ft (about 460 m).

▶ The mineral-rich geysers of water that come from the seabed are called black smokers, and can reach temperatures of 750°F (400°C).

Oasis undersea

The deep sea is a poor habitat for most wildlife, but some places are able to support some of the world's strangest fauna. Fueled by volcanic heat that escapes from cracks in Earth's crust, hydrothermal vents can sustain colonies of limpets, shrimps, starfish, tube worms, and fish.

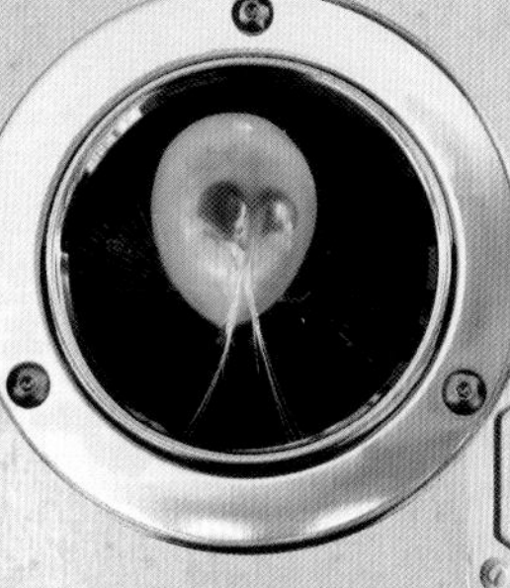

Giant ostracod
Location: Mid-Atlantic Ridge
Depth: 2,356–6,115 ft (718–1,864 m)

The future

Researching the deep ocean remains one of the great challenges facing science. It is such a perilous environment that humans rarely venture there. ROVs (remotely operated vehicles), such as *Jason*, and AUVs (autonomous underwater vehicles), such as *Sentry*, are now used to enable scientists to explore the seabed from the safety of a ship's deck above.

◀ This image uses colors to show the uneven nature of the Pacific Ocean seabed. The deepest areas appear blue and green. Underwater peaks appear as red and yellow, and mark the East Pacific Rise.

ZONES OF THE DEEP

0 ft

Light Zone Sunlight travels through the water at this level, so plants can photosynthesize (make food), supporting a large range of life-forms.

650 ft

Twilight Zone Dim levels of light can pass through the water, but there is not enough light to support photosynthesis.

3,300 ft

Dark Zone Many animals survive in the inky depths. The seabed is home to sponges, shelled animals, sea cucumbers, and worms.

13,000 ft

Abyssal Zone Fewer animals can survive as the water gets deeper. A great pressure of water bears down on those that do.

20,000 ft

Hadal Zone This is the most mysterious place on Earth, and some strange creatures manage to survive here. Little is known about them.

WILD Winds

Wind is little more than moving air. It is invisible and almost weightless—yet it is impossible to control and is one of the planet's most destructive forces. When winds become high-energy storms, they can develop into hurricanes more than 500 mi (800 km) across—and wreak total havoc.

A spinning tornado collects dirt and grit from the land, turning it into a brown funnel of air.

ON APRIL 3, 1974, THE U.S. ENDURED WHAT IS THOUGHT TO HAVE BEEN ITS WORST EVER TORNADO OUTBREAK, DURING WHICH 150 TORNADOES CAUSED MORE THAN 300 DEATHS AND 6,000 STORM-RELATED INJURIES.

Twisting tornadoes

Tornadoes can be deadly, but short-lived. They begin when warm, wet air encounters cool, dry air. In the right circumstances, a vertical column of rotating air forms, which causes a "supercell" that can transform into a vortex of violently rotating wind.

A supercell storm, such as this one in Nebraska, U.S., can produce several tornadoes during a few hours of activity.

On the move

Air moves because it becomes warm in some places, and cool in others. Warm air molecules have more energy, and move faster, than cold ones. When air moves faster, it expands and rises above cold air, setting up weather systems that sometimes have extreme outcomes.

Storm chasers

Tornado Alley in the Great Plains region of the U.S. is famous for its wild winds, and the storm chasers that pursue them for the thrill, or to gather scientific data. Storm chasers don't just watch the twisters—their goal is to actually go inside them. They follow computer weather models and search for brewing storms. Once in the middle of a tornado, storm chasers rely on their vehicles for protection against high-speed winds, torrential rain, lightning, and giant hailstones.

Hurricanes

The world's greatest storms are called hurricanes, typhoons, or tropical cyclones. They begin at sea and can inflict terrible damage if they move onto land. The worst hurricanes have winds that swirl at more than 155 mph (250 km/h). At this velocity, winds have the strength to rip the roofs off buildings and cause storm surges, when seawater is picked up and hurled inland.

On August 29, 2005, Hurricane Katrina hit land, causing devastating damage in areas such as Kenner, Louisiana, U.S.

IN 1900, A HURRICANE BARRELED THE TEXAN CITY OF GALVESTON, FLATTENING IT AND CAUSING A STORM SURGE AND ONE OF THE U.S.'S WORST NATURAL DISASTERS. AS MANY AS 10,000 PEOPLE DIED IN ONE NIGHT.

Freaky WEATHER

Weird weather events have long been features of biblical tales and folklore, and have often been attributed to a divine intervention in earthly matters. Scientists have sought to uncover the genuine causes of these oddities, and today they are more likely to be explained by rare, but entirely natural, weather systems.

Cloud art

The study of clouds is called nephology, and for many people it is more of an art than a science. These airborne masses hold water droplets or ice crystals and, owing to climatic conditions, can form some strange shapes. Freaky cloud formations include mushrooms, jellyfish, and donuts!

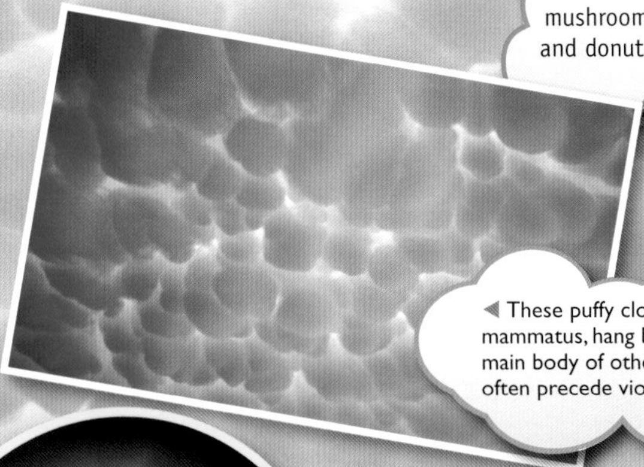

◀ These puffy clouds, known as mammatus, hang beneath the main body of other clouds and often precede violent storms.

Sun halo

Also called a sundog, this strange atmospheric phenomenon is caused by ice crystals inside high, thin clouds. The crystals reflect light, causing it to shine in a ring, and creating a rainbow that looks as if it is wrapped around the Sun.

Raining fish and frogs

For centuries there have been reports of strange things falling from the sky during storms. These bizarre events are caused by tornadoes, or their watery equivalents—waterspouts. Animals, especially fish or frogs, are swept up into the air, carried some distance, and then dropped during a rainstorm.

▶ A waterspout forms and touches down alongside the Mekong River in Cambodia.

A CHUNK OF ICE MEASURING 7 IN (NEARLY 18 CM) ACROSS FELL FROM THE SKY DURING A STORM IN AURORA, NEBRASKA, U.S., IN 2003.

◀ Lightning striking through a column of volcanic ash produces a dazzling display.

Blue Moon

The Moon may appear blue when forest fires or volcanic ash send tiny particles into the atmosphere where they mix with droplets of water. The mixture is carried by winds and refracts moonlight, causing a blue haze to form.

Fiendish fireballs

About 100 lightning strikes occur around the world every second, slashing through the sky with awesome electrical energy. Balls of lightning, however, are rare events. Fireballs can be the size of a beach ball and they have been seen to pass through windows and walls, hiss, and even explode.

BLUE AND RED FLASHES OF LIGHT ARE KNOWN AS BLUE JETS AND RED SPRITES AND ARE SOMETIMES SEEN ABOVE STORMS. THEY ARE PROBABLY CAUSED BY LIGHTNING IN THE UPPER REGIONS OF THE EARTH'S ATMOSPHERE.

▼ In 2010 parts of Queensland, Australia, were hit by flood waters that covered an area larger than France and Germany put together.

Freak floods

Flooding is one of the most common natural disasters on Earth, but flash floods take everyone by surprise. Often caused by a break in flood defenses or riverbanks, following unusually heavy rains or ice-melts, flash floods swamp large areas. In low-lying areas, the effects can be particularly catastrophic.

Ultra FREEZE

Soft, fluffy snow can transform a landscape into a stunning, white wilderness. Yet in its most extreme forms, snow can also bring disaster and destruction. From raging blizzards to colossal avalanches that crash to the ground with the impact of solid rock, the power of snow should never be underestimated.

MOUNT BAKER IN WASHINGTON STATE IN THE U.S. HAD A TOTAL SNOWFALL OF 95 FT (29 M) IN THE WINTER OF 1998–1999.

What is snow?

In cold places—mostly near Earth's poles or at high altitude—rising water vapor can freeze as tiny ice particles in the air. Ice crystals stick together to form snowflakes. The simplest snowflakes are six-sided prisms, but these can branch to create more complex structures. The shape and size of a snowflake depends on the temperature, pressure, and amount of water that is held in the air.

Is every snowflake unique?

Probably yes, although how would anyone ever know? If several trillion ice crystals fell every year, the chance of two identical crystals forming in the lifetime of the Universe is virtually zero.

AVALANCHE SURVIVAL

Mountain rescuers recommend some simple steps to increase the likelihood of survival when out in avalanche-prone areas.

* Check avalanche hotlines and assess the avalanche risk before going into an area.
* If you are skiing or snowboarding, carry an avalanche rescue beacon, which transmits a message to rescue teams.
* You can't outrun an avalanche, but you may be able to run to the side of one.
* If you are knocked off your feet, grab hold of a tree or a rock, or stick your ski pole into the snow.
* Being caught by an avalanche is like being caught in river rapids—the snow will start to pull you under. Try to "swim" through it, and keep trying to make your way to the top of the snow pile.
* When you stop tumbling, clear an area in front of your face so you can breathe.
* Push your arm upward for the best chance of being spotted by someone.
* If you see someone being caught by an avalanche, mark the last point you saw them, so that you—or a rescue team—have a better chance of finding them.

A SEASON OF BLIZZARDS IN WESTERN U.S. IN 1949 LASTED FOR SEVEN WEEKS. DURING THAT TIME MORE THAN 100 PEOPLE, AND ONE MILLION CATTLE, DIED.

Whiteout

A blizzard is a snowstorm driven by winds of 30 mph (48 km/h) or more, where visibility is reduced to 650 ft (200 m) or less. In a severe blizzard or "whiteout," visibility is near to zero.

Hundreds of tons of snow coursing down a hillside can fell trees, crush cars, and demolish houses.

Alpine avalanche

Heavy snow in Chamonix, France, in 1999 caused an avalanche of more than 10.6 million cubic ft (300,000 cubic m) of snow. The flow traveled at 60 mph (97 km/h) until it hit a small hamlet below, destroying buildings and burying people under 100,000 tons of snow. Twelve people died.

The Ends of THE EARTH

The Arctic is a frozen ocean surrounded by continents. During the height of summer in the Arctic Circle, daylight continues for 24 hours. In winter, there is at least one day when the Sun does not rise.

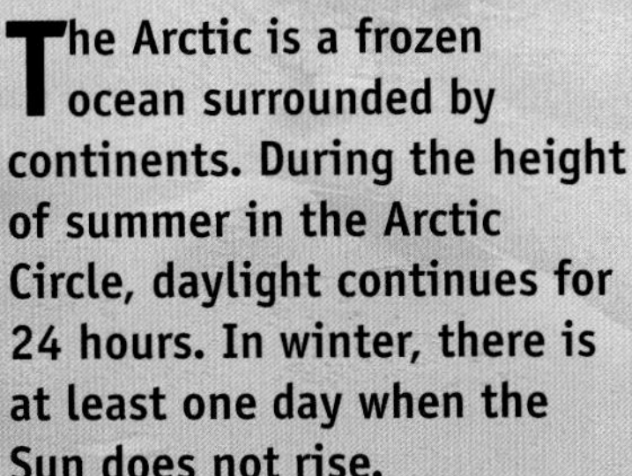

◀▲ Animals that can survive within the Arctic Circle include Arctic foxes and polar bears. The foxes often follow the bears, to feed on the leftover bits of their kills.

▲ Divers explore under Arctic ice, discovering wildlife that survives at the Earth's extreme ends.

▶ Animals that can survive in the Antarctic include penguins, seals, whales, and albatross. Shrimplike krill live in the Southern Ocean and are among the most numerous animals on the planet.

The South Pole is on a massive continent—Antarctica—which is covered by the world's largest icecap. With an average area of 5.3 million sq mi (13.7 million sq km), the icecap is one-and-a-half times bigger than the U.S., and holds about 70 percent of the world's fresh water.

▼ Scientists explore ice caves in Antarctica to uncover the region's mysterious past.

A time-delay photograph captures the midnight sun and its reflection in the Arctic Ocean, as it appears to move across the sky.

Temperatures in northern Greenland can fall to –94°F (–70°C).

IN 1958, A SUBMARINE SAILED BENEATH THE FROZEN ARCTIC OCEAN, PROVING THE ICE SHEET RESTS ON WATER, NOT ON LAND.

NORTH POLE

SOUTH POLE

IN PARTS OF THE ANTARCTIC THE SUN REMAINS BELOW THE HORIZON FOR 105 DAYS DURING THE WINTER, LEAVING THE LAND IN NEAR-TOTAL DARKNESS.

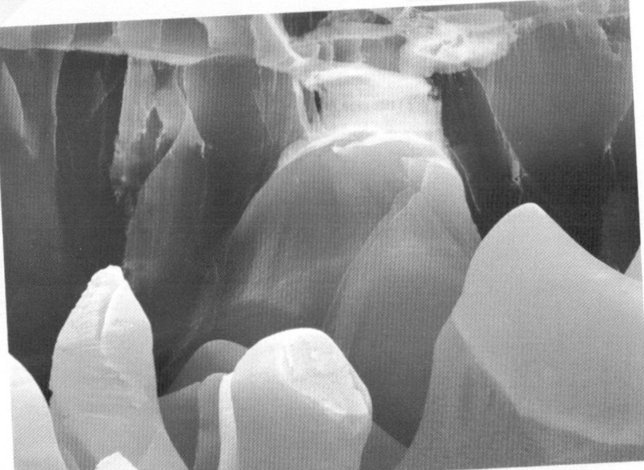

In winter, the Antarctic ice sheet spreads into the ocean, forming layers called ice shelves. Huge ice blocks break off the shelves to form massive icebergs.

The coldest temperature ever recorded was at Vostok in the Antarctic. It was –128.6°F (–89.2°C).

Super DRY

Deserts are the world's driest places, where years may pass with no rain at all. They can also suffer extremes of temperature, with hot days and freezing nights. Even the icy Antarctic is classed as a desert. These super-dry places are desolate and often barren—without access to water, few living things can survive.

EARTH'S HOTTEST PLACES

1. Al'Azízíya, Libya 135.9°F (57.7°C)
2. Greenland Ranch, Death Valley, U.S. 134°F (56.7°C)
3. Ghudamis, Libya and Kebili, Tunisia 131°F (55°C)

Las Vegas is a city of excess, but scientists warn it could run dry in the next 50 years.

The desert city

Despite the harsh and inhospitable environment of deserts, one of the world's most successful cities was built in one. Las Vegas, in the American Mohave Desert, is home to 1.8 million people and accommodates 30 million tourists a year. Water is supplied by nearby Lake Mead, but the city is growing too fast for the supply.

In Los Angeles, 140 gal (530 l) a day is required per person—in Las Vegas that figure swells to an unsustainable 307 gal (1,165 l).

A fast-moving wall of Saharan sand and dust, called a haboob, advances on a market in Sudan.

Scorched Sahara

The giant Sahara Desert covers an area equivalent to the U.S., and it is growing all the time. Huge dunes form, reaching heights of 970 ft (300 m), and winds can whip up sandstorms and dust devils. Dust is lighter than sand, and can travel enormous distances.

ARICA IN THE CHILEAN ATACAMA DESERT EXPERIENCED LESS THAN 0.03 IN (0.75 MM) OF RAIN DURING ONE 59-YEAR PERIOD.

Burning up

Wildfires are often started by human activity or lightning strikes, and when they take hold in areas that have endured long, dry periods they can spread by leaps and bounds. Australia has about 15,000 wildfires a year. In 1997, strong winds followed a severe drought in Indonesia, and the result was a massive inferno that raged across 2,900 sq mi (7,500 sq km).

◀ Known as bushfires in Australia, these infernos can rampage through 12 mi (20 km) of vegetation in just one hour.

EARTH'S DRIEST PLACES

RAINFALLS, ON AVERAGE

1. ARICA, CHILE
   ONE DAY EVERY SIX YEARS
2. ASYÛT, EGYPT
   ONE DAY EVERY FIVE YEARS
3. DAKHLA OASIS, EGYPT
   ONE DAY EVERY FOUR YEARS

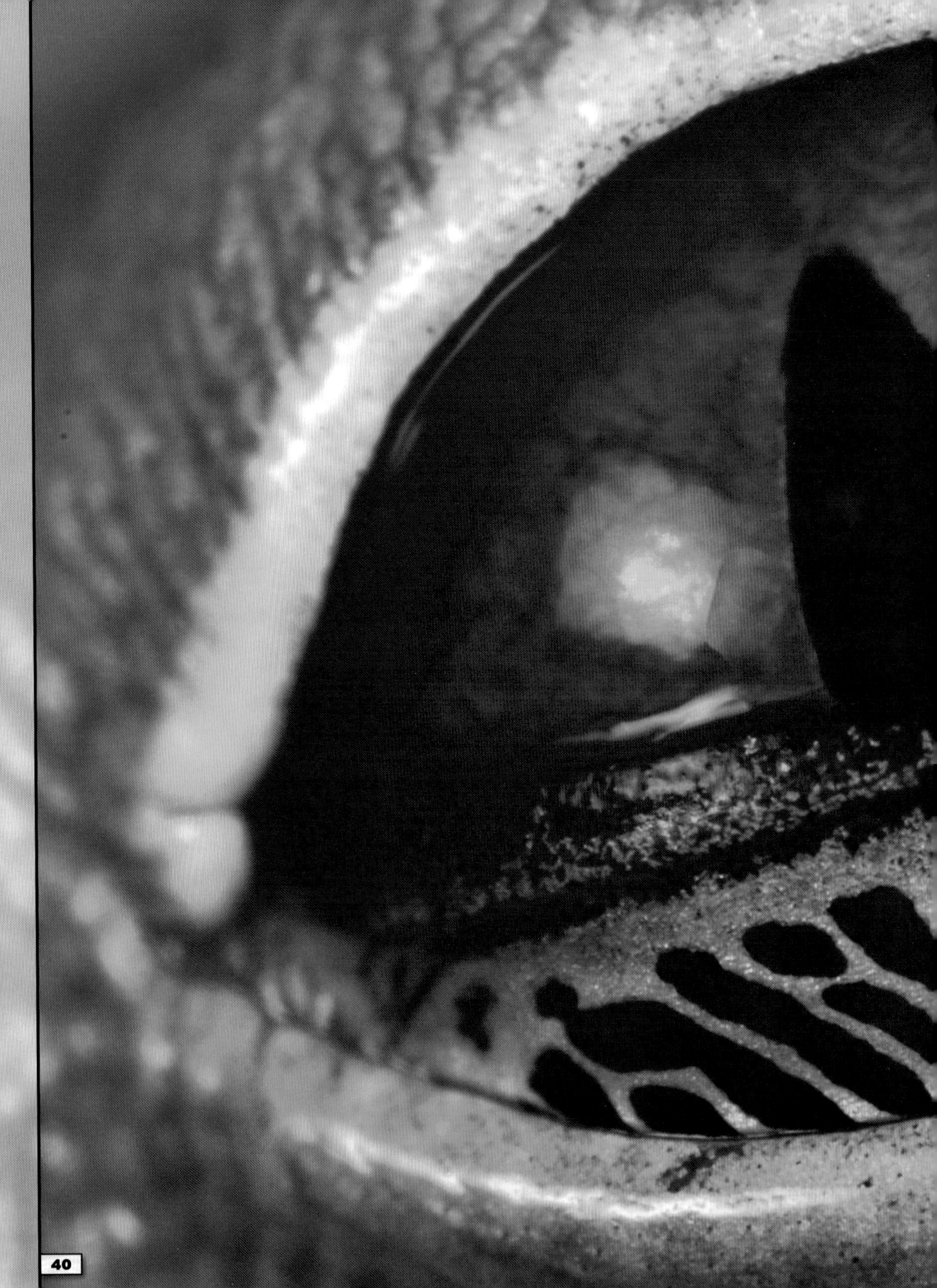

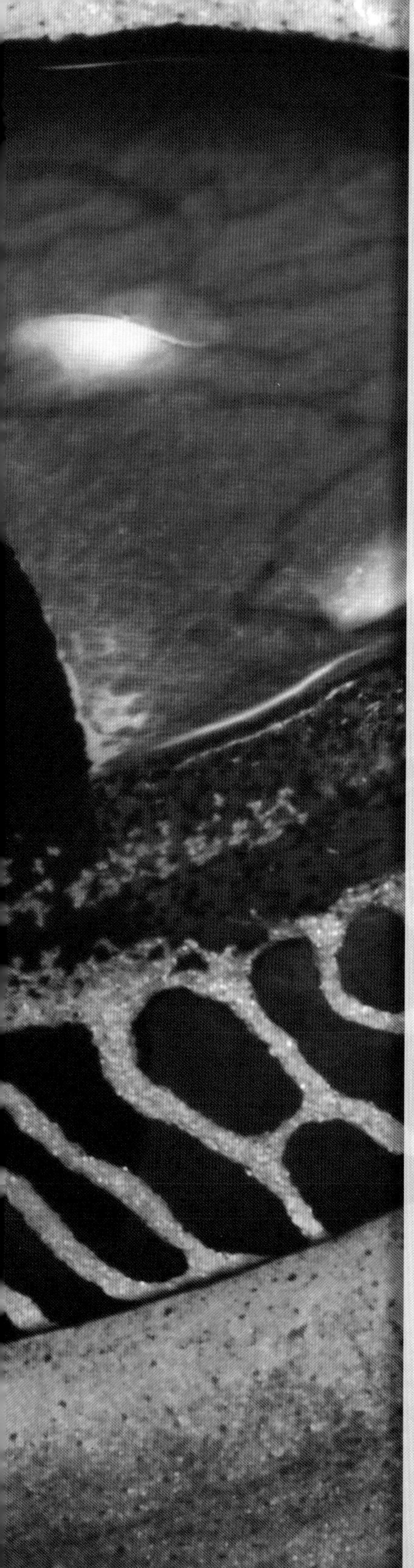

Awesome ANIMALS

In the wild, a fight for survival is taking place, and many creatures go to extremes to rise above the rest.

◀ The red-eyed tree frog has a thin membrane that partly covers its brightly colored eye. This allows the frog to see while remaining camouflaged.

Unusual

All animals need to move to find food, seek shelter, escape enemies, and of course link up with breeding partners. Most creatures walk, run, fly, or swim, depending on their habitat, but some use unusual and unexpected ways of moving—such as flying with their feet!

Feet feats

From cheetahs and deer to ostriches and cockroaches, long, slim legs are a sure sign of speedy sprinters. There are many ways to get about on foot—kangaroos hop, grasshoppers leap, fleas jump, and some lizards and bugs even walk on water. However, few creatures are bipedal (move around regularly on two legs). A lizard may rear up briefly in fear, and an orangutan might amble along a branch, but only a select few—birds and humans—have the upright posture and delicate balance for bipedal walking.

▲ The sifaka, a large Madagascan lemur, holds out its arms for balance while it moves using short, sideways hops.

▲ The mudskipper uses its muscular armlike pectoral fins to haul its body across the tidal ooze. If in danger, this bizarre fish flips its whole body into the air to move to safety.

Emergency aerobats

There's a massive difference between actual flying, like a bird, and a perilous leap into midair with just flaps of skin preventing a fatal plummet to the ground. "Flying" squirrels, lizards, frogs, and snakes don't actually fly, but glide. Their aerial ability is mainly used for emergencies. They create a broad surface, often by opening out flaps of skin, which encounters air resistance to slow their fall. A tilt or twist gives some control over direction, and a few bruises on landing are preferable to being gobbled up by a predator.

◀ Frogs usually use their webbed feet to provide a powerful push when swimming. However, the flying frog of Southeast Asia sails through the air using its webs like mini-parachutes to increase drag, slowing its descent.

CLOCKED AT MORE THAN 65 MPH (105 KM/H), THE SAILFISH IS THE FASTEST SWIMMER IN THE WORLD.

▶ Using its partly webbed toes and fast strides, the basilisk lizard races on its hind legs across water—with no time to sink.

Water sports

Muscle-packed bodies and thrashing fins give fish speed—the fastest species, such as the sailfish, have stiff, narrow, crescent-shaped tails. However, fins are adaptable and can be used for out-of-water movement, too, such as in the goby and walking catfish. Bird wings are similar in shape to fins and some birds use them to thrust through water rather than air. Kingfishers and dippers can "swim" briefly, but penguins have given up air flight completely and only "fly" underwater.

▲ The kingfisher, using its wings as both rudders and underwater brakes, strikes with astonishing accuracy.

COOL Senses

All around are more light rays, sounds, and smells than humans could ever imagine. Animals of all kinds can tune into this abundance of sensations with their amazing supersenses. Often an animal is almost entirely dependent on just one dominant sense—block a bat's ears or an anteater's nostrils and they cannot survive.

▶ Giant anteaters sniff out their tiny quarry from more than 150 ft (45 m) away.

Sniff, snort, snuffle

A polar bear can sniff out a seal carcass up to 4.5 mi (7 km) away, while a human would need to be within 300 ft (90 m) to detect even a trace of this rotting stench. Bears, wolves, and dogs far exceed a human's capacity because they have more than 200 million microscopic smell cells in their noses, compared to a human's five million. The sense of smell is not just for finding food. Without it, elephants would die of thirst, lions would not be able to mark their territory, and many moths and beetles could never detect scents released by potential mates that tell them they are ready to breed.

▼The male cockchafer beetle's feathery antennae (feelers) detect scent particles, called pheromones, from females up to several miles away. These pheromone messages tell the male that the females are ready to mate.

ANIMALS VS HUMANS

RHINO Sight estimated at five times poorer than a human's—it cannot distinguish between another rhino and a jeep at 300 ft (90 m) away. However, its sense of smell is ten times better than a human's.

EAGLE Sight is at least ten times better than a human's—it can see a rabbit more than 2 mi (3 km) away.

BAT Hearing can pick up vibrations ten times faster than a human—so it can hear a tiny gnat's flapping wings.

MOTH Sense of smell is more than 10,000 times more sensitive than a human's—it can scent nectar from a blossom that a human could not even see in daylight!

▲ A bat finds its way around using echolocation—it squeaks and then listens to the echoes to work out where objects in its path are. Large ears help a bat to gather these sounds. If a human's ears were relative in size to the long-eared bat's, they would be bigger than trashcan lids!

Hear, hear!

A noise that sounds quiet to a human might deafen an owl or a bat. They have far more microsensors in their ears, and they move their ears or head much more carefully to receive the maximum number of sound waves and pinpoint an object's position. Ears are not always on the head. Insects such as grasshoppers and crickets have them on their knees, and some fish "hear" with their swim bladders.

▲ Finding and attacking prey is no problem for a jumping spider. They have two huge eyes to see objects in great detail and color. The remaining six eyes detect movement and create a large field of vision.

Seeing the invisible

Animal eyes can see infrared and ultraviolet light—both of which are outside the spectrum of light that is visible to humans. Insects in particular are highly tuned to these invisible wavelengths. To a bee, plain-looking petals are covered with ultraviolet lines that point to the sweet nectar inside. Some fish have an amazing sense of sight, too. Piranhas can see the warm, infrared glow of a mammal—then launch their mass attack.

The GROSS Factor

Animals have some disgusting habits. To deter predators, they spray vomit or excrement, spit saliva, and even squirt blood from open vessels. When it comes to feeding, they certainly have no manners—tearing at flesh and creating a bloody mess. Some animals even tuck into excrement for a tasty snack.

THE HORNED LIZARD SQUIRTS A BLOODY FLUID FROM ITS EYES—MORE THAN 5 FT (1.5 M)—AT A THREAT.

Disgusting defense

Vomit, slime, urine, droppings, spit, and pus can sting, cause infection, and create an off-putting stench. Some animals capitalize on this by using their bodily fluids to make enemies recoil and retreat. The innocent-looking sea cucumber throws up its super-sticky guts over an attacker, while several kinds of seabird projectile vomit more than 3 ft (1 m) at an enemy.

▼ The world's largest lizards have big appetites. Komodo dragons feast on a rotting dolphin carcass, enjoying the fatty blubber and the guts filled with semidigested fish. Male komodos can reach lengths of 10 ft (3 m).

Feeding frenzy

Even before a huge pile of food becomes available, predators and scavengers wait in the wings. A dying whale is tracked by sharks, orcas, and seabirds, while a sick elephant lures hyenas, jackals, and vultures. As soon as one plucks up the courage to move in for a mouthful, the rest rush to grab what they can. The feeding frenzy that follows is rough, gory, and urgent as they push and scrap to get the best share before it's all gone.

Animal babies can be born in the most disgusting conditions. Some parasitic wasp grubs hatch in the guts of a caterpillar, and proceed to eat the host alive. Dung beetle grubs emerge from their eggs into balls of excrement. Surinam toad tadpoles develop inside their mother's back, under her skin. Other frogs whip up a foam using a cocktail of their saliva, skin slime, sperm fluid, and excrement, and lay their eggs here.

▼ A group of male gray foam-nest tree frogs cluster around one female and whip their bodily fluids into a froth, in which she deposits her spawn.

Nasty nourishment

Dung, droppings, and excrement might look and smell horrible. However, the digestion of most animals is not very efficient, so feces often still contain plenty of nutrients. Dung eaters usually like to get it while it's fresh, before molds, germs, and flies arrive to contaminate the rotting mass.

▲ This turkey vulture quickly devours fishy feces from a fur seal.

Wicked ASSASSINS

Natural born killers are feared for their deadly weapons. These fearsome animals mercilessly slay their prey with lethal teeth, claws, and fangs, devouring flesh, bones, and blood with ease—no morsel is spared.

Wolfie the Wolffish

Last seen in the waters of the Atlantic Ocean, the wolffish is 5 ft (1.5 m) long and can be recognized by its vast number of teeth. It has about 100 of them—fanglike at the front, broad for crushing at the back, and continuing into its throat. Its typical victims are shellfish, starfish, crabs, and urchins, which the wolffish crushes to death with great power.

WANTED

Terminator the Alligator

This 15-ft- (4.6-m-) long 'gator is wanted for drowning prey by dragging it underwater. Victims include turtles, snakes, waterbirds, and mammals up to the size of deer. Beware—the alligator is armed and dangerous, with 50 cone-shaped teeth and amazingly strong jaw muscles. Do not approach.

WANTED

REWARD $2,000

JAWS THE GRIZZLY BEAR

Towering up to 10 ft (3 m) tall, the grizzly is a formidable hunter. Its weapons include powerful teeth and jaws, plate-sized paws, and curved claws. These features, combined with enormous weight, power, and stamina, mean that nothing is safe. The grizzly will attack anything up to the size of moose and never lets go.

FANG THE GABOON VIPER

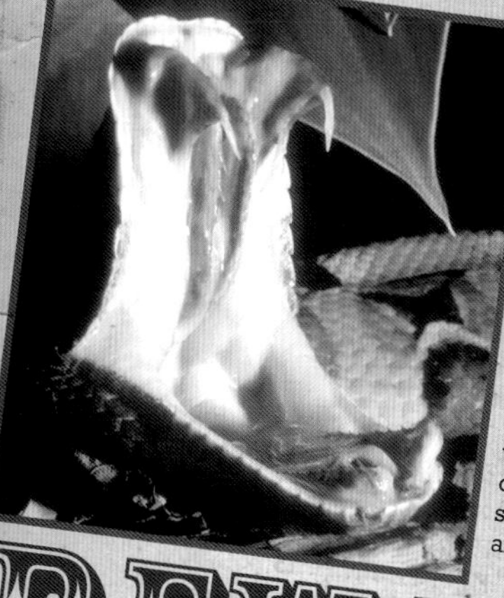

The Gaboon viper is a massive 6 ft (2 m) long. Mice, rats, birds, and similar small creatures have been found dead, marked with puncture wounds. This cold-blooded killer strikes at lightning speed, using its long, foldout front fangs to stab the victim's flesh and inject deadly venom. It then waits for the victim to die of shock as the heart stops beating (cardiac arrest).

WANTED

DEAD OR ALIVE

SMILER THE SAND TIGER SHARK

Lurking in the shadows of the deep, the 11-ft- (3.5-m-) long sand tiger shark charges suddenly, taking its victim by surprise. Fish, squid, shellfish, and crabs have all suffered from this menace's slashing bite.

MOST WAN

A master of stealth, this 8-ft- (2.4-m-) long assassin camouflages itself among the grass, stalking before the sudden rush of attack. Armed with huge canine teeth and slicing back teeth, victims are killed with a throat-crushing bite, before the lion tears its flesh apart using sharp, curved claws. An experienced killer, no "hit" is too big or small for this ferocious feline. Its kill list includes gazelles and antelope, as well as rats and beetles.

CLAWS THE LION

BABOONS OFTEN KILL OTHER BABOONS TO BECOME THE BOSS OF THE TROOP.

Deadly DEFENSE

The forest is nearly dark and almost quiet. A creature sneaks up on the juicy meal it has been tracking. It steadies itself, preparing to pounce... WOAH! Suddenly two huge eyes appear, glaring in the gloom. A big cat? A snake? An owl? No, they're eyespots (false eyes)—one of many animal self-defense tactics.

Terrible taste

Having horrible-tasting or poisonous flesh deters predators and works as a great group defense strategy. After biting one foul-tasting animal, a hunter learns to recognize its warning signs, such as colors and patterns, and stays away from all similar-looking prey.

◀ The African foam grasshopper shows its nasty taste by blowing noxious bubbles from tiny breathing holes, called spiracles, along its body.

Animal armor

Some creatures lack speed to escape enemies, or foul-tasting defenses to deter them. Instead they use simple physical protection. Tough-shelled animals include crabs, clams, and snails, as well as armadillos and pangolins. They simply shut up tight and wait for the danger to pass.

▶ The three-banded armadillo has bony plates within its skin, covered by outer scales of horny keratin. Its armor is so flexible that it can curl into a tight ball that will completely defeat predators.

PLAYING DEAD

When under threat, the Virginia opossum flops onto its side, puts out its tongue, leaks foul-smelling anal fluid, and emits a rotting stench. By acting "dead," no hunter will try to eat it.

◀ A rear view of the peacock katydid (a type of grasshopper) shows how its suddenly raised wings display enormous eyespots to startle a potential attacker.

Guns blazing

Camouflage is a great defense tactic. An animal that matches the background color of its habitat can just sit still and hope to go unnoticed. But what if it's spotted? The next tactic is to make a grand show of defense—rear up, look big, reveal your weapons, make a noise, wave and shake, and generally try to look as frightening and inedible as possible.

▶ If its disguise is rumbled, the dead-leaf mantis raises its body and extends its wings and fearsome, spiked, jackknife forelegs to appear super-fierce.

Young and Old

Why do elephants live longer than flies? These creatures are at two ends of a whole spectrum of life strategies. One is to develop slowly, and take great care of just a few young. The other is to live fast and die young, mating frequently and producing lots of offspring but providing no parental care.

Labord's chameleon

Shortest-lived of any four-legged vertebrate, this lizard's life cycle is perfectly adapted to Madagascar's seasonal changes. It lives for a single year, spending eight months in an egg and just four months in its adult form.

1 DAY!

Have a Great Day!

happy birthday!

1 TODAY!

Brine shrimp

Old shrimps lay tough-cased eggs before their salt lake dries up for summer. When it starts to rain in fall, the eggs hatch, and the next generation begins to feed.

Mayfly

The mayfly spends a year or two as an underwater nymph. Then it emerges, molts to reveal its wonderful wings, mates in midair, and dies—all within 24 hours.

Worker honeybee

Day after day of nonstop toil means the worker honeybee's body suffers immense wear and tear. The egg-laying queen might make it to five years old.

Macaw

Several parrot species may reach the half-century mark. Intelligence—along with their powerful beaks and claws—help these birds to survive.

BIRTHDAY GREETINGS!

Elephant

Size and power provide protection against lions and other foes, and family ties mean younger and more vulnerable members of the herd are well-guarded by the females of the group.

giant birthday!

Giant tortoise

Life in the slow lane, with a reptile's unhurried body chemistry, plentiful food, few natural predators, and a thick, protective shell, is a great recipe for reaching a great age.

HAPPY BIRTHDAY

Quahog clam

This shellfish holds the record for the longest life (and perhaps the most boring—it spends all of its many days lying on the dark seabed).

400 TODAY!

Koi carp

These precious and pampered ornamental fish are popular pets because they reach a great age, in addition to their beautiful coloration.

Dinner TIME

In the wild, animals rarely know where their next meal is coming from, so any snack is greedily gobbled up. If a glut of food appears, some species will eat until they are almost bursting—the opportunity to devour their fill may not come again.

▶ The Bryde's whale spends all day filtering tiny creatures such as krill and small fish from the water. Its daily diet can weigh 3 tons—equivalent to the amount of food eaten by a human over a period of seven or eight years.

▼ This African bullfrog has no teeth and cannot tear up or chew its mouse victim. Instead, frogs and toads feed by stretching their head-wide mouths and gulping prey whole.

Down in one

The bodies of many creatures are adapted for eating huge amounts in a single feeding session. Features range from a stretchy stomach to a dislocating jaw. With scavengers and enemies lurking everywhere, fast food is best—rapid gulps or the all-in-one swallow. After gorging their fill, these gluttons can hide away from danger while they digest.

Leave it in the larder

Some animals store excess food for later, to avoid waste and prepare for periods when food is scarce. Squirrels bury nuts, crocodiles wedge gazelles beneath underwater rocks, and tigers scrape leaves and soil over deer carcasses. These clever methods mean these creatures are less likely to die of starvation when times are hard.

▶ The leopard can haul a kill three times its own weight up into a tree, away from scavengers such as jackals.

▼ These white-backed vultures rush to peck the juiciest morsels from a dead giraffe, before a pack of hyenas arrive on the scene.

Scavenger hunt

Old meat is still a valuable source of nourishment, so a large carcass attracts a multitude of scavengers. The first (airborne vultures) and the fiercest (hyena clans) get the richest pickings. Lesser scavengers such as jackals soon follow.

Bite to kill

Any predator must make careful decisions about which prey to tackle, and how. If an animal has just eaten, it may feel full and sluggish, and this might put it off tackling another large victim. A predator will also assess the fitness of potential prey—is it strong and healthy, or (preferably) too young, old, or sick, for its defenses to prove a problem? The attack itself must be swift and decisive, since in the wild even a slight injury makes a hunter far less capable.

▶ After a lightning, twist-and-turn chase, the leopard seal strikes with its viciously sharp canine teeth. The seal moves in as the penguin weakens, and chomps away at the fatty blubber and tasty flesh.

The Perfect **Animal?**

Every species is superbly adapted to its habitat and way of life. But some creatures' features are super-adapted, compared to other, similar animals. If we could bring together all these extreme adaptations into one combi-creature, surely it would instantly be crowned king of the animal kingdom?

Ringtailed lemur's TAIL

Not only an excellent balance aid, the lemur's tail is used to convey signals about mood and intention. The male sprays a nasty scent on its own tail and waves it at opponents to mark its territory. The tail also indicates an individual's rank within the group, and attracts a mate.

Cheetah's BODY

Slim and streamlined, the fastest land animal's body is lithe yet muscular and flexible, and ideal for out-sprinting prey.

Gerenuk's HIND LEGS

Slim and strong, this antelope rears up on its hind legs to reach juicy leaves in tall trees—food that few other animals can reach.

Elephant's EARS

Not only brilliant for catching faint sounds, the world's biggest ears can flap both to lose internal heat and to fan cooling air over the body.

Tarsier's EYES

The tarsier hunts by grabbing passing moths and bats, so its massive eyes have a fabulous ability to follow fast motion, as well as superb vision even on the darkest nights.

Tiger's MOUTH

Huge, sharp teeth and one of the biggest, strongest bites of any land animal ensures that any victim is fatally wounded in an instant.

Proboscis monkey's NOSE

Long and drooping, this remarkable nose amplifies hoots and calls, and also offers a superior sense of smell compared to other monkey species.

Giraffe's NECK

As well as reaching far higher food than any other ground-bound animal, a giraffe's excellent vantage point gives it an all-round aerial view—so it can spot approaching predators from a long way off.

Kangaroo's LEGS

The kangaroo's hind legs offer an energy-efficient, bouncing gait, with the added extra of huge leaps 26 ft (8 m) long and 13 ft (4 m) high.

The natural world is both nice and nasty, when animals of two different species live together in a symbiotic relationship. Here, both partners help each other in some way for mutual benefit.

Best of friends

Sea anemones and clownfish work together in harmony. Although anemones feed by paralyzing small fish with their stinging tentacles, the clownfish's slimy coating resists the venom. The anemone recognizes this and rarely attempts to attack. In return for this safe haven, the clownfish eats debris and pests among the tentacles to keep the anemone clean. The anemone also scares off animals that may prey on clownfish, while the clownfish lures in other fish to be eaten by the anemone.

▶ As the clownfish swims around the anemone, water circulation increases, which helps the anemone to breathe.

▶ Ants crowd around the aphids and "milk" them so they secrete sweet, sugar-rich honeydew.

Buddies vs Baddies

Sometimes partnerships are horribly one-sided. One benefits, while the other gets hurt—the parasite-host situation. But being a parasite is a balancing act. If you are too successful, all your hosts die out and you have nowhere to live and nothing to eat.

Eaten alive

Some of the nastiest parasites are small wasps that lay their eggs in living caterpillars and other larvae. The wasp stings and paralyzes the caterpillar, then deposits its eggs inside the host's body. The wasp grubs hatch and proceed to eat the helpless host bit by bit.

▼ This tomato hornworm caterpillar is covered with parasitic wasp eggs. Its death will be slow as the hatched grubs chomp away until all that's left is an empty skin.

Protection for food

Aphids (greenfly and blackfly) are tiny, soft, and defenseless—except when they are in the care of an ant colony. While the aphids feed on plant sap with their sucking mouthparts, ants from a nearby nest patrol the region and keep away aphid enemies, such as ladybugs. In return for their protection, the ants feed on a sugary liquid, called honeydew, produced by the aphids.

▼ This impala is being "cleaned" by red-billed oxpeckers. Although they get rid of pests, oxpeckers may also peck at their host's skin, keeping wounds open—making this bird both a helper and a parasite.

A quick cleanup

The oxpecker doesn't only peck oxen—it may debug antelope, gazelles, giraffes, zebras, rhinos... as well as many more. The bird feeds on pests, such as lice, fleas, and ticks, especially in hard-to-reach places, as well as blood from any open wounds.

▶ This common cuckoo fledgling dwarfs its eager dunnock foster parent. The dunnock's instinct to feed its young is so strong, it fails to recognize that this giant youngster is an imposter.

Crafty cuckoo

A brood parasite takes advantage of other animals at breeding time, using them to raise its own offspring. The female cuckoo lays her egg in another bird's nest. The chick hatches, pushes out the other eggs, and demands food from its new parents. Other brood parasites include cowbirds, whydahs, and honeyguides.

SHOWTIME Spectacular!

Rivals for attention

Impressing partners is only a part of courtship. Animals may also have to compete with rivals who want to get in on the action and steal their partner.

Most creatures spend their time keeping a low profile, trying to stay unnoticed by predators. But there are times when an animal needs to make itself known, showing off any special features, either to attract a mate or to discourage a rival or enemy from approaching.

FLICKER, FLASH

The female ***glowworm*** *is actually a wingless beetle and glows to attract a winged male for mating.*

DRESS UP

A male ***ruff*** *erects his beautiful soft collar of pale feathers as he struts and calls when breeding.*

KICK, PUNCH

A female ***hare*** *plays hard to get as she "boxes" with a male to test his health, speed, reactions, and vigor.*

BLOW UP

A male ***greater frigate*** *stretches his gular (throat) pouch to show his potential as a mating partner.*

Courting couples

Animal courtship is not just a quick flirt for fun—it's a serious test. Each partner checks the other is the correct species, strong and healthy, and will pass on good genes to any offspring.

FAN OUT

A ***peacock*** *fans out his shimmering, green tail to impress a peahen. The brighter the colors, the more attractive his tail appears.*

FEED ME

A ***European bee-eater*** *pair give each other food morsels as they flutter like butterflies when courting.*

PUFF OUT

The male ***hooded seal*** *impresses potential partners by inflating a balloon of skin out of its nose.*

FLAG UP

A courting male ***anole lizard*** *flicks out his colorful throat fan, or dewlap, to attract a mate.*

Bright SPARKS

Q: What do chimps, dolphins, octopuses, elephants, parrots, dogs, and monkeys have in common?

A: They are some of the animal world's smartest cookies. Their range of talents—including tool use, problem solving, and teamwork—make them top of the class.

Using tools

Many animals have developed incredible techniques to obtain food otherwise unattainable for them. The Egyptian vulture uses a stone as a hammer to crack a tough egg, while the woodpecker finch extracts grubs from tree holes with a cactus spine. The master is the chimp—it not only uses tools, but also modifies them. For example, it chews the end of its termite "fishing stick" to make it sleeker and easier to poke into the mound.

The Egyptian vulture drops a stone onto an ostrich egg to break it open and feed on the nutritious contents.

Chimps have developed a clever way to collect termites. They poke a stem into a termite nest, then simply withdraw it and lick off the termites.

This veined octopus carries a discarded cockle shell for shelter.

Problem solving

Problem: if you are soft-bodied, how do you guard against hungry enemies? Solution: borrow someone else's protection. The hermit crab uses this technique and will try on several old whelk shells for size to find the best fit. Small fish and octopuses also take advantage of empty seashells as temporary shelters.

SPECIAL STORAGE

The acorn woodpecker slots acorns and other nuts into purpose-pecked bark cracks, adding more holes each year.

Dolphins "talk" using clicks and squeaks as they corral sardines into a baitball, where they can be picked off easily.

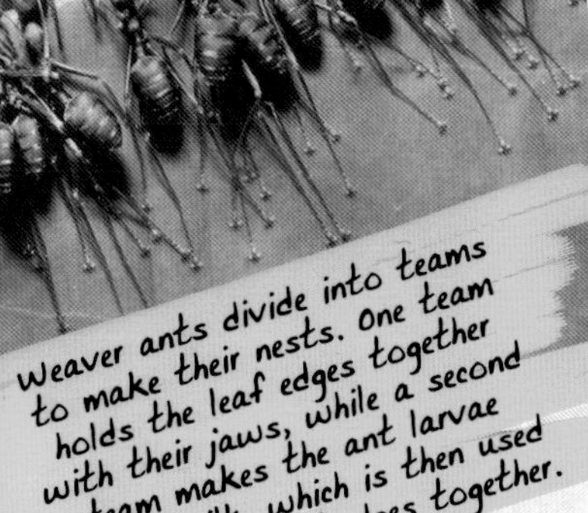

Weaver ants divide into teams to make their nests. One team holds the leaf edges together with their jaws, while a second team makes the ant larvae produce silk, which is then used to "sew" the leaf edges together.

Dream team

Each member of an animal team knows its place and its purpose within the group. Ants are preprogrammed to only follow a few simple instincts, so rarely adapt to new situations. With a decreasing fish population in the oceans, dolphins, however, have developed new methods of finding food—such as chasing trawler nets laden with fish, to feed on any escapees.

abcdef $2 \times 2 = 4$

Strength in NUMBERS

Living and working together in a group can offer some species many advantages. With more animals, there is a greater number of resources—more eyes on the lookout, more defensive weapons to protect the young, and more teeth and claws to attack prey.

Mighty migration

Animals go on annual or seasonal journeys, called migrations, usually due to changes in climate or a seasonal lack of food. Every year, at the start of the wet season (October–November), Christmas Island red crabs move across the shore like an unstoppable red tide, marching into the sea to lay eggs in their millions.

Body building

An inconvenient gap in the path is no problem for a swarming ant colony, especially when they are army ants on the march. The ants simply build a bridge from their own bodies. Neighboring ants lock legs as more climb over them to lengthen the interlinked chains. The bridging ants may stay like this for hours, and even die, as their fellow workers surge over and resume the search for fresh food.

Hound dogs

African wild dogs can take down large prey, up to 20 times their own size—using teamwork. The lead dog picks out a young, old, or sick quarry such as a wildebeest. With dogged determination the pack hounds the desperate victim for many miles, until it is so weak from exhaustion that they can move in for the kill.

Savage swarms

Locusts require a few months of good conditions to breed and build up their numbers. Gradually, they form an enormous gathering, capable of completely consuming vegetation across an entire region. Continuously in search of fresh greenery, swarms containing hundreds of millions of locusts can quickly ravage farm crops.

ANY HINT OF BLOOD IN THE WATER SENDS A GROUP OF RED-BELLIED PIRANHAS INTO A FEEDING FRENZY. WITH DOZENS OF SETS OF RAZOR-SHARP SLASHING TEETH, THEIR FEROCIOUS ATTACK IS IMMEDIATE AND OFTEN FATAL.

Strange Babies

Many animal parents have strong caring instincts, and will even risk their lives to save their babies. Some creatures go to extremes to give their offspring the best chance of survival. The young of some species are born while still at an early stage of development, when they are vulnerable and require constant care. They also look nothing like their parents—in fact, some animal babies look very odd indeed.

▼ A female giant panda gives birth to a single cub, which may stay with her for two years or more. Once a cub is weaned (after the first year), the mother may leave it for days at a time, while she forages for food.

Mini me or metamorphosis?

Some animal offspring, such as seal pups and tiger cubs, are unmistakable mini versions of their parents. Others, such as tadpoles and caterpillars, change dramatically from birth to adulthood. These drastic changes in shape, called metamorphoses, allow the youngsters to live in different environments and eat different foods from the parents, to avoid competing against each other.

Pink and hairless

Many newborn mammals and birds are born when they are still pink and hairless. Their eyes and ears are closed, and they can only feed and sleep. The mother can leave them to find food for herself—once the youngsters are hidden in a nest or a burrow. Her offspring are entirely dependent on her for protection and food.

◀▲ Most caterpillars hatch from eggs a few days after they are laid. They consume vast amounts of leaves before pupating inside a chrysalis and emerging in their adult form to feed on flower nectar.

▼ Seal cubs look just like their parents, except they are born with white fur. They feed on their mother's rich milk and grow faster than any other mammal of their size.

▶ A newborn kangaroo doesn't have proper arms or legs. Yet straight away it has to climb from the birth opening and through its mother's fur to her pouch. Then it attaches to a teat, and stays there for six months until ready to leave the pouch.

Born at an early age

Marsupial mammals such as kangaroos, koalas, wombats, and possums are born at a very early stage of development. Many do not even have recognizable eyes or ears, and their limbs are just flaps or "buds" on the featureless body. These newborns do little except wriggle to the mother's pouch, or marsupium, latch onto a teat with their barely formed mouth, and feed on her milk. Within the protection of the pouch, they continue the stages of development that other mammals go through while still in the womb.

▶ The Virginia opossum may have more tiny pink babies (below) than she has teats. Some die so that the survivors can grow big enough for a ride (above).

Brilliant Builders

Animals create some amazing structures, whether building alone or in groups. Everything they build is for a purpose—a nest to protect their young, a bridge to get from one place to another, or a trap to capture prey. Building methods can vary, depending on what materials are available in a particular habitat.

Supersize it

Some creatures make massive constructions compared to their size. Termites are insects that are only the size of peas, yet their mounds can tower more than 32 ft (10 m) high—that's equivalent to a skyscraper more than 1.5 mi (2.5 km) tall. Other outsizers dig down deep. A network of tunnels built by prairie dogs in Texas, U.S., covered 23,000 sq mi (60,000 sq km) and housed 400 million of these rodents—20 times more people than in the largest cities.

Actual-size termite

Adult human

20-ft termite mound

◀ Much of the termite mound above the ground is hollow chimneys, made of sun-baked earth. They provide air-conditioning to the main nest below ground level.

◀ The masked weaver tears leaves and stems into strips and delicately intertwines them to create its ball- or flask-shaped nest.

Perfect homemakers

Animals often build nests or burrows to live in for just a short time, usually to raise their young. Most of their behavior is instinctive, but skills and techniques improve greatly with practice. Nests can be made out of a wide range of natural materials, such as grass and mud, as well as materials from other animals, such as feathers and fur.

▶ The breeding nest of the harvest mouse is hardly larger than a tennis ball. It is built in between stems, high above the ground, to protect the young from danger.

◀▼ A beaver lodge can reach up to 65 ft (20 m) wide and 16 ft (5 m) high.

My home is my castle

The beaver's house, or lodge, is a solid construction of branches, rocks, twigs, and mud. Each generation of beavers carefully fells trees, gnaws off boughs, and adds reinforcements to make an amazing fortress that even hungry wolves and bears cannot break into.

Super STRENGTH

Heavyweight

Elephants can lift logs and other objects weighing up to one ton with their trunks—but the elephant has a great body weight, too, at 5 tons. So a fairer measure of strength is to compare weight moved against body weight—for an elephant, this is just 1/5.

◀ Elephants are the strongest of all land animals, but that's mainly due to their great size.

Human weightlifters can hoist more than three times their body weight, but that's puny compared to some insects. We are weaklings in other ways too, like our jumping ability, pulling power, or bite strength. But we are champions in one way—as athletic all-rounders.

Weasels are the world's smallest carnivores, with some individuals weighing little more than one ounce (30 g). They must eat at least one third of their own body weight every day to survive, and can bring down rabbits weighing 35 oz (one kilogram) or more.

A DUNG BEETLE CAN PULL MORE THAN 1,000 TIMES ITS OWN BODY WEIGHT.

▶ Dung beetles can roll balls of fresh dung up to 30 times more than their own body weight.

ANTS CAN LIFT UP TO 50 TIMES MORE THAN THEIR OWN BODY WEIGHT AND CAN CARRY THE LOAD OVER A DISTANCE OF MANY FEET.

Rolling home

Dung beetles roll excrement—from animals including rhinos, wolves, antelopes, elephants, and cats—into balls. While the dung is still moist, the beetles roll the balls to a suitable place, lay eggs inside them, and bury them. The grubs then feed on the dung when they hatch.

Bite size

Bite power depends on whether the biter is angry or relaxed, and whether it uses all its teeth and jaws. Lions, hyenas, sharks, and crocodiles are all super-crunchers, able to crush the bones of prey with ease. However, the extinct dinosaur *T rex* probably had the strongest bite of any animal that has ever lived.

A SHARK CAN BITE 60 TIMES HARDER THAN A HUMAN.

▶ Great white sharks have a strong bite, but the real damage comes from its razor-sharp teeth that can easily saw through flesh and bone.

Can You See Me?

One of the oldest tricks in the animal world is for your body shape, color, pattern, or texture to mimic your surroundings. Camouflage is all about visual trickery and blending in, whether it's to stay unnoticed by enemies or lurk unseen near prey.

A broken-off tree stump merits no second look. Just as well for the great potoo, a night-hunting bird that must stay completely still by day.

Acting the part

Camouflage depends not only on colors, patterns, and shapes, but on movements, too. It's no good merging perfectly into the surroundings, if a sudden movement gives the game away. To be successful, camouflaged creatures must move with extreme care. If the leaf it is resting on blows in the wind, the animal must hang on and sway with it, or risk discovery.

The imperial moth is highly camouflaged on the forest floor, and must rustle and flip with the real leaf litter.

To remain concealed, the leaf-tail gecko must mimic the random motion of a dead leaf—whether remaining motionless or moving with the breeze.

Peering faces

Some predators are not so much well camouflaged as well hidden. Forest frogs, desert toads, and soil-dwelling spiders burrow into the ground, leaving only their eyes and ears exposed to detect passing prey. They must stay like this for hours, until their victim relaxes and strays within reach of their lightning strike.

The Chacoan horned frog almost buries itself in soil, waiting for a beetle or grub to pass by.

A SHARK'S COLORING HELPS IT TO SNEAK UP ON PREY—ITS DARK BACK BLENDS WITH THE SEABED, WHILE ITS PALE BELLY MATCHES THE LIGHTER WATER ABOVE. THIS IS KNOWN AS "COUNTERSHADING."

The nose and eyes of the sidewinding adder match the grains of desert sand around it, hiding it almost completely from view as it waits patiently for its next victim.

Lurking danger

The bigger you are, the more difficult it is to hide from your prey. Big cats have some of the best camouflage colors and patterns, with each species well adapted to its main habitat. Lions are tawny to match the African savanna's dry grasses and dusty soils. Tiger stripes blend in with undergrowth and shrubs, and are particularly effective in the half-light when they are usually out hunting. Leopards and jaguars tend to stay among trees, and their spots mimic the dappled shadows cast by the twigs and leaves above.

A lion peers through the African grassland, perfectly color-matched to its surroundings, on the lookout for food—and danger.

The Big Lineup

Monster creatures are thriving all over the planet. A big animal can usually see off predators easily, and is likely to be strong and able to reach food that others can't. On the downside, these giants have to find and eat lots of food to get the energy they need to survive.

BLUE WHALE

Largest animal ever known

105 FT (32 M) Length of its body

198 TONS Weight of its body

3.5 TONS Weight of food it eats in one day

25 FT (7.6 M) Width of its tail

6 TONS Weight of its tongue

30 MPH (48 KM/H) Top swimming speed

1,300 LB (600 KG) Weight of its heart

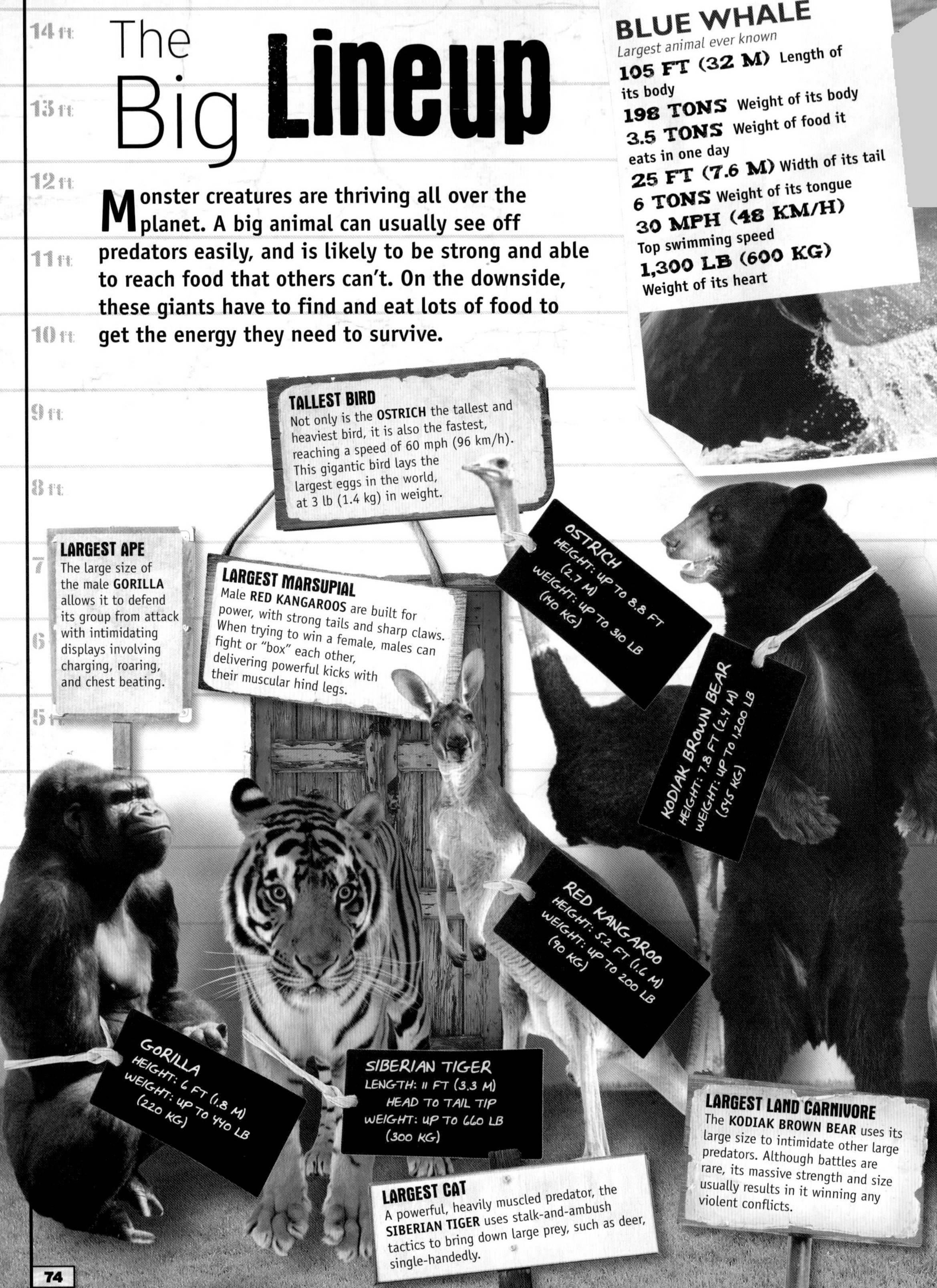

TALLEST BIRD

Not only is the **OSTRICH** the tallest and heaviest bird, it is also the fastest, reaching a speed of 60 mph (96 km/h). This gigantic bird lays the largest eggs in the world, at 3 lb (1.4 kg) in weight.

LARGEST APE

The large size of the male **GORILLA** allows it to defend its group from attack with intimidating displays involving charging, roaring, and chest beating.

LARGEST MARSUPIAL

Male **RED KANGAROOS** are built for power, with strong tails and sharp claws. When trying to win a female, males can fight or "box" each other, delivering powerful kicks with their muscular hind legs.

LARGEST LAND CARNIVORE

The **KODIAK BROWN BEAR** uses its large size to intimidate other large predators. Although battles are rare, its massive strength and size usually results in it winning any violent conflicts.

LARGEST CAT

A powerful, heavily muscled predator, the **SIBERIAN TIGER** uses stalk-and-ambush tactics to bring down large prey, such as deer, single-handedly.

LARGEST LAND MAMMAL
An angry or frightened **AFRICAN ELEPHANT** can bulldoze anything in its path. A single tusk can reach 10 ft (3 m) long.

LARGEST SEAL
A well-fed male **ELEPHANT SEAL** is as heavy as a real elephant. Dominant males, known as "beachmasters," fight fiercely to defend their territories.

TALLEST LAND MAMMAL
The muscular neck of the **GIRAFFE** is as long as a human is tall, and can be swung around like a battering ram to bash predators.

Incredible SCIENCE

Discover the breakthroughs that have shaped the world, and what science can reveal about our remarkable Universe.

◀ The power of a scanning electron microscope (SEM) homes in on the head of a tiny fruit fly, showing the 800 separate lenses that make up each of its two compound eyes.

Big BANGS

Explosions are the most powerful events in the Universe, capable of suddenly blasting apart anything from a rock to an entire giant star. They occur when heat, chemical, or nuclear reactions cause a dramatic and almost instantaneous expansion of gases. Some giant explosions, such as supernovae and volcanoes, occur naturally, but man-made explosions can also be very powerful.

Exploding star

The biggest explosion in the Universe is a supernova—the explosion that ends the life of a supergiant star. It may only be visible for a week, but can be seen far across the Universe, as bright as a galaxy of 100 billion stars.

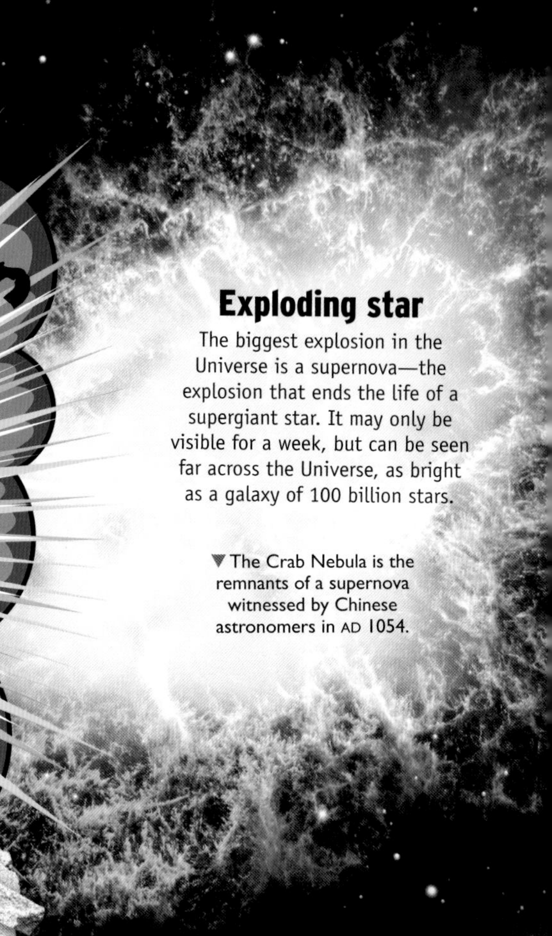

▼ The Crab Nebula is the remnants of a supernova witnessed by Chinese astronomers in AD 1054.

Blow me down!

To demolish a building without damaging anything nearby, engineers have to make it implode (explode inward). To do this, they place explosive charges in carefully chosen weak points in the building, then set them off in a particular sequence.

▲ Experts need to place explosives very carefully to bring down an unwanted building, such as this 18-story apartment block in Shenyang, China.

Death trap

Land mines are bombs that can be buried just beneath the surface of the ground. Packed with a chemical called Trinitrotoluene (TNT), a land mine explodes by detonation—a powerful shock wave rushes through it, turning all the TNT almost instantly to gas. The gas expands violently, causing terrible damage. A detonator (a tiny explosive device inside the mine) triggers the explosion. Detonators are designed to be triggered when someone steps on the mine or drives a vehicle nearby.

EXPLOSIVE STRENGTH

The power of explosions is often measured in comparison to TNT by weight.

ITEM	POWER
1. Large hand grenade	3 oz (85 g) TNT
2. World War II bomb	6 lb (2.7 kg) TNT
3. "Bunker-buster" bomb	1 ton TNT
4. Hiroshima atom bomb	15 kilotons (15,000 tons) TNT
5. Hydrogen bomb	50 megatons (25 million tons) TNT
6. Mount Toba eruption	85 megatons TNT
7. Supernova	1,000 trillion trillion tons TNT

▶ An entire rock face in a quarry is blasted away by a line of simultaneous explosions.

Volcanic violence

The VEI (Volcanic Explosivity Index) rates the power of explosive volcanic eruptions on a scale from 0 to 8. The Mount St. Helens eruption of 1980 had a VEI of 5. When Mount Toba in Indonesia erupted around 75,000 years ago, it had a VEI of 8, so it was 10,000 times more powerful than Mount St. Helens and was one of the largest explosions on Earth, ever.

▼ Volcanic eruptions are the most powerful natural explosions on Earth.

Rock blast

To blast rock from the ground, quarries usually use dynamite. Invented by Swedish chemist Alfred Nobel (1833–1896), dynamite was the first High Explosive, and consists of sticks of sawdust soaked in nitroglycerin and wrapped in paper. Nitroglycerin contains so much oxygen that it detonates easily when heated. Typically, the heat source is a current of electricity running through a wire set into the dynamite.

Chemical Clash

When a candle burns, metal goes rusty, or a cake rises in the oven, a chemical reaction is taking place. When chemicals meet and react, they change each other to form new chemicals. But not all chemical encounters are quite so gentle.

CHEMICAL REACTIONS ARE CONSTANTLY TAKING PLACE WITHIN THE 100 TRILLION OR SO LIVING CELLS INSIDE YOUR BODY, SO THERE MAY BE MORE THAN 400 BILLION REACTIONS TAKING PLACE INSIDE YOU EVERY SECOND!

Exploding pop

Dropping Mentos mints into cola makes the drink suddenly fizz up in a fountain of froth. The Mentos react chemically with the cola, instantly creating bubbles of carbon dioxide gas, which turn the cola into a gushing foam. Other substances create bubbles in soft drinks, but the chemicals in Mentos make the reaction especially dramatic.

▲ Rusting corrodes tough steel into flaky, brown iron oxide as it reacts with oxygen in the air.

Acid danger

Strong acids are dangerous chemicals because they react so powerfully. Acids contain hydrogen, and when mixed with water the hydrogen atoms are turned loose as highly reactive "ions." Splashed on skin, acids can cause terrible burns by absorbing water in a reaction that creates a lot of heat. Strong acids can also dissolve metals.

▲ Mentos are covered in minute pits that act as nucleation sites—places that concentrate gas formation.

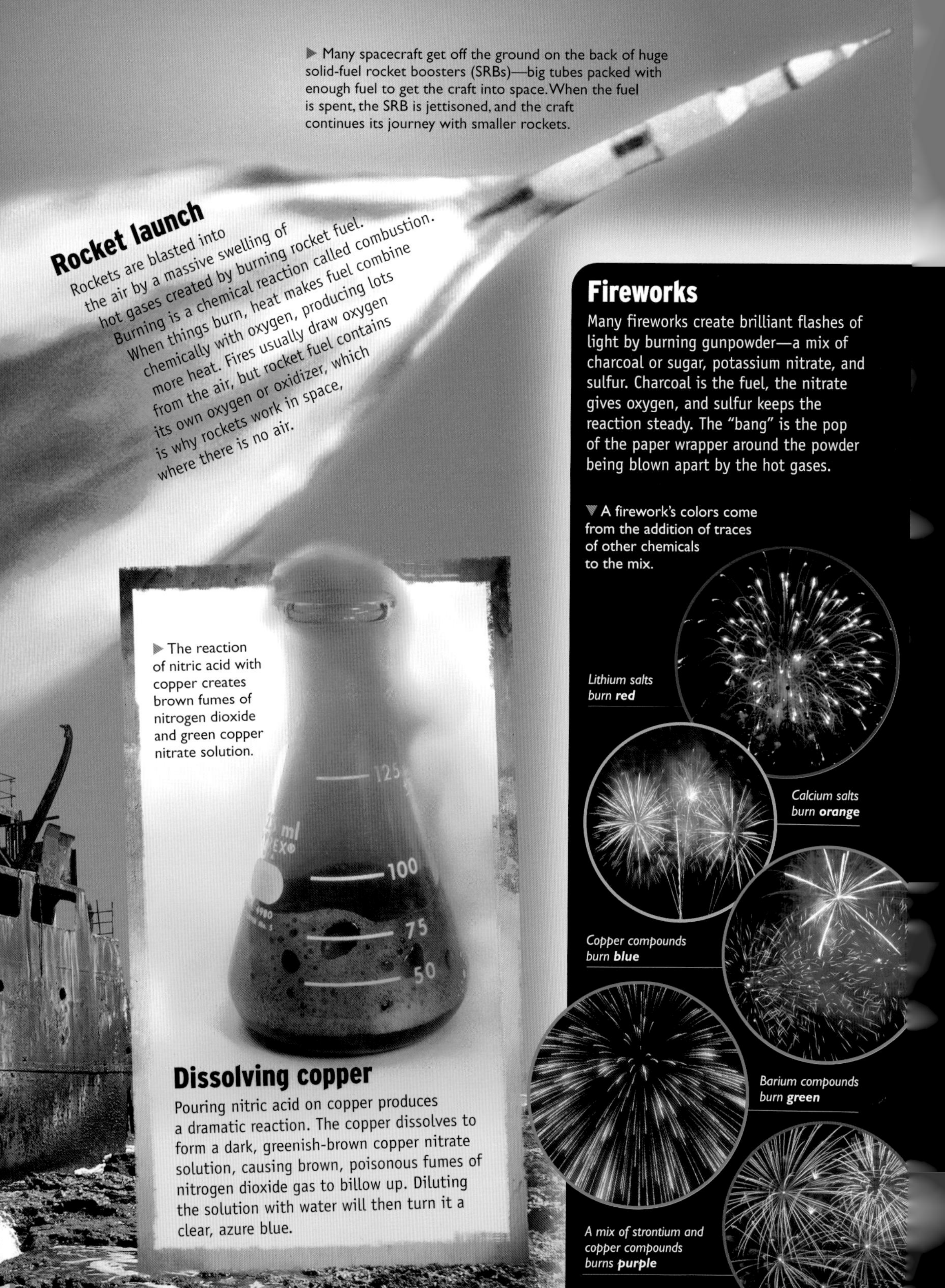

Many spacecraft get off the ground on the back of huge solid-fuel rocket boosters (SRBs)—big tubes packed with enough fuel to get the craft into space. When the fuel is spent, the SRB is jettisoned, and the craft continues its journey with smaller rockets.

Rocket launch

Rockets are blasted into the air by a massive swelling of hot gases created by burning rocket fuel. Burning is a chemical reaction called combustion. When things burn, heat makes fuel combine chemically with oxygen, producing lots more heat. Fires usually draw oxygen from the air, but rocket fuel contains its own oxygen or oxidizer, which is why rockets work in space, where there is no air.

Fireworks

Many fireworks create brilliant flashes of light by burning gunpowder—a mix of charcoal or sugar, potassium nitrate, and sulfur. Charcoal is the fuel, the nitrate gives oxygen, and sulfur keeps the reaction steady. The "bang" is the pop of the paper wrapper around the powder being blown apart by the hot gases.

A firework's colors come from the addition of traces of other chemicals to the mix.

Lithium salts burn ***red***

Calcium salts burn ***orange***

Copper compounds burn ***blue***

Barium compounds burn ***green***

A mix of strontium and copper compounds burns ***purple***

The reaction of nitric acid with copper creates brown fumes of nitrogen dioxide and green copper nitrate solution.

Dissolving copper

Pouring nitric acid on copper produces a dramatic reaction. The copper dissolves to form a dark, greenish-brown copper nitrate solution, causing brown, poisonous fumes of nitrogen dioxide gas to billow up. Diluting the solution with water will then turn it a clear, azure blue.

Wonder MATERIALS

Natural materials such as diamond and silk can be incredibly tough. But now scientists are creating a range of entirely man-made wonder materials. Some are incredibly light, others are incredibly strong, and some are both.

◀ The high-strength carbon fibers inside CRP help to absorb pressure. In a pole-vaulter's pole, CRP's combination of strength and flexibility gives a vaulter extra lift as it springs straight.

Carbon power

By embedding long fibers made of carbon in plastics, scientists make a material called carbon reinforced plastic (CRP). The plastic keeps it very light, but the fibers give it both strength and flexibility—perfect for the light, strong springiness needed for a pole-vaulter's pole. CRP is known as a "composite" because it combines plastic and carbon.

Jelly light

Aerogels are materials so light that they almost seem to float. Gels are jellylike materials that are mostly liquid. Aerogels are made by sucking liquid out of a gel and replacing it with gas. The gas filling not only makes aerogels amazingly light, but also very good barriers to heat.

▶ Aerogel stops the heat of the bunsen burner flame reaching the flower entirely.

CARBON FIBERS ARE FOUR TIMES STRONGER THAN STEEL WHEN PULLED, YET JUST ONE QUARTER OF THE WEIGHT.

▶ The LCROSS mission smashed a rocket with a wurtzite boron nitride nose into the Moon deliberately to throw up dust for scientists to analyze.

Tough titanium

Alloys are created by adding materials to a metal. Alloys of aluminum and magnesium are tough and light—which is why they are used to build aircraft. But the heat generated as high-speed jets tear through the air may be too much for aluminum alloys. So the fastest jets, such as the *F22 Raptor*, are made mostly from incredibly tough, superlight titanium alloys.

Super strong

Wurtzite boron nitride is the world's hardest material—harder even than diamond. It is used wherever materials need to be really, really tough and cost doesn't matter—from the heads of oil drills to the tips of "bunker-busting" bombs.

▲ With a superlight, superstrong titanium alloy fuselage (main body), the *F22 Raptor* can fly at speeds of up to 1,500 mph (2,400 km/h).

▶ The *Seabreacher* is a submersible made of Kevlar. It is so light and strong that it can burst out of the water like a dolphin.

The toughest threads

In 1961, DuPont chemist Stephanie Kwolek (b. 1923) discovered how to spin fibers from liquid chemicals such as oil. These "aramid" fibers are amazingly strong—threads of the aramid fiber Kevlar are five times stronger than steel. Kevlar has many applications, from helping to make puncture-resistant bicycle tires to strengthening cables used in suspension bridges.

▶ The fibers of Kevlar (a modified form of nylon) are incredibly tough for their weight, so they are used to make stabproof and bulletproof vests.

Deep

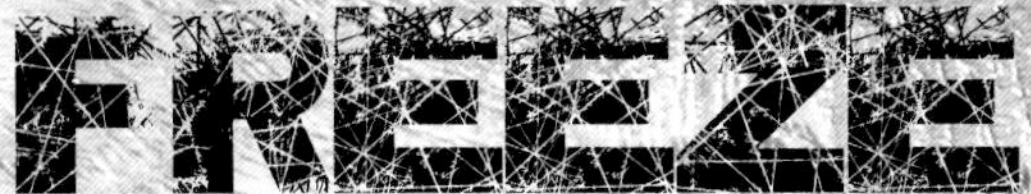

Freezing point, when water turns to ice, might seem pretty cold, but it can get much colder in locations such as Siberia and Antarctica. Elsewhere in the Solar System there are places that make Antarctica seem scorching. And in laboratories, scientists can create temperatures so cold that even atoms nearly freeze up.

1 Maximum chill

The coldest temperature possible is known as Absolute Zero. This is 0 Kelvin, or –459.67°F (–273.15°C). At this temperature atoms have no energy at all and do not even vibrate.

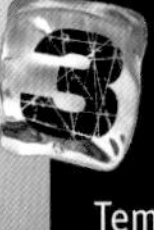

3 Supercold boomerang

Temperatures near Absolute Zero might only be achieved in a lab, but there is at least one place in the Universe that comes pretty close. In a cloud of gas known as the Boomerang nebula, the temperature is thought to be just 1K (–457.87°F, or –272.15°C).

2 Coldest ever

In 2003, scientists cooled sodium gas inside a magnetic container to the coldest temperature ever achieved on Earth. It was just half a nanokelvin—half a billionth of a degree—above Absolute Zero!

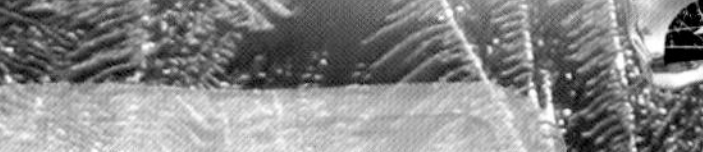

MEASURING UP

Temperature is measured on three scales. In everyday life, people use degrees Fahrenheit (°F) or degrees Celsius (°C). You can convert from °F to °C using a simple formula: subtract 32, divide by 9, and multiply by 5. To convert from °C to °F, divide by 5, multiply by 9, and add 32. Scientists may prefer to use the Kelvin scale, which is identical to Celsius but starts at a different place. While 0°C is the freezing point of water, 0K (–459.67°F, or –273.15°C) is the lowest temperature possible and is called Absolute Zero.

Chilled matter

Substances normally exist in one of three states—gas, liquid, or solid—depending on the temperature. But at 17 nanokelvins above Absolute Zero scientists can push gases into another state, known as a Bose-Einstein condensate (BEC). In a BEC, atoms have so little energy that if a beam of light is passed through them then it will come to a complete standstill.

▶ Ultracold rubidium atoms (top) briefly condense into a BEC (center) before evaporating again (bottom).

Inside this flask, helium gas has been cooled to the point where it turns liquid.

▶ Antarctica experiences the coldest natural temperatures on Earth.

6 Ice station

The coldest outside temperature ever recorded on Earth was –128.6°F (–89.2°C) at the Russian Vostok Station in Antarctica on July 21, 1983.

4 Helium liquefies

Helium remains a gas until incredibly low temperatures. It finally becomes a liquid at 4K (–452.2°F, or –269°C).

7 Brrrr!

On February 6, 1933, the temperature in one of the world's coldest towns, Oymyakon, in Siberia, plunged to a bitterly cold –90 °F (–67.7°C).

-269°C | -235°C | -89.2°C | -67.7°C | 0°C

-452.2°F | -315°F | -128.6°F | -90°F | 32°F

5 Icy moon

The coldest place in the Solar System is Neptune's moon, Triton. It is so far from the Sun that it receives none of its heat, and temperatures on its surface drop to –315°F (–235°C).

▼ Uniquely, water expands when it freezes, making it less dense, which is why icebergs float.

Neptune

Triton

8 Freeze!

Water normally freezes solid to become ice at 273.15K (32°F, or 0°C). The addition of salt or pressure keeps it liquid at slightly lower temperatures.

Super SCORCH

The more energy things have, the hotter they get. Our bodies get their warmth from the energy released by reacting chemicals. The Sun and stars get their immense heat from the energy released when atoms are forced together by the tremendous pressures in their cores.

▶ Beneath the pale clouds, the surface of Venus is almost hot enough to melt tin.

3 On the boil

A liquid's boiling point is the hottest it can get without becoming a gas. The boiling point of water is normally 212°F (100°C). Beneath geysers, underground pressure allows water to be "superheated" to higher temperatures.

4 Trapped heat

Venus' thick atmosphere traps the Sun's heat, causing temperatures on the planet's surface to reach 896°F (480°C).

37°C 41°C 100°C 480°C 827°C

98.6°F 106°F 212°F 896°F 1,521°F

▲ This thermogram is created using infrared radiation. It indicates differences in temperature by color, from hot (white) to cool (blue).

2 Hot spots

In Dallol, Ethiopia, maximum daily temperatures averaged more than 106°F (41°C) for six years between 1960 and 1966!

5 Hot coals

The temperature of coal fires can vary, but coal can burn at up to 1,521°F (827°C).

1 Body heat

Your body temperature is normally around 98.6°F (37°C), except when you have a fever. Even then it only reaches 104°F (40°C)—much hotter would kill you.

◀ These sulfurous volcanic pools lie in a region that experiences some of the hottest temperatures on Earth: Dallol, in Ethiopia.

Molten metal

The bonds between atoms in a metal are very strong, so most metals don't melt until they get very hot. Some steels melt at around 1,517°F (825°C), while tungsten doesn't melt until around 6,170°F (3,410°C).

8 Blue star

The hottest known star in the Universe is Eta Carinae. Its surface reaches more than 72,000°F (40,000°C), which is why it glows blue-hot.

▼ In 2005, astronomers realized that superhot Eta Carinae is not one star but two.

10 Hottest ever

In February 2010, scientists working deep underground in New York, U.S., in the tunnels of the Brookhaven National Laboratory's RHIC (Relativistic Hadron Ion Collider) created the hottest temperatures since the beginning of the Universe. In the RHIC's tunnels, gold atoms smash into each other at almost the speed of light, briefly creating temperatures of 7 trillion°F (4 trillion°C).

▼ The Sun's atmosphere, or corona, reaches a blistering 1,800,000°F (1,000,000°C).

7 Sun burned

The temperature on the surface of the Sun is about 9,900°F (5,500°C). This extreme heat gives sunlight its yellow color—if the Sun were cooler, it would be more reddish. At the center of the Sun, temperatures reach more than 24 million°F (15 million°C)!

9 Big Bang heat

The hottest natural temperature was at the very start of the Universe, during the Big Bang, when temperatures briefly reached 3–5 trillion°F (2–3 trillion°C).

▶ Variations in microwave radiation in this computer map of the sky reveal the lingering glow of the Big Bang.

GIGANTIC Universe

To us tiny humans, Earth seems pretty big. A few centuries ago people thought it was the biggest thing in the Universe. But as telescopes reveal more, it's becoming clear that Earth is seriously small. Some things in space are so huge, they make our entire galaxy seem like a grain of sand on a beach.

1 Biggest planet

At 142,984 km across, Jupiter is the biggest planet in the Solar System. Its diameter is 11.2 times larger than Earth, and its volume is 1.43×10^{15} km^3, so you could cram over 1,300 Earths inside Jupiter and still have room to spare!

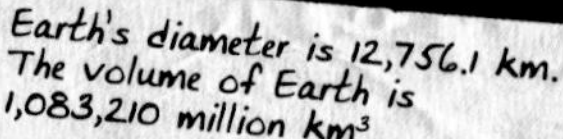

Earth's diameter is 12,756.1 km. The volume of Earth is 1,083,210 million km^3.

2 The Sun

The Sun dwarfs Jupiter. It is 1.4 million km across—109 times bigger than Earth. Its volume is $1{,}412 \times 10^{16}$ km^3, which means you could get 1.3 million Earths inside the Sun.

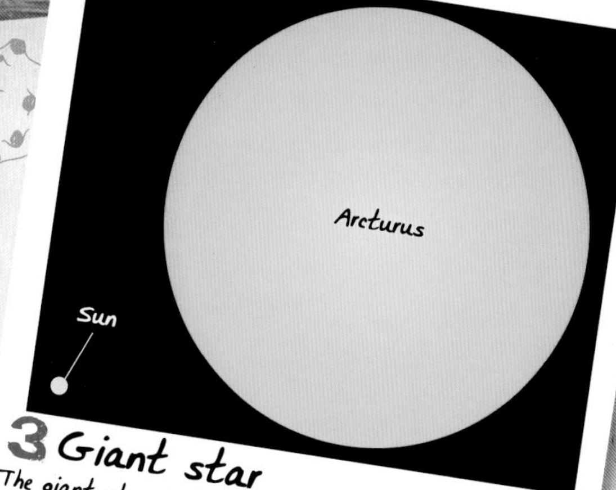

3 Giant star

The giant star Arcturus is 25 times the diameter of the Sun, and is the third brightest star in the night sky.

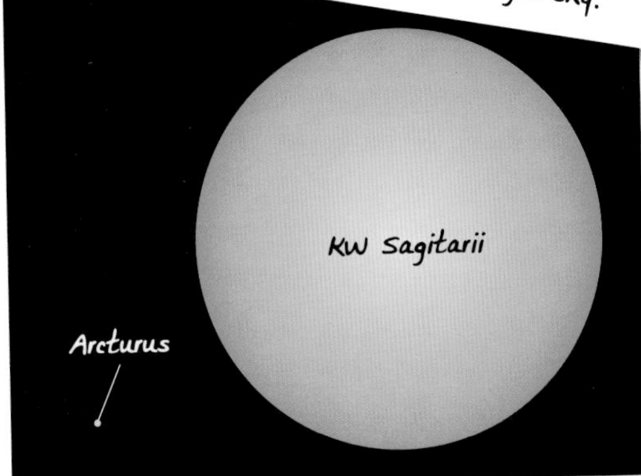

4 Biggest star

The biggest star we know of is the hypergiant KW Sagitarii. At almost 2 billion km across it is 60 times bigger than Arcturus and more than 1,500 times bigger than the Sun!

LIGHT-YEARS

Dimensions in space are so vast that it's not practical to measure them in kilometers. Instead, astronomers measure things in light-years. Light always travels at the same speed—299,792 km/sec—so distances can be measured by the number of years it takes for light to cross them. A light-year is the distance light travels in a year, which is 9,460 billion km.

Milky Way galaxy

If the Sun were the size of a grain of sand, the Milky Way would be the size of the Sun!

5 Our galaxy

Our Sun is just one of about 400 billion stars in the Milky Way galaxy. The Milky Way is 100,000 light-years across—a million trillion km.

6 Biggest galaxy

The IC 1101 galaxy is 5 million light-years across—50 times as big as the Milky Way.

7 Supercluster

The Milky Way is one of more than 2,000 galaxies in the cluster of galaxies known as the Virgo Cluster. But this cluster is tiny compared with superclusters such as the Perseus-Pisces supercluster, which is more than 300 million light-years across—3,000 times as wide as the Milky Way. If the Sun were the size of a grain of sand, this supercluster would be almost as big as the Solar System.

8 Sloan Great Wall

The Universe is arranged like a gigantic spider's web. All the stars, galaxies, and clusters are concentrated in vast, thin walls. The biggest is the Sloan Great Wall, which is 1.37 billion light-years long—more than 12,000 times as wide as the Milky Way.

Mega IDEAS

As scientists explore the extremes of our world, they often need to use huge, complex pieces of equipment. Exploring the vastness of the Universe requires massive telescopes and research stations in space. Strangely, some of the biggest and most elaborate machines have been built to study things that are so tiny, they are invisible to the naked eye.

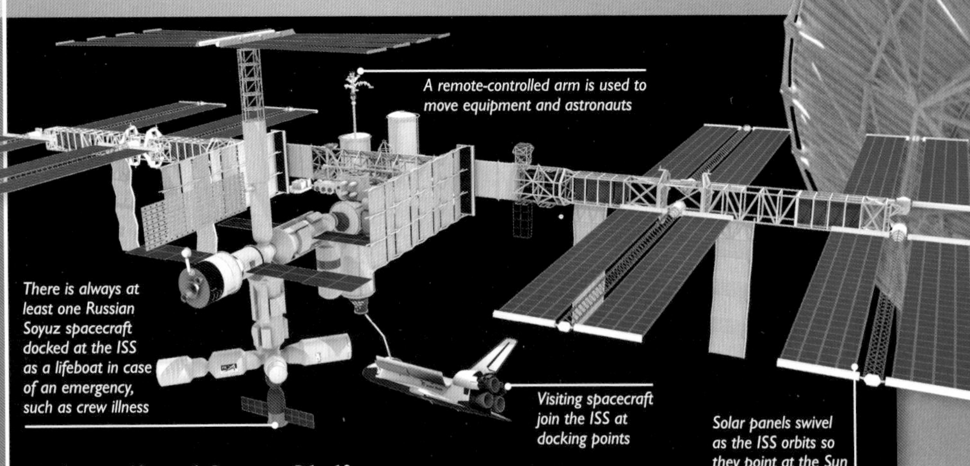

A remote-controlled arm is used to move equipment and astronauts

There is always at least one Russian Soyuz spacecraft docked at the ISS as a lifeboat in case of an emergency, such as crew illness

Visiting spacecraft join the ISS at docking points

Solar panels swivel as the ISS orbits so they point at the Sun

International Space Station

The biggest space station ever built, the ISS orbits between 173 mi (278 km) and 286 mi (460 km) above Earth. It is so big, it can be seen from the ground with the naked eye. Its parts were carried up bit by bit by dozens of space flights, then assembled in space by astronauts in more than 130 separate space walks.

▲ The ISS hurtles around Earth at an average speed of 17,239.2 mph (27,743.8 km/h), completing 15.7 orbits per day.

Human Genome Project

Every cell in your body carries instructions to keep you alive (and create your children), all contained on a tiny string of the chemical DNA. The instructions are in the form of thousands of chemical sequences called genes. The Human Genome Project was a huge international program to map the human genome (identify exactly where on human DNA every single gene occurs). The project began in 1990 and was completed in 2003.

▲ A computer image shows a tiny part of the map of DNA, with each bar showing one of the four chemical bases that make up the code.

Millennium Run

The Millennium Run is one of the biggest computer simulations ever created. The idea behind it was to create a computer model of every particle in a section of the Universe to test theories on how the Universe developed. In 2005 the first run traced what happened to every single one of ten billion particles, involving 20 million galaxies in a region of space 2 billion light-years across. Images generated by the simulation show how dark matter—a form of matter that cannot be detected by telescopes as it does not emit any radiation—is distributed across the Universe.

▼ A computer image generated by the Millennium Run shows how dark matter is distributed in the local Universe—an area 206 million light-years in distance across.

Very Large Array

Radio waves are very long, so capturing radio signals from distant stars and galaxies effectively requires huge radio dishes. Instead of a single big dish, they can use an array (series) of linked dishes spread over a vast area. The Very Large Array (VLA) on the Plains of San Augustin, New Mexico, U.S., has 27 dishes arranged in a "Y" shape up to 22 mi (36 km) apart.

▲ Each of the 27 dishes in the VLA measures 82 ft (25 m) across.

RADIO TELESCOPES SUCH AS THE VLA HAVE MAPPED CLOUDS OF GAS SHOWING THE SHAPE OF THE MILKY WAY, AND DISCOVERED WHAT SEEMS TO BE A MASSIVE BLACK HOLE AT ITS CENTER.

Small **WORLD**

Looking at your skin through a magnifying glass reveals all kinds of details invisible to the unaided eye. However, scientists have now developed microscopes that allow us to see a world that is on a much smaller scale. Even a good magnifying glass only magnifies objects by a few times. The most powerful scanning tunneling microscopes (STMs) magnify things billions of times, and can reveal particles smaller than atoms.

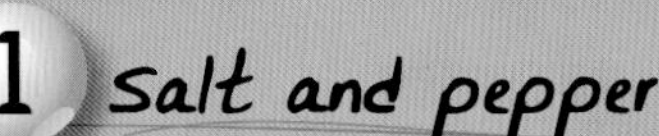

1 Salt and pepper

10^{-3} m (1 mm)

To the unaided eye, pepper looks pretty much like salt, only dark brown. But a good light microscope shows just how different they are. Pepper is, of course, the seed of a plant. Salt is a mineral crystal.

2 Human hair

10^{-4} m (100 micron)

Your hair may feel pretty smooth and fine, but under a microscope you can see that each hair has a rough surface, and looks rather like a tiny tree trunk.

3 Red blood cells

10^{-5} m (10 microns)

The most powerful light microscopes can show the tiny red cells in blood, but to see their shapes clearly you need a scanning electron microscope (SEM). SEM pictures show that when red blood cells are healthy, they are a neat button shape.

4 Bacteria

10^{-6} m (1 micron)
You can just about see bacteria with light microscopes, but SEM pictures can show detailed close-ups.

◀ Bacteria such as *Helicobacter pylori* live in many human stomachs, and can cause stomach upsets.

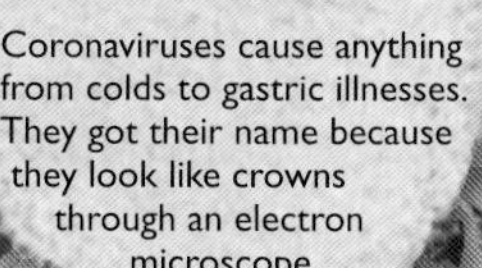

5 Virus

10^{-7} m (100 nanometers)
Viruses are much tinier than bacteria and can only be seen with electron microscopes, such as the transmission electron microscope (TEM).

Coronaviruses cause anything from colds to gastric illnesses. They got their name because they look like crowns through an electron microscope.

SCIENTISTS CAN MAKE ELECTRONIC DEVICES AS SMALL AS A SINGLE ATOM. VERY SOON, A POWERFUL COMPUTER NEED BE NO BIGGER THAN A GRAIN OF SAND.

6 Molecule

10^{-8} m (10 nanometers)
Atomic force microscopes (AFMs) and the most powerful TEMs can show actual strands of DNA.

◀ DNA can be seen clearly with a TEM, magnified almost half a million times.

7 Atom

10^{-9} m (1 nanometer)
To see an atom, you need a scanning tunneling microscope (STM).

MICROSCOPES

Light or optical microscopes use combinations of lenses to magnify things. They can magnify up to about 2,000 times. The smallest thing they can see is about 500 nanometers (500 billionths of a meter).

Electron microscopes can show things up to 20,000 times smaller. They don't use lenses at all—they fire electrons at their subjects and record the way the electrons bounce off. Instead of seeing an object directly, you look at a picture of it that builds up on a screen.

Scanning tunneling microscopes (STMs) and atomic force microscopes (AFMs) work by touch. AFMs run a sharp point that looks similar to an old-fashioned record needle over the subject. These microscopes can show atoms.

Microscopic Zoo

In recent years, scanning electron and tunneling microscopes have homed in on the world of insects and microbes to reveal them in amazing detail and clarity. Even the tiniest bugs appear as large and monstrous as creatures from another world. There are many, many more different species of these microscopic organisms than there are in all the rest of the living world put together.

◀▲ A tiny fruit fly seen through an SEM with a close-up of the "talons" on its leg (inset left).

Small fly

Magnified more than 800 times, this SEM image shows the two birdlike talons on the end of a fruit fly's leg. The hairlike stalks beneath the talons are covered with adhesive pads or "pulvilli." These allow the fruit fly to cling to vertical surfaces such as glass, which appear completely smooth to the naked eye. Scientists are hoping to develop artificial nanomaterials that adhere in a similar way.

Stomach bug

Transmission electron microscopes (TEMs) reveal the microscopic zoo living inside the human stomach. This is the bacteria *Helicobacter pylori* magnified 7,700 times. These bacteria get their name, "pylori," from the fact that they live in the pyloric (lower) part of many people's stomachs. Fortunately, they usually have no effect.

▲ *Helicobacter pylori* can move around by whipping its tail or "flagella."

Living jewels

Diatoms are algae that float in water and get their energy from the Sun, like plants do. They are so small, they can only be seen properly with an SEM. But SEMs reveal them to be astonishingly beautiful geometric "jewels." There are more than 100,000 different species.

▲ These fantastic, beadlike diatoms are only one hundredth of the width of a human hair.

▶ The spiny surfaces of these minute pollen grains help them stick to feathers and fur.

Plant packet

SEMs reveal the huge variety of different forms of pollen. Pollen is the dusty substance that flowers spread to help them reproduce. Each grain is a tough case holding male sex cells that must be delivered to the female ova or egg to create a seed for a new flower. Grains are so tough, they last tens of thousands of years, so archeologists can use SEM pictures of ancient pollen to identify plants that were growing long ago.

▼ A magnified head louse appears monstrous as it climbs along a human hair.

MICROSCOPIC NEMATODE WORMS MAKE UP 90 PERCENT OF ALL LIFE ON THE OCEAN FLOOR.

High life

In close-up, a head louse clinging to a human hair looks like a monster crawling along a tightrope. Head lice are tiny, wingless insects that live in the hair of living humans, lay their eggs on hair shafts, and feed entirely on human blood, sucked from the scalp.

▼ Protozoa such as this amoeba may be microscopic, but they are animals that can move around of their own accord.

The smallest animals

Protozoa are the smallest of all animals, made from just one cell. Most can only be seen under a microscope, yet they breathe, move, and reproduce like bigger animals. They live in water or damp places. Some protozoa can cause serious diseases. Others are helpful because they eat harmful bacteria and are food for fish and other animals.

Light FANTASTIC

In the last 50 years, scientists have come to understand light and radiation so well that they can now do things with it that might once have seemed like magic. The most exciting effects, such as the creation of holograms and measurements of astonishing accuracy, are achieved with laser light, but other kinds of light can be used for anything from seeing a living brain in action to spotting an invisible thumbprint at a crime scene.

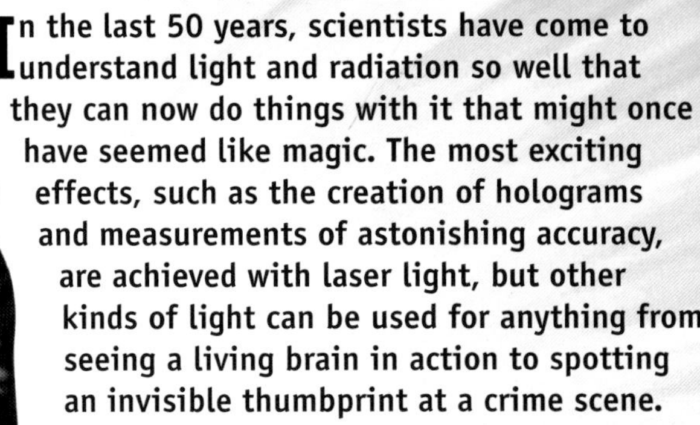

◀ A magnetic resonance image (MRI) scan "sees" inside a living body, showing both skeleton (white) and lungs (orange) in 3-D.

Body scan

Doctors and scientists use magnetic resonance imaging to take 3-D pictures that show the inside of the human body. It works by using powerful magnets to draw the nuclei (centers) of all the body's atoms into alignment. The magnet is then switched off. As the nuclei twist back to their normal position, they send out photons (particles of radiation). Detectors pick up the photons and a computer can then build up the 3-D image.

▼ This hologram shows Lindow man, a body preserved for 2,000 years in an English marsh.

Hologram magic

Holograms are 3-D images made by splitting a laser beam in two. One half, the reference beam, goes to the camera. The other bounces off the subject, breaking up the neat pattern of laser light waves. The camera records how this broken pattern interferes with (differs from) the reference beam, and this data can be used to project a 3-D image using lasers.

Nonmoving holograms have been around for half a century, but scientists are developing solid-looking moving holograms. In time, they may be able to create holograms that look like the real object.

▼ Ultraviolet (UV) light shows up otherwise invisible traces of blood and other body fluids splashed on a wall at a crime scene.

Spotting the crime

Criminals may think they've left no trace of their crime, but ultraviolet (UV) light can reveal all kinds of invisible evidence. Fingerprints and traces of body fluids at the crime scene that cannot otherwise be seen show up clearly under UV—light made of waves slightly shorter than violet light, just too short to be visible.

Laser precision

The precision of a laser beam means it can be used to take incredibly accurate measurements. For example, geologists can bounce lasers off satellites to measure the distance between continents an ocean apart to within a few millimeters. LiDAR (Light Detection and Rangefinding) is an amazing way of building up an instant 3-D map, in which a survey plane or satellite moves over a target and scans it with pulses of laser light. Detectors then pick up the reflections and use them to build up a 3-D image.

LASER LIGHT

The first laser beams were created in 1960 by Theodor Maimann. Laser light is like no natural light in the Universe. All natural light is said to be "incoherent" because it is a chaotic mix of lots of photons (particles of light) of different wavelengths. In laser light, the photons are all identical and in sync. The result is an intense beam of light of just one color, which is much harder to scatter than ordinary light. In fact, laser light can be bounced off the Moon and back and still stay in a single, tight beam.

Making stars

Shifting dust in the air makes it hard to get a clear view of space beyond. That's why stars appear to twinkle. Astronomers use computers to adjust telescope images for the dust, using bright stars as a reference—a technique known as Adaptive Optics (AO). But there aren't always bright stars in the part of the sky astronomers need to study, so instead they create their own guide star using a laser. As the laser is shone up into the sky it creates a little "star" where it hits sodium gas and makes it glow.

◀ An observatory sends out a beam of laser light to create a sodium laser guide star in the sky for astronomers.

Extreme Conditions

Some scientists learn about the world in laboratories, but others venture into the most extreme conditions to gather data and make observations. To find out more, some scientists will fly into the heart of a hurricane, endure months in the bitter chill of the Antarctic, walk into an active volcano, crawl into deep caves, dive to the depths of the ocean, climb towering rain forest trees, and much more. Where there is something to be learned, scientists will go.

Hot and hazardous

Volcanoes are incredibly dangerous up close. Although a protective suit provides a shield against the heat and fumes, it will not save a person in the event of an eruption. The two most famous volcanologists (volcano experts) of all time, Maurice and Katya Krafft, were killed, along with 41 journalists, when they were filming on Japan's Mount Unzen in 1991. Without warning, the volcano blasted out an avalanche of searingly hot gas and ashes that engulfed them in seconds.

Volcanologists test material from a live volcano.

DANGEROUS DINNERS

Cooking in chemist Helen Maynard-Casely's kitchen is a dangerous business. She uses ordinary ingredients such as cream, sugar, and bread, but she subjects them to extreme pressures and temperatures to see what happens to them. She might chill cream with liquid nitrogen at –274°F (–170°C), or squeeze burnt toast hard enough to turn the carbon it contains into diamonds. Her colleague, Colin Pulham, at the Edinburgh Centre for Science Under Extreme Conditions, in Scotland, makes diamonds by blasting carbon with dynamite!

Scientists wearing breathing masks brave the poisonous air of a cave to collect samples.

Storm chasers

Tornadoes are incredibly powerful storms. Their twisting funnels of winds can blast a building apart or whip a truck into the air. But they are localized and very brief, rarely lasting more than 15 minutes. Scientists such as Chuck Doswell and Dr. Josh Wurman have to chase the tornadoes they study at high speeds—and risk being caught in the storm themselves. The chase is so exciting that many people now pursue tornadoes just for the thrill, but authorities fear someone may soon be killed.

Going underground

Professor Hazel Barton is willing to go into Earth's depths to pursue her studies of bacteria that live in extreme conditions. Bacteria such as these can only be found in the most inaccessible caves. To study them, Professor Barton has to squeeze through narrow passages and swim through underwater lakes where visibility is practically zero and the air is often poisonous.

A storm chaser hurriedly sets down a weather probe in the path of an oncoming tornado.

The probe will measure conditions right in the heart of the tornado.

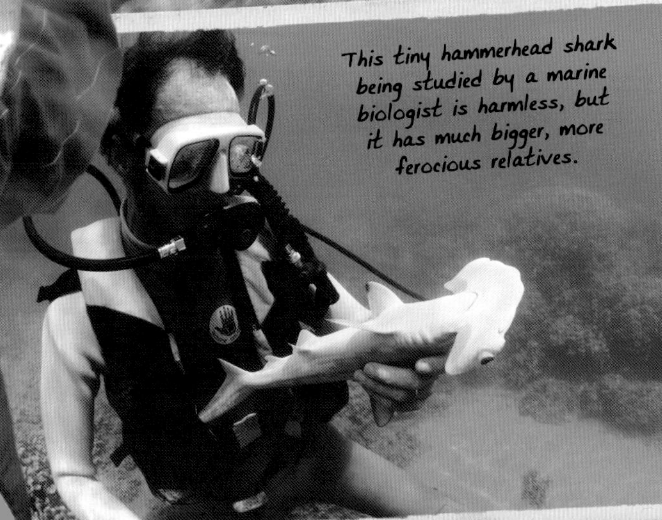

This tiny hammerhead shark being studied by a marine biologist is harmless, but it has much bigger, more ferocious relatives.

Ocean peril

Exploring the ocean can be difficult and even life threatening. In the surface waters, there is not only the danger of drowning, but also the threat of serious injury from potentially lethal creatures such as sharks, jellyfish, and stonefish. Deeper down, the water is bone-chillingly cold and pitch-dark—and the pressure is enough to crush a car.

Feel the FORCE

Force is what makes things happen. It can push things or pull them, speed them up or slow them down, draw them together or split them apart. Without forces, nothing would start or stop. Some forces—such as the force required to move your eye across this page—are tiny, while others are incredibly strong. Machines give us much more force than our bodies are capable of alone, but the most extreme forces are natural.

Muscle cars

Power is a measure of not only force but also how fast it is delivered. A kilowatt (kW) of power is a force of one newton delivered at one meter every second. A small family car can get by with less than 50 kW of power, but to accelerate quickly, high-performance cars need a lot of force, very fast. That's why the *SSC Ultimate Aero TT*'s engine generates an incredible 960 kW of power.

▼The *Emma Maersk* dwarfs any passing craft, and is powered by an engine that weighs more than 2,500 tons.

Ship power

The more weight that must be moved, the more force you need, so the world's most powerful motors are on the world's heaviest ship—the *Emma Maersk*, which is driven through the ocean by the mighty Wärtsilä-Sulzer RTA96 diesel. It produces more than 83 megawatts (million watts) of power—as much as 10,000 high-performance cars!

MEASURING FORCE

One newton is the force that makes a mass of one kilogram accelerate at one meter per second every second. It's roughly equivalent to the force you'd use if you threw a big pebble into the sea.

45 N	The force required to push an adult over
670 N	The force of a karate chop breaking a plank
300–730 N	The gravitational force holding you on the planet
2,000 N	A good kick on a football
2,900 N	The force of a karate chop breaking a concrete slab
7,000 N	The force of an accelerating car
500,000 N	The force of a large locomotive
770,000 N	The thrust of a jumbo jet's engines
33,000,000 N	The thrust of the *Saturn V* rocket
200 million trillion N	The gravitational pull between the Moon and the Earth
350 billion trillion N	The gravitational pull between the Sun and the Earth

ONE OF THE STRONGEST FORCES EVER MADE BY HUMANS WAS FOR THE SATURN V ROCKET THAT LAUNCHED THE APOLLO SPACECRAFT TO THE MOON. THE FIRST STAGE OF THE ROCKET GENERATED A THRUST OF 3.4 MILLION N.

The *SSC Ultimate Aero TT* is the most powerful sports car ever, and can reach a speed of more than 270 mph (430 km/h).

Fundamental forces

There are many kinds of force. "Contact" forces directly push or pull, for example when someone hits a ball. Others act "at a distance," with no direct contact. All the fundamental forces of the Universe—gravity, electromagnetism, and the two nuclear forces that hold atoms together—act at a distance. Forces like this depend inversely on the distance between the affected objects—that is, they get weaker the further apart they are.

Star quake

There are forces in the Universe that make anything on Earth look minuscule. On December 27, 2004, a flash of energy burst from the star SGR 1806-20 in what is called a "star quake." This quake had a power of 10,000 trillion trillion trillion watts. If the star had been even 10 light-years away from Earth it would have shaken the Earth to bits. Luckily, it was much further away!

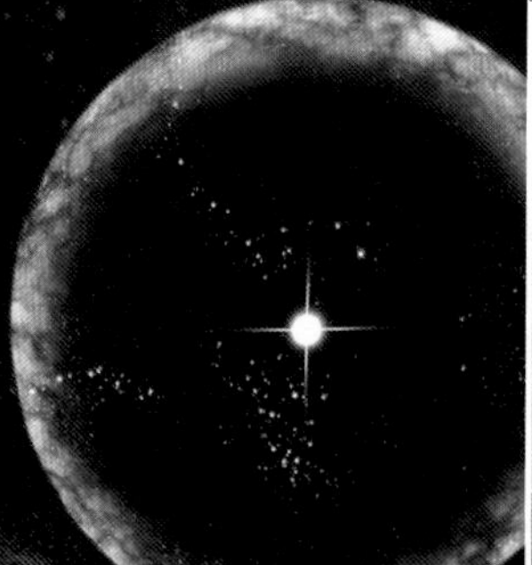

The energy burst from the star SGR 1806-20 in 2004 was so huge, it was visible from Earth.

Buildings were sent crashing down by the San Francisco quake of 1989.

MOUNTAIN SHAKING

Even the thrust of a rocket such as the mighty *Saturn V* is dwarfed by the natural forces involved in earthquakes. The faintest tremor has 60 million watts of power, while the most powerful earthquake ever, which hit Chile in 1960, generated 11 million billion watts. With this kind of force, earthquakes can lift up and knock down entire mountains.

STRANGE Brains

Most scientists are sensible, rational people, but sometimes they are working on ideas too complictated for most regular people to understand, so they can come across as being a bit peculiar. A few scientists become so obsessed with their research that their behavior seems truly eccentric (to put it mildly). Here are a few of the strangest scientists ever.

Elixir of life

The German alchemist, physician, and theologian Johann Konrad Dippel (1673–1734) was convinced he could find an elixir that would give people eternal life—and bring dead people back to life. He lived in Castle Frankenstein in Germany and tales of his experiments with corpses inspired Mary Shelley's famous story of Doctor Frankenstein and his monster. Dippel also invented Prussian Blue, the first of the chemical dyes that are used to give most clothes their colors today.

▲ Johann Dippel thought he could find a liquid that would bring the dead back to life.

He's electric

Serbian-born American Nikola Tesla (1856–1943) was the genius who gave us our modern electricity supply by pioneering the use of Alternating Current (AC) to send power over huge distances. However, some of Tesla's theories were slightly more eccentric. His idea of transmitting energy through the air without wires is now becoming a reality, but thankfully his plans for a giant death ray have not come to fruition.

▶ Nikola Tesla's many unusual ideas included using magnetic coils to turn Earth into a huge steerable spaceship.

I CAN FLY!

Some of the bravest—or craziest—scientists have been those who attempted to fly. There are many who tried strapping on wings to jump from high places and never lived to tell the tale. One of the most daring and successful was German flier Otto Lilienthal (1848–1896). Lilienthal made more than 2,000 pioneering hang glider flights in the 1890s. Sadly, a flight in 1896 proved fatal, but his experiments were crucial to the Wright brothers' famous first plane flight seven years later in 1903.

▶ Otto Lilienthal in 1893 on one of his glider flights in the hills near Berlin, Germany.

▶ Kevin Warwick shows off the cyborg arm that responds to his thoughts.

The cyborg

Cyborgs are creatures of science fiction—they are half-human and half-robot. But British scientist Kevin Warwick (b. 1954) is turning himself into a cyborg for real. He isn't mad, though—he wants to experiment on himself to find ways of helping disabled people. He has implanted electronic devices into his arm that link his nervous system directly to a computer, so that he can operate the computer just by thinking.

ROCKET MAN

One of the pioneers of space technology, German-born American engineer Wernher von Braun (1912–1977) was obsessed with rockets from a very young age. Aged 12, von Braun packed his toy wagon with firecrackers and lit them, causing him to shoot across the street while his neighbors looked on in horror. The incident resulted in him being arrested by the police. However, von Braun was not so much mad as just dedicated to his science.

▶ Wernher von Braun was responsible for the development of the V2 rocket in Germany, and went on to become a leading figure in the American space program after World War II.

BLACK Hole

Black holes are places where gravity is so strong that it sucks everything in, including light. They form when a star or part of a galaxy gets so dense that it collapses under its own gravity, shrinking to an infinitely small point called a singularity. Gravity around the singularity is so ferocious that it sucks in light, space, and even time.

WE CAN'T STUDY THE POINT AT WHICH LIGHT DISAPPEARS IN A BLACK HOLE IN SPACE, BUT SCIENTISTS AT THE UNIVERSITY OF ST. ANDREWS, SCOTLAND, CREATED A VIRTUAL BLACK HOLE IN THE LABORATORY USING PULSES OF LASER LIGHT.

Old supernova

Some black holes form when an old giant star collapses into a supernova. Astronomers can't actually see black holes, but sometimes they can detect their presence from their effect on other objects. Stars often form pairs, or binaries. If one star is a black hole, astronomers might be able to see the effect of its gravity on the visible companion star. They may also spot X-rays bursting from matter ripped off the companion star by the power of the black hole.

▶ An artist's impression of a black hole (right) ripping matter off its companion star (left) in a binary pair.

Supermassive

In the center of the Milky Way, in a region called Sagittarius A*, 20 million stars are packed into a space just 3 light-years across, and hurtling round at incredible speeds. Calculations show they must be in the grip of the gravity of an object two to three million times as heavy as the Sun yet only twice as big. It must be what astronomers call a "supermassive black hole." There is thought to be one at the heart of every spiral-shaped galaxy.

▲ Astronomers think the pink cloud near the galaxy NGC 4438 may be a bubble of gas belched out by a supermassive black hole at the galaxy's center. NGC 4438 is one of a pair of galaxies known as the Eyes Galaxies.

▲ The powerful magnetic forces created by a black hole inside the galaxy Pictor A shoot out an X-ray jet thousands of light-years long.

Jet propulsion

Black holes don't just suck things in. As they mash up the matter they draw in, they can spew out giant jets of the remnants—electrons and other subatomic particles. The gigantic black hole at the heart of the M87 galaxy is shooting out an astonishingly brilliant beam of these remnants for thousands of light-years into the darkness, like some kind of galactic searchlight.

INSIDE A BLACK HOLE

In every black hole there is a point of no return, called the event horizon. Beyond this point, time has no meaning and not even light can get out.

If you saw someone falling into a black hole, you would never see them reaching the event horizon. Instead, you would see them going slower and slower and getting redder and dimmer until they finally faded away altogether.

If you fell into a black hole, you would be stretched out like spaghetti because the pull of gravity on your feet would be so much stronger than on your head. Astronomers believe you'd become so "spaghettified" that you would eventually be ripped apart.

As you are being ripped apart, time would speed up dramatically—you'd see the future flashing by outside the black hole. But you couldn't get out, or get a message out, since even light cannot escape a black hole.

Tunnel through time

Some scientists think black holes may be linked to white holes. White holes, if they exist, would be the opposite of black holes—places where matter and radiation spew out into space like a fountain. A few scientists think that black holes and white holes could be linked by a tunnel through space and time called a wormhole. If there are such things as wormholes, it might be possible to slip through them to travel vast distances through space instantly, or even to travel through time to the future or the past.

A MASSIVE Mystery

Deep beneath the countryside on the border of Switzerland and France is a circular tunnel more than 16 mi (27 km) long. Inside it is the world's largest machine—the Large Hadron Collider (LHC). It is basically a long, ring-shaped tube in which hadrons (subatomic particles) are accelerated round and round, reaching incredible speeds, and then smashing together. What scientists hope to see in the smashed bits may answer fundamental questions about the Universe, such as why things have mass, momentum, and inertia.

▼ The LHC has to run at incredibly low temperatures. This is the refrigeration or cryogenics unit.

▶ This computer simulation of the detector screen in the LHC shows what may happen if a Higgs boson (see far right) is found, sending out a spray of subatomic particles as it breaks up.

◀ The LHC uses powerful magnets to accelerate particles through a tube in opposite directions at high speeds and then smash them together head-on. Special sensors track the new particles created briefly as the smashed particles break up.

▼ A crash test shows the effects of momentum dramatically—the car starts to crumple just before the test dummy is catapulted forward.

THE SEARCH FOR THE HIGGS BOSON

Forces such as electromagnetic radiation are transmitted by tiny "messenger" particles known as bosons. But scientists don't really know what mass is, or why things have inertia and momentum. It may all be down to a particle called the Higgs boson. This is how it might work:

Imagine a celebrity arriving at a party. As she swans in, fans (the Higgs bosons) crowd round her, giving her mass. The crowd makes it hard to get her moving, so she has inertia, but once they all start moving it's hard to stop them, so they give her momentum, too.

The mysterious Higgs boson is one of the things scientists are hoping to see among the smashed bits of particles in the LHC.

Momentum

Once an object is moving, it won't stop unless forced to because its mass propels it on. This is called momentum. It's what keeps the planets orbiting the Sun, and what carries a speeding roller coaster up the next incline. There's no more convincing demonstration of momentum in action than a crash test. When the test car slams into a wall, the momentum of the car and the dummy try to carry them on, which is why they smash into the wall with such force.

Inertia

It takes force to get something moving, because an object's mass keeps it rooted to the spot. This is called inertia. That's why a shot-putter has to be so strong to get the heavy shot moving.

◀ In order to throw the heavy shot, the shot-putter has to overcome all its inertia.

Mass

Momentum and inertia both depend on mass—the amount of matter involved. The heavier something is (the more massive it is), the more momentum and inertia it has.

Energy UNLEASHED

The nucleus of most atoms is fairly stable—but not always. Sometimes nuclei can partly disintegrate (radioactivity) or split in two (nuclear fission). Under severe pressure, different nuclei may fuse together (nuclear fusion). When any of these things happen, it unleashes matter and energy, known as radiation. The Universe is filled with natural radiation, and it's the energy of nuclear fusion that makes stars shine. Humans have learned to harness this energy, both to generate power and to create nuclear bombs—the most devastatingly powerful weapons of all time.

Solar power

The Sun shines because it is so big that the pressure in its core is huge—enough to force the nuclei of hydrogen atoms to fuse to make helium. The energy released by each individual fusion may be tiny, but there are so many atoms involved that the heat generated is enormous. This nuclear fusion drives temperatures in the Sun's core to 27 million°F (15 million°C) and makes the surface glow white-hot.

RADIOACTIVITY

The nucleus of an atom is made of two kinds of particle—protons and neutrons—and there are three main kinds of radioactivity:

Alpha decay is when an alpha particle (two neutrons and two protons) breaks away from the nucleus.

Beta decay is when a neutron splits to form a proton, emitting a beta particle (an electron) and a particle called an antineutrino.

Gamma rays are not emitted from the nucleus, but are a kind of electromagnetic radiation emitted from electrons like light, but they are very energetic and dangerous.

NUCLEAR FISSION

Conventional fuel is too bulky for submarines to carry for long voyages underwater, so many big subs are now powered by nuclear reactors. The reactors generate heat from the fission (splitting) of uranium atoms, which are large and easily split. The heat creates steam to drive the submarine's turbines. Just a few small rods of uranium fuel power a sub for many long voyages.

◀ Nuclear power allows submarines to stay on patrol underwater for long periods.

▼ Radiocarbon dating has helped scientists work out that Tollund man, whose preserved remains were found in a Danish bog, dates back to the 4th century BC.

THE BIGGEST BOMB EVER EXPLODED WAS THE 50 MEGATON RUSSIAN H-BOMB KNOWN AS THE TSAR BOMBA, WHICH WAS DETONATED IN OCTOBER 1961 IN NOVA ZEMLAYA, EASTERN SIBERIA.

Carbon dating

Some variations of atoms, called isotopes, are more likely to disintegrate radioactively than others. The radioisotope carbon-14, for example, is present in all living things, but when they die, the isotopes begin to disintegrate. The rate of disintegration is so steady that by measuring the proportion of carbon-14 isotopes left in remains of once living things, scientists can tell exactly how long they have been dead. This process is called radiocarbon dating and it is one of the most valuable archeological techniques.

▶ Thermonuclear bombs use a small fission bomb to set off a massive hydrogen fusion bomb. It starts with a gigantic fireball, such as this one in a test in the Pacific in 1958.

H-bomb

The nuclear bomb that destroyed Hiroshima in Japan in 1945 depended on the fission of big atoms such as uranium and plutonium. But even more terrible bombs were created by the fusion of tiny hydrogen atoms. The hydrogen was encased in a small bomb that was exploded first to create the pressure to fuse the hydrogen atoms. These hydrogen or H-bombs are now known as thermonuclear weapons.

Radiation danger

Exposure to radiation can be very dangerous. Gamma radiation is the most dangerous because the particles are small enough to penetrate the skin. The larger particles of alpha and beta radiation are less immediately dangerous, but if you eat any food containing them, they can also cause illnesses from nausea to cancer, and may even result in death.

◀ The accident at the Chernobyl Nuclear Plant, Ukraine, in 1986 was one of the worst ever, releasing radiation that was carried by wind far across Europe. The red color in this satellite image of the area around the nuclear plant indicates radioactivity.

Birth of the UNIVERSE

10^{27} °C	10^{12} °C
10^{-32} sec	3 min

0 seconds
First the Universe was a tiny hot ball that grew as big as a football, then cooled to (just) 10 billion billion billion°C.

10^{-43} seconds
In the "Planck" era, the four basic forces (gravity, electromagnetism, and the two nuclear forces) were joined as a single force.

10^{-32} seconds
The forces split into four and space swelled quadrillions of times in less than a fraction of a second, from something smaller than an atom to bigger than a galaxy. This is known as inflation.

10^{-12} seconds
The Universe became a sea of particles such as quarks and gluons, which began to gain mass.

3–20 minutes
Gravity and the other forces began to pull things together. Quarks and gluons joined to form the nuclei of the smallest atoms, hydrogen. Then hydrogen nuclei joined to make helium nuclei.

300,000 years
The first atoms formed and made gases.

One million years
After one million years or so, the gases began to curdle like sour milk into long strands called filaments with vast dark holes called voids in between.

Galaxies are flying out and away from each other in all directions. This means the Universe must be expanding rapidly, so in the past it must have been much smaller. Indeed, it is now thought that long ago—about 13.5 billion years ago—the Universe was tinier than an atom. That was when it burst into being in what is often called the Big Bang. After the Big Bang, the Universe began swelling with such force and speed that astronomers are not sure if it will ever stop.

2,726 °C	253.15 °C	-270 °C
300,000 years	1 billion years	Today (13.7 billion years)

SCIENTISTS HAVE WORKED OUT THAT THE BIG BANG WAS ACTUALLY MORE LIKE A DEEP HUM OR THE ROAR OF A JET PLANE THAN A BANG.

OLD AND YOUNG

When astronomers observe galaxies 13 billion light-years away, it is as if they are staring into ancient history. But the galaxies they are seeing are (relatively) very young. The oldest stars we can see are quite close to us, in globular clusters, which are groups of a few million stars within the Milky Way. Stars in the NGC 6397 cluster are 13.4 billion years old.

0.5–1 billion years

The filaments gradually clumped into clouds. Eventually, these clouds formed stars and galaxies.

4.567 billion years

The Solar System was born—the Earth and other planets were formed from a ring of dust around the Sun.

Today

The Sun is almost halfway through its life today, but new stars and planets are forming all the time throughout the Universe.

S/C
NITROUS

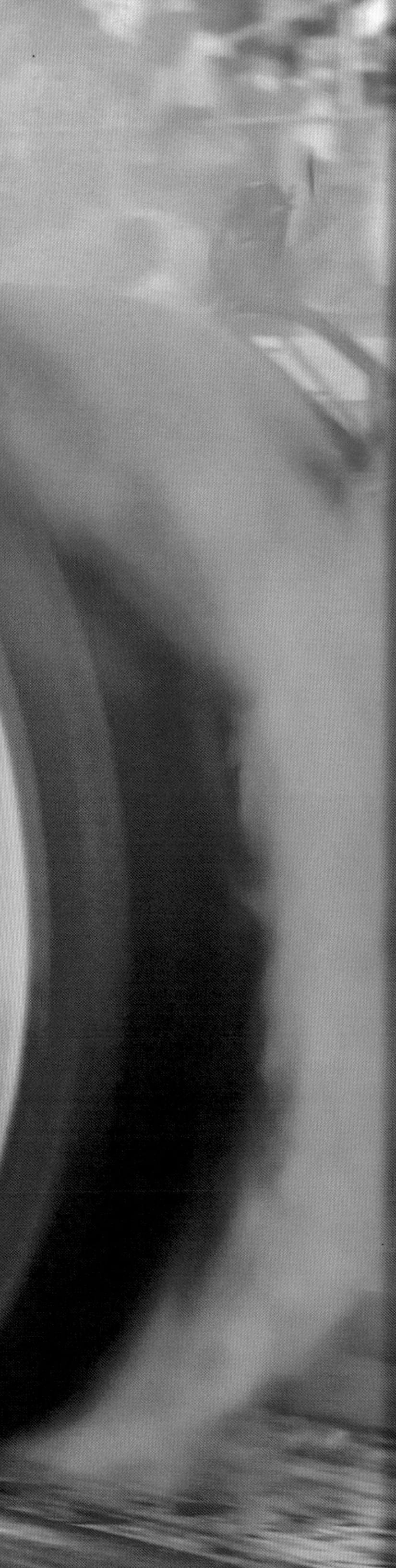

Ultimate MACHINES

Today's technological marvels are tomorrow's old news—welcome to the supersonic world of machines.

◀ A Top Fuel dragster burns rubber, spinning its rear tires on the drag strip before starting the race. Reaching 200 mph (320 km/h) in less than 2.5 seconds, this is the fastest accelerating car in the world.

ROCKETING Away

Rockets are the ultimate escape artists. Not only do they leave Earth, overcoming its strong pull of gravity, they also carry their own weight, huge amounts of fuel, and a payload—the satellite, astronauts, or probe that needs to be taken into space. In order to achieve this astounding feat, rockets need to generate awesome amounts of power.

◀ The space shuttle, *Columbia*, blasts off, propelled by its pair of gigantic rocket boosters. The boosters drop away from the shuttle about two minutes after liftoff.

Preparing for liftoff

After being carefully assembled and triple-checked, a rocket is carried on a large, slow-moving crawler transporter to its launchpad. Raised upright, beside a tall launch gantry, the rocket is filled with fuel and its launch sequence is programmed. As the final countdown finishes, the rocket engines start. They use fuel at an alarming rate. An engine on *Saturn V* used 1,738 lb (788 kg) of fuel every second—enough to power 260 *Boeing 747* airliners—as well as 3,945 lb (1,789 kg) of liquid oxygen.

TOP 5 TALLEST ROCKETS

SATURN V (USA)
363 ft (110 m)

N1 (SOVIET UNION)
345 ft (104 m)

ARES I-X (USA)
327 ft (100 m)

DELTA IV HEAVY (USA)
235 ft (72 m)

ANGARA A5/KVRB (RUSSIA)
209 ft (64 m)

NASA'S NEW ATLAS V ROCKET STANDS 191 FT (58 M) HIGH AND WEIGHS 737,400 LB (334,500 KG).

▼ A new solid-fuel *Ares I* rocket engine is tested on the ground, generating an awesome 3.6 million lb (1.6 million kg) of thrust. The rocket is 154 ft (47 m) tall and consumes about 700,000 lb (320,000 kg) of fuel per minute.

GETTING A BOOST

One way to give spacecraft a push at liftoff is to use boosters—solid-fuel rockets containing a mixture of fuel and oxidizer that fire up at launch time. Each booster is used up quite quickly—*Ariane 5*'s boosters lasted for just 130 seconds. The boosters then eject from the main spacecraft, reducing its weight as it heads into space.

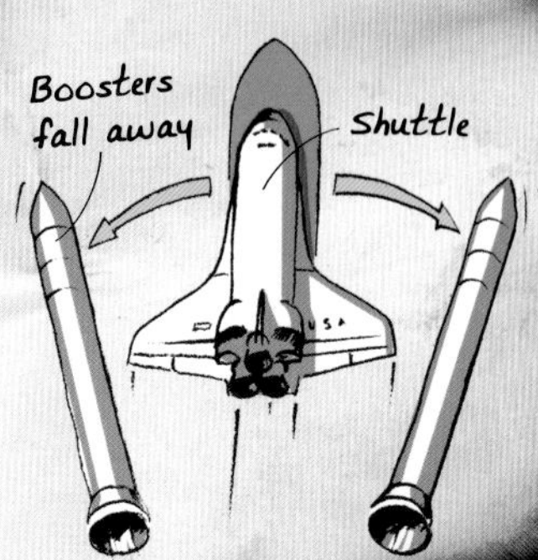

Massive engine thrust

Rocket engines can generate huge power. *Saturn V* sent U.S. astronauts to the Moon between 1969 and 1973. Its five F1 rocket engines each produced 1.5 million lb (700,000 kg) of thrust—roughly the same amount of power created by half a million sports cars! The F1 engines ran for just 2.5 minutes, but in that time they blasted *Saturn V* to a height of 42 mi (68 km) above Earth. As their fuel ran out, the engines were jettisoned with the spacecraft zooming at more than 6,160 mph (9,915 km/h).

Saturn V, carrying the Apollo 15 lunar mission, lifts off from Kennedy Space Center. The rocket burned 4.4 million lb (2 million kg) of fuel during the first 150 seconds of operation.

ROBERT GODDARD LAUNCHED THE FIRST LIQUID-FUELED ROCKET IN 1926. IT WAS 11.2 FT (3.4 M) TALL AND WEIGHED JUST 6 LB (2.7 KG).

Mixing it up

A rocket engine needs oxygen to work but there is no oxygen in space. When they are in Earth's atmosphere, rockets cannot draw in air like a jet engine does. Rockets solve this problem by carrying thousands of gallons of oxidizer (oxygen-making substances). When oxidizer is mixed with fuel and burned, huge amounts of hot, high pressure gases leave the rocket nozzles, often at speeds of more than 12,000 ft (3,800 m) per second.

Droids in DANGER

Some robots work in locations or situations too risky or difficult for humans to explore or perform tasks. These include places where poisonous chemical spills, radioactive leaks, or crumbling earthquake-damaged buildings would harm or even kill people.

▼ A British Army bomb disposal bot moves closer to a car that is suspected to contain a real bomb.

Bomb bots

Sent to investigate unexploded ordnance such as mines or bombs, bomb disposal bots take measurements and close-up photos, and send them back to human experts a safe distance away. Their extendable arms can be fitted with a range of tools, including claws to lift and carry a suspicious package, and water disrupters, which blast water into a bomb to scramble its circuits before it can detonate.

Rescue robots

When disaster strikes, robots help to locate survivors and investigate the most risky parts of an accident site. Some robots can wriggle their way through pipes or rubble. They can detect dangerous gases or spot signs of life among wreckages. Their microcameras send images to rescue workers on the surface. Rescue robots were used to seek out victims after the 2001 World Trade Center disaster and after Hurricane Katrina struck in New Orleans, U.S., in 2005. They also helped after the Crandall Canyon mine disaster in Utah, U.S., in 2007.

◀ A rescue robot clambers over rubble using its jointed sets of tracks, and a CCD camera sensor scans the terrain in front of it.

IN 2004, THE SCORPIO AND SUPER ACHILLES ROBOTS RECOVERED FLIGHT RECORDER INSTRUMENTS IN THE RED SEA FROM A CRASHED BOEING 737.

▶ Robot submersibles can deploy bait cages to attract animals for observation and research.

Deep divers

Unmanned machines can dive for long periods of time—without having to supply large amounts of oxygen for any crew to breathe. They can be built small to get into difficult areas and are used to examine dangerous parts of the ocean floor, such as undersea volcanoes and plane and ship wreckages. The *Jason* ROV (Remotely Operated Vehicle) explored the wreck of *Titanic* more than 2.5 mi (4 km) below the surface of the Atlantic Ocean.

Fire! Fire!

Heat, toxic smoke, and the threat of a burning building crashing down makes fighting fires one of the most dangerous jobs in the world. Robots are being developed to tackle blazes alongside human firefighters. Some robots, such as *Firerob* and *FFR1*, are designed to get close to major infernos. *Firerob* can withstand temperatures that would fry people—up to 2,280°F (1,250°C).

▲ *Guardrobo D1* patrols buildings, detecting changes of temperature and smoke to find small fires. It can then put them out with its own fire extinguisher.

Dramatic DRAGSTERS

No cars accelerate faster than dragsters. Pairs of these speed machines race each other down a long, narrow ribbon of track called a drag strip. Races are over a distance of either a quarter of a mile (402 m) or an eighth of a mile (201 m). With the fastest dragsters, the race is over in under five seconds. Blink and you really will miss it.

▶ Two Top Fuel dragsters power down the strip at Las Vegas Motor Speedway, U.S. Drivers have to steady their vehicles, which shudder under the extreme power.

Top Fuel machines

The National Hot Rod Association is where the top dragster operators race, and the fastest of all are Top Fuel machines. These long, thin vehicles are made of a tubular steel frame with a wheelbase (the distance between the front and rear wheels) of 180–300 in (457–762 cm)—three times the length of a normal car. The powerful engines are mounted between the large rear wheels and are fueled by racing alcohol, which is an explosive mixture of nitromethane and methanol. This mixture generates more than three times the power of regular gasoline. About 16 gal (60.5 l) of fuel is used in one race.

ALMOST 8,000 HORSEPOWER IS GENERATED BY A TOP FUEL DRAGSTER ENGINE—THAT'S MORE THAN TEN NASCARS ON THE STARTING GRID OF THE DAYTONA 500.

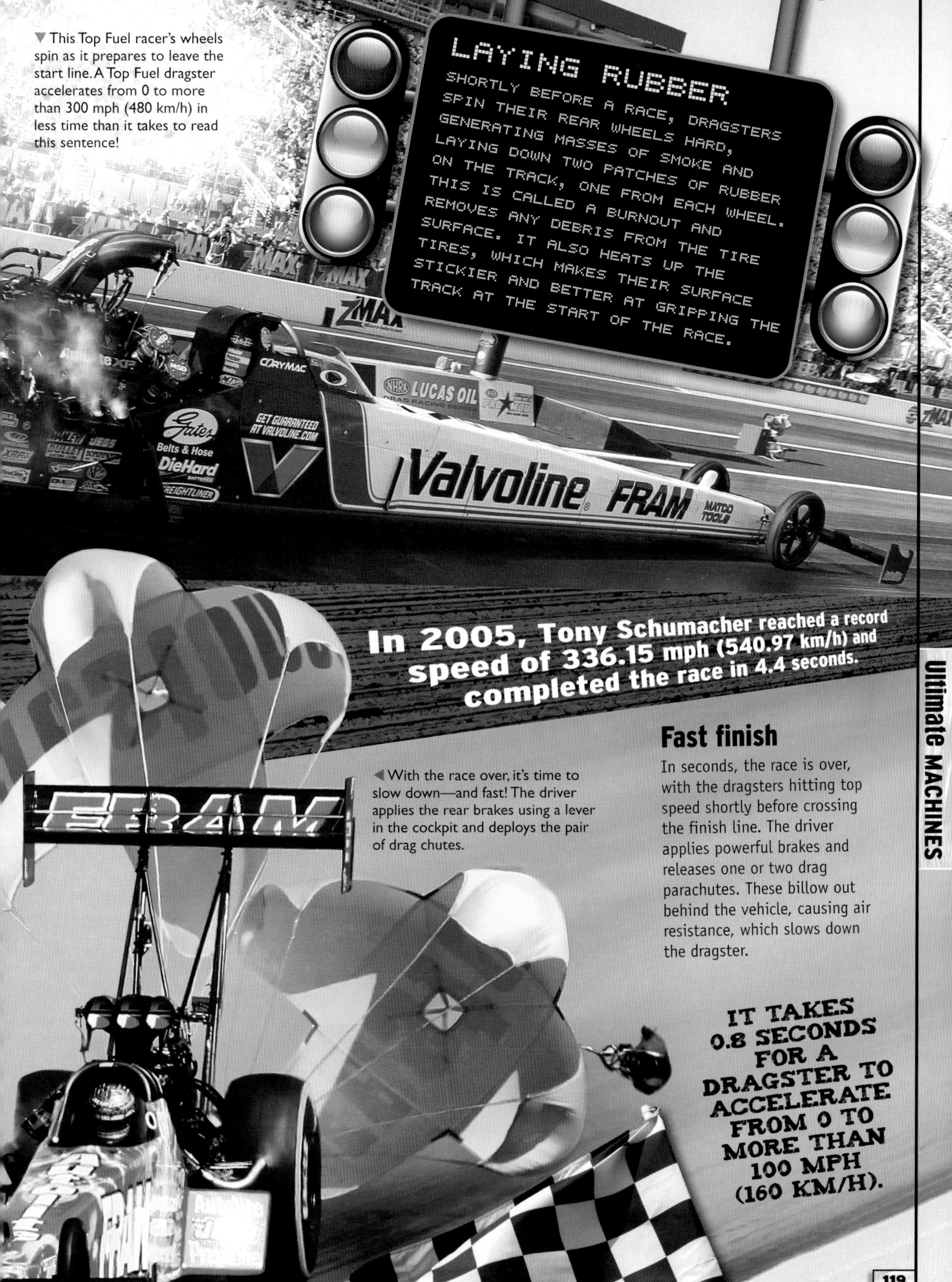

▼This Top Fuel racer's wheels spin as it prepares to leave the start line. A Top Fuel dragster accelerates from 0 to more than 300 mph (480 km/h) in less time than it takes to read this sentence!

LAYING RUBBER

SHORTLY BEFORE A RACE, DRAGSTERS SPIN THEIR REAR WHEELS HARD, GENERATING MASSES OF SMOKE AND LAYING DOWN TWO PATCHES OF RUBBER ON THE TRACK, ONE FROM EACH WHEEL. THIS IS CALLED A BURNOUT AND REMOVES ANY DEBRIS FROM THE TIRE SURFACE. IT ALSO HEATS UP THE TIRES, WHICH MAKES THEIR SURFACE STICKIER AND BETTER AT GRIPPING THE TRACK AT THE START OF THE RACE.

In 2005, Tony Schumacher reached a record speed of 336.15 mph (540.97 km/h) and completed the race in 4.4 seconds.

◀With the race over, it's time to slow down—and fast! The driver applies the rear brakes using a lever in the cockpit and deploys the pair of drag chutes.

Fast finish

In seconds, the race is over, with the dragsters hitting top speed shortly before crossing the finish line. The driver applies powerful brakes and releases one or two drag parachutes. These billow out behind the vehicle, causing air resistance, which slows down the dragster.

IT TAKES 0.8 SECONDS FOR A DRAGSTER TO ACCELERATE FROM 0 TO MORE THAN 100 MPH (160 KM/H).

ROBO-ZILLA!

Some machines are not built to save lives or provide transport, they are purely for entertainment. Many such robots come in the form of pets such as Sony's *AIBO*, a robotic dog that responds to voice commands. Other machines are built to be more brutal. They are designed to stun, surprise, and even shock people. These are the extreme entertainment machines.

Robosaurus stands a massive 42 ft (13 m) high

The spiked tail is 30 ft (9 m) high

VICTIM LIST

- CARS
- BOATS
- JETS
- TRUCKS
- LIGHT AIRCRAFT

DREADFUL DINOSAURS

A number of robotic dinosaurs have been built to wow and scare visitors to theme parks, museums, and other attractions. Some are remote controled, meaning that a human operator guides their movements from a short distance away. Others might be preprogrammed to repeat a series of movements.

The crushing force of the jaws is equal to 20,000 lb (9,000 kg)

Flamethrowers project fire up to 20 ft (6 m)

Smashed AND fried—this car is history

Robosaurus

There is little doubt about which robotic dinosaur is the biggest and baddest of all. *Robosaurus* is 42 ft (13 m) tall and weighs 30 tons (27,000 kg). The beast's large steel head contains the cockpit, where a human pilot sits and controls the giant dinosaur's movements. Signals sent to the machine's 20 hydraulic motors enable *Robosaurus* to prowl an arena, rear up, and grasp and lift cars and trucks in its two large claws.

Awesome claws can grasp and crush cars and aircraft

Car-nivorous

What really wows audiences is *Robosaurus'* appetite for destruction. Powerful hydraulic pistons and cylinders enable its claws to close with around 24,000 lb (10,900 kg) of force—enough to crush a car or even a plane. Further hydraulics power *Robosaurus'* mouth, which contains 12-in- (30-cm-) long metal teeth that can tear through trucks or chew up an aircraft wing. It was sold in 2008 for $575,000 (£350,000).

Monster Features

* Fly-by-wire for robot movements
* Super flamethrowers
* Confetti cannon
* Light and sound show
* Earsplitting roars and growls
* Burps from the 10,000-W sound system, powered by ten car batteries

Diving DOWN

Submersibles and submarines are able to dive down, carrying people and scientific equipment to explore the ocean depths. Many submersibles have found treasure, bombs, or parts of planes. The deeper they dive, the higher the water pressure, so the tougher subs need to be. At 7,000 ft (2,100 m) down, an unprotected submarine would be crushed like a tin can.

Titanic explorer

One of the most traveled submersibles of all, *Alvin* is a veteran of more than 4,000 dives. It has explored *Titanic* and also located an unexploded hydrogen bomb accidentally dropped into the Mediterranean Sea. With its strengthened hull, it can carry three people in cramped conditions on a journey to depths of up to 2.8 mi (4.5 km) below the ocean surface. Each dive lasts between six and nine hours.

Name: *Alvin*
Deepest dive: 14,764 ft (4,500 m)
Size: 23 ft (7 m) x 8.5 ft (2.6 m) x 12 ft (4 m)
Used for: Deep-ocean exploration

Name: *Scubster*
Deepest dive: 19.7 ft (6 m)
Size: 13.8 ft (4.2 m) x 7.8 ft (2.4 m)
Used for: Shallow water scuba diving operations

Pedal power

This amazing French mini-sub has no engine. Instead, it is pedal-powered by its pilot. Hard pedaling turns the two sets of fan blades, which can move the craft forward at a cruising speed of 6 mph (10 km/h). A large, clear canopy gives wonderful underwater views.

Searching the deep

Deep Flight 1 carries just one person who lies face down. It can stay underwater for up to four hours. Its six external lights brighten the murky depths, allowing the craft's four cameras to take amazing images of ocean life.

IN 1960, THE TRIESTE SUB REACHED THE BOTTOM OF THE DEEPEST PART OF THE PACIFIC OCEAN, A DEPTH OF ABOUT 35,800 FT (10,900 M).

Name: *Deep Flight 1*
Deepest dive: 3,000 ft (914 m)
Size: 13 ft (4 m) x 8 ft (2.5 m)
Used for: Deep-ocean exploration and photography

Flying through water

Most submarines have large ballast tanks that are either filled with water to dive down or emptied to rise up. However, *Deep Flight Aviator* uses upside-down wings! The wings work like the wings of a plane, but in reverse, driving the sub down through the water at speeds up to 330 ft (100 m) per minute. This two-person submersible also has twin cockpits, allowing a navigator or trainee pilot to practice their skills.

Name: *Deep Flight Aviator*
Deepest dive: 1,500 ft (457 m)
Size: 22 ft (7 m) x 12 ft (4 m) x 6 ft (2 m)
Used for: Submersible pilot training and research

Name: *Typhoon*
Deepest dive: 1,312 ft (400 m)
Size: 560 ft (170 m) long
Used for: Carrying nuclear ballistic missiles

Mega subs

Built in the 1970s, the Soviet Union's *Typhoon* Class Submarine wasn't the deepest diver, but at more than 560 ft (170 m) long, it was definitely the largest. Completely empty of fuel, crew, and supplies, it weighed a staggering 44 million lb (20 million kg). Housing 150 crew, the submarine was powered by two nuclear power reactors and carried 20 missiles, as well as torpedoes, which could be used against enemy ships. The submarine could stay underwater for 120 days at a time.

BLISTERING Bikes

Motorbikes are one of the most versatile types of motor vehicle. They can be built to cruise long distances on roads in comfort, race around tracks, or climb and jump over rough offroad terrain. The fastest bikes, such as MotoGP machines, can race at speeds close to 200 mph (322 km/h).

IN 2009, MOTOGP'S DANI PEDROSA REACHED A RECORD SPEED OF 217.037 MPH (349.288 KM/H) ON A HONDA BIKE.

▼ Two MotoGP bikes roar around a fast turn on a race circuit. The riders' knee hovers just fractions of an inch above the track surface.

Lean angle

Motorbike riders learn to shift their body weight on their motorbike saddle to control their machine and stay balanced. Riders lean into corners so that the bike turns with them. In motorcycle racing, riders take corners at high speed so have to lean close to the track, with their knees protected by plastic or metal guards called knee sliders.

Muddy machines

Motocross machines are tough enough to survive an offroad bashing. Racing over muddy or dirt circuits with hills, ditches, bumps, and tight turns, a motocross bike has a rugged frame and a powerful suspension system to keep the wheels on the ground as much as possible, while a cord called a kill switch attaches the rider to the bike's engine ignition. Should the rider fall off, the bike's engine is cut and stops.

▶ A staggering 1,250 motocross riders take part in the Weston beach race in the U.K. The bike tires have a rough, knobbly outer surface to help them grip in the loose sand.

THE SUZUKI HAYABUSA CAN GO FROM 0 TO 60 MPH (96 KM/H) IN JUST 2.7 SECONDS. THE BIKE HAS A TOP SPEED OF AROUND 186 MPH (299 KM/H).

Ice Speedway

Motorcycle speedway sees four bikes race around a tight oval dirt track. The action is intense and the bikes have no brakes, but that isn't extreme enough for some speedway riders. They choose to race on ovals covered with a layer of frozen ice. Ice bikes can reach a speed of 80 mph (130 km/h).

An Ice Speedway rear tire has 200–300 spikes that are one inch (2.5 cm) long to grip the ice.

Secret SPYBOTS

▼ *Global Hawk* cruises on a mission, which can last more than 24 hours between takeoff and landing.

Human spies are used for missions that depend on gaining the trust of other people. However, sometimes machines are better. Spying robots can be built to travel into dangerous territory, observe people and locations, and send their findings back to their human controlers. And if a robot is captured, it holds no secrets itself—unlike human spies.

Sky spies

Unmanned aerial vehicles (UAVs) are the most common type of robospy. They vary greatly in size—*Sentry Owl* can be fitted into a solider's backpack, put together in a few minutes, and then launched using a large elastic catapult. *Global Hawk*, with a wingspan of 116 ft (35.4 m), is much larger. Whatever their size, UAVs can spy from the sky with powerful zoom cameras and thermal imagers that detect heat from people or vehicle engines at night. Some UAVs can patrol for days at a time. In 2008, *QinetiQ Zephyr* took off and flew for 14 days in a row without landing.

▼ *Cypher* hovers through a mocked-up city street at Fort Benning, Georgia, U.S. The flying robot's 4-ft- (1.2-m-) long internal rotor blades give the robot a top speed of 60 mph (97 km/h).

Hover, no bother

Flying robots can hover at a set height, taking photos and video footage of suspicious activity in tall buildings. *Cypher* is a donut-shaped robot, which looks like a UFO. It is able to hover for an hour at a time while its cameras snap away. Future hovering spies may also be able to monitor Internet activity and access Wi-Fi hotspots inside buildings to snoop on emails and messages.

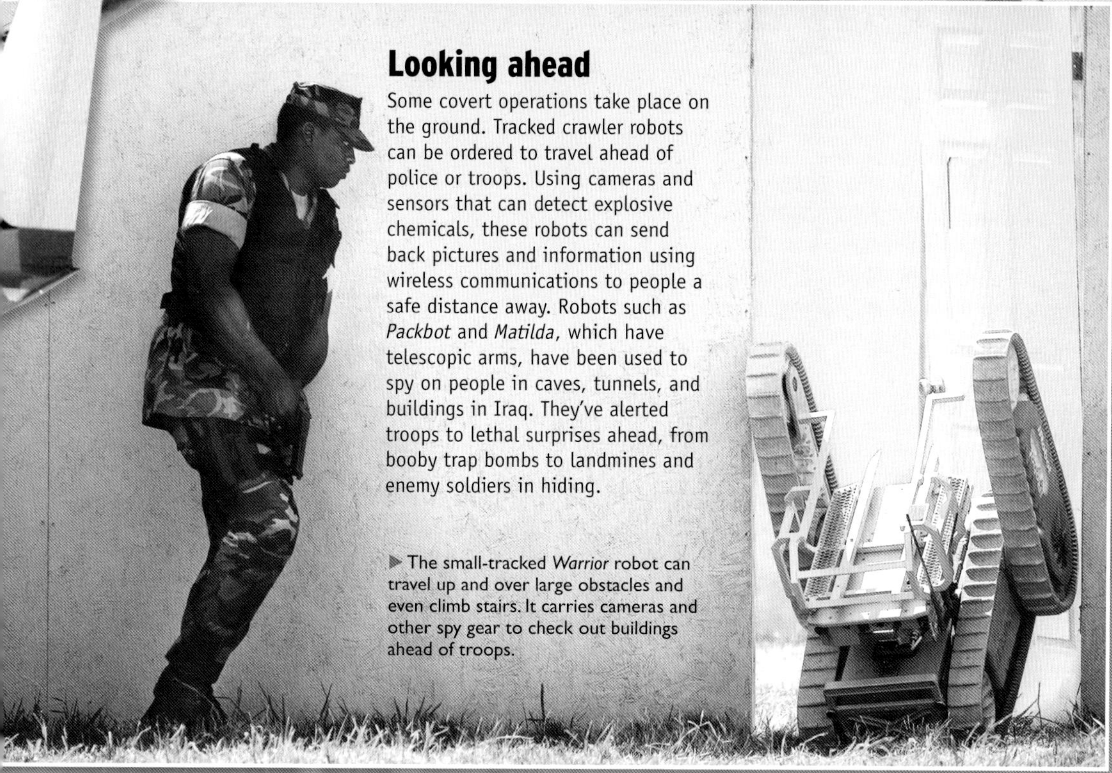

Looking ahead

Some covert operations take place on the ground. Tracked crawler robots can be ordered to travel ahead of police or troops. Using cameras and sensors that can detect explosive chemicals, these robots can send back pictures and information using wireless communications to people a safe distance away. Robots such as *Packbot* and *Matilda*, which have telescopic arms, have been used to spy on people in caves, tunnels, and buildings in Iraq. They've alerted troops to lethal surprises ahead, from booby trap bombs to landmines and enemy soldiers in hiding.

► The small-tracked *Warrior* robot can travel up and over large obstacles and even climb stairs. It carries cameras and other spy gear to check out buildings ahead of troops.

▼ Using cameras and microphones, a *WowWee Rovio* transmits what it sees and hears to its owner, who can be hundreds of miles away.

Home alone?

Having your own home spy is no longer science fiction. Robots including *Fujitsu Maron-1*, *Tmsuk Banyru*, and *WowWee Rovio* can act as spies at home. Their sensors can detect unexpected movement, while cameras can film intruders, record what they say, and then transmit this information over the Internet to the homeowner.

Insect agents

Micro Aerial Vehicles (MAVs) are flying robots made to the scale of living insects. They are capable of carrying both tiny cameras and listening devices that are able to record conversations and relay them back to their base via radio signals. Built cheaply and in large numbers, future squadrons of MAVs might be able to swarm over large areas, searching for particular chemical substances or a person whose face matches the one held in their memories.

◄ The *Delfly* robot carries a tiny camera and weighs just 0.1 oz (3 g). It flaps its wings to keep airborne.

White-knuckle RIDES

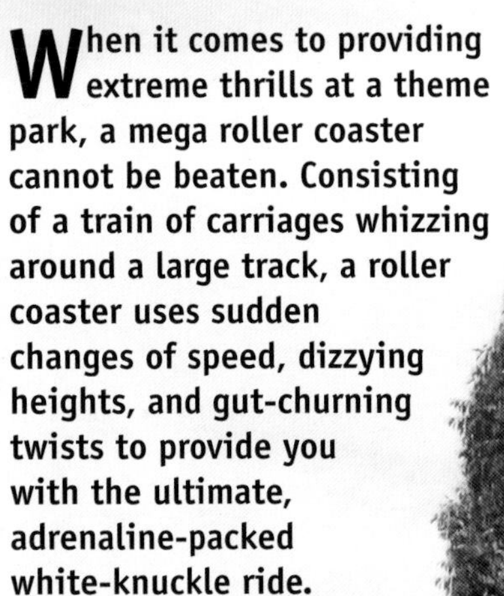

When it comes to providing extreme thrills at a theme park, a mega roller coaster cannot be beaten. Consisting of a train of carriages whizzing around a large track, a roller coaster uses sudden changes of speed, dizzying heights, and gut-churning twists to provide you with the ultimate, adrenaline-packed white-knuckle ride.

▲ Hundreds of thrillseekers can ride the twisting, looping *Colossus* roller coaster at Thorpe Park, U.K., every hour.

▲ The 2,260-ft- (690-m-) long *Infusion* in Blackpool, U.K., suspends passengers in chairs hanging from the track.

Hanging around

On some rides such as *Anaconda* in Virginia, U.S., the cars hang from below the track. This can give an exhilarating and scary view of the ground below. On the *Superman Ultimate Flight* roller coasters in New Jersey and Georgia, U.S., the cars tilt so that passengers hang facedown, their bodies parallel to the ground, as they race along at 60 mph (96 km/h)—just like flying superheroes.

Power trips

Roller coasters use a variety of different power systems to launch the ride and build up speed. Modern roller coasters, such as *Kingda Ka* in New Jersey, U.S., use a hydraulic launch mechanism, in which mighty hydraulic pumps power a winch that pulls the roller coaster train at fearsome speed. People on the ride find themselves hurtling down the track at an extreme speed of 128 mph (206 km/h). And all that takes place in just 3.5 seconds!

▼ Mean and green, the *Kingda Ka* ride takes just 59 seconds from start to finish.

Twist and turn

A roller coaster track loops and turns through various types of bend. Some are sharply banked (angled in or out) to make it feel like you are falling over the edge of the track. Others are tight hairpin turns, which the train whizzes through at high speed. The ultimate turn, called an inversion, takes you upside down. The simplest of these is a loop-the-loop, where the track travels in a vertical circle. *Colossus* at Thorpe Park, U.K., is not particularly long at 2,789 ft (850 m), but it contains a world-record ten inversions in the one minute and 45 seconds it takes to get from start to finish.

KINGDA KA'S 418-FT (128-M) DROP IS THE BIGGEST IN THE WORLD.

VIEW FROM THE TOP

Big drops

A roller coaster is carefully designed to give the maximum number of safe thrills as possible along its length. Many roller coasters have giant vertical or almost vertical drops from the top of the hill (the highest points on the ride) down to almost ground level. *Top Thrill Dragster* in Ohio, U.S., has a 400-ft (122-m) drop.

DODONPA IN JAPAN IS THE WORLD'S FASTEST ACCELERATING ROLLER COASTER. IT TAKES JUST 1.8 SECONDS TO REACH 106.8 MPH (171.9 KM/H).

Monster TRUCKS

Trucks perform many tasks, such as shifting building materials around construction sites and hauling freight on roads between cities. Some trucks, however, are just built to entertain. Monster trucks appear in arenas and stadiums to perform stunts and jumps, car crushing, and to race over obstacle courses against each other.

▼ Two monster trucks trample old cars in an exciting showdown. Most monster trucks have a top speed of 50–85 mph (80–137 km/h), but some go faster.

HOW BIG IS BIGFOOT 5?

HEIGHT 15.5 ft (4.7 m)

WIDTH 13 ft (3.9 m)

WEIGHT 28,000 lb (12,701 kg)

TIRE WEIGHT 2,400 lb (1,087 kg)

Super stunts

Monster trucks perform some amazing stunts, often in quite small arenas. In 1999, *Bigfoot 14* roared off a ramp and jumped over a *Boeing 727* airliner, recording a massive 202-ft- (61.6-m-) long jump. Drivers wear helmets and flame-retardant racing suits and are strapped securely into their seat with harnesses. Windshields are often made of a clear plastic called Lexan, which does not shatter.

Mighty movers

Monster trucks are built from a tubular steel frame covered in body panels. The body perches high above its giant wheels, riding on a strong suspension system to allow the truck to climb over other vehicles. All four wheels are driven by the engine, and the tires are 5.5 ft (1.7 m) in height and 3.6 ft (1.1 m) wide. The entire vehicle weighs 10,000 lb (4,536 kg).

▼ *Bigfoot 5*'s tires are so big, at 10 ft (3 m) in diameter and 4 ft (1.2 m) wide, that children can stand inside the wheels.

▼ *Liebherr T 282B* can carry an enormous load of up to 720,000 lb (327,000 kg).

Big rigs

Even bigger than *Bigfoot* are the giant tipper trucks used in the mining industry to move rock and rubble from place to place. The *Liebherr T 282B* dump truck measures 48 ft (14.5 m) long and 29 ft (8.7 m) wide. Its engine alone weighs more than 20,000 lb (9,091 kg).

A bunch of dummies

Crash test dummies are models of real people placed inside cars or on motorbikes so that testers can record and analyze the effects of a crash on people. Dummies come in all different sizes, representing different ages and genders. Inside each dummy is a rigid structure that mimics parts of the human skeleton. The latest crash test dummies can cost up to $200,000 (£150,000).

CRASH! BANG!

CRASH! Metal crumples, glass shatters, and fabrics shred. There are thousands of car crashes around the world every day. But motor vehicles are getting safer and that's partly down to the work of crash testing centers. They test vehicle models before they go on sale to research how to make them safer.

Crash test benefits

In the past, crash testing has revealed cars that do not protect drivers and passengers, stopping unsafe vehicles going on sale. It has also helped lead to major safety innovations such as side impact bars in car doors and air bags, which inflate rapidly on impact to protect the head of both the driver and the frontseat passenger.

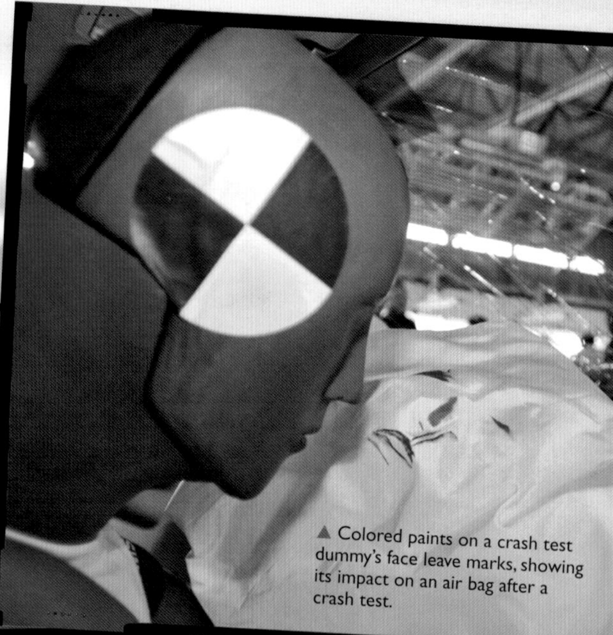

▲ Colored paints on a crash test dummy's face leave marks, showing its impact on an air bag after a crash test.

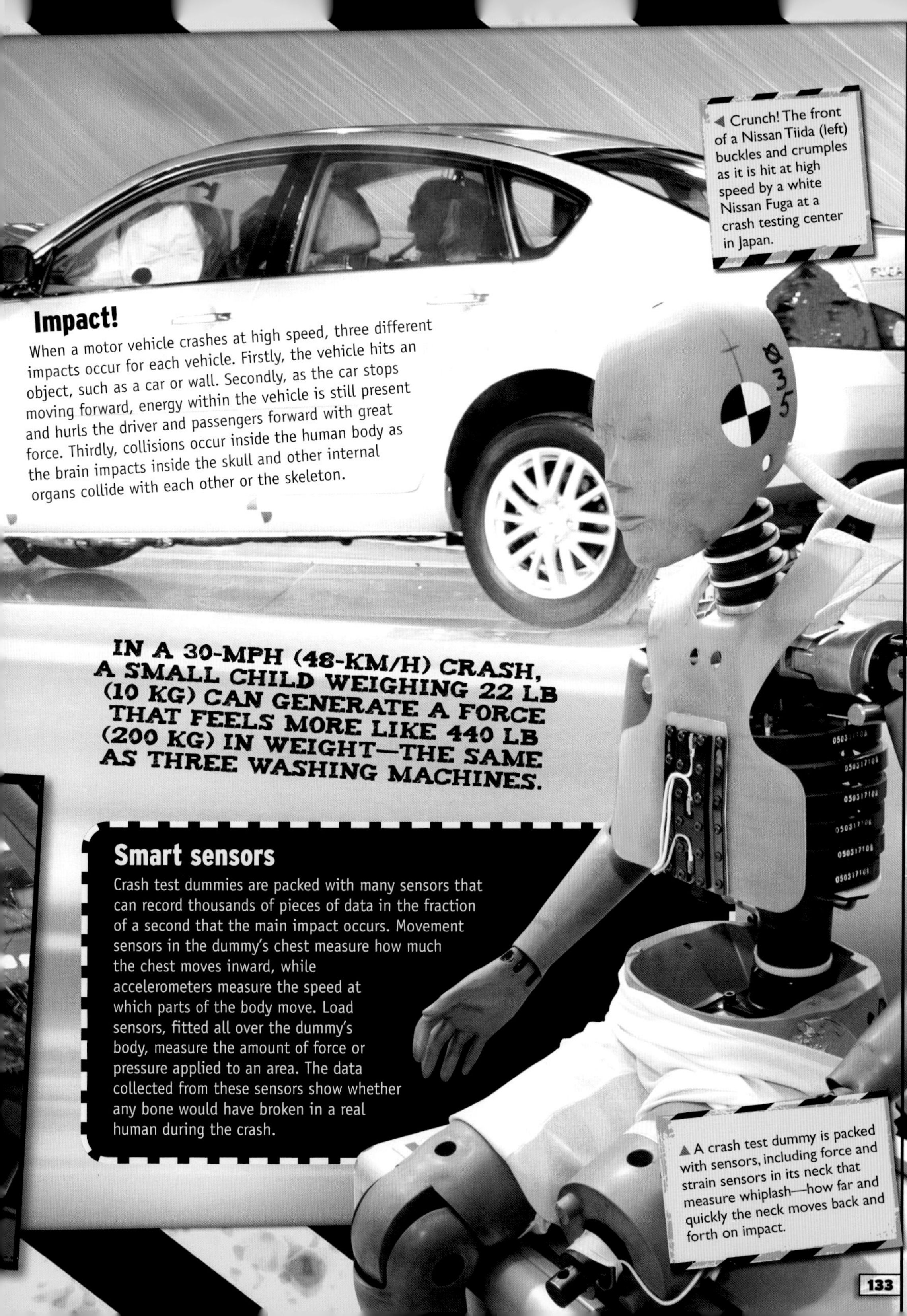

◀ Crunch! The front of a Nissan Tiida (left) buckles and crumples as it is hit at high speed by a white Nissan Fuga at a crash testing center in Japan.

Impact!

When a motor vehicle crashes at high speed, three different impacts occur for each vehicle. Firstly, the vehicle hits an object, such as a car or wall. Secondly, as the car stops moving forward, energy within the vehicle is still present and hurls the driver and passengers forward with great force. Thirdly, collisions occur inside the human body as the brain impacts inside the skull and other internal organs collide with each other or the skeleton.

IN A 30-MPH (48-KM/H) CRASH, A SMALL CHILD WEIGHING 22 LB (10 KG) CAN GENERATE A FORCE THAT FEELS MORE LIKE 440 LB (200 KG) IN WEIGHT—THE SAME AS THREE WASHING MACHINES.

Smart sensors

Crash test dummies are packed with many sensors that can record thousands of pieces of data in the fraction of a second that the main impact occurs. Movement sensors in the dummy's chest measure how much the chest moves inward, while accelerometers measure the speed at which parts of the body move. Load sensors, fitted all over the dummy's body, measure the amount of force or pressure applied to an area. The data collected from these sensors show whether any bone would have broken in a real human during the crash.

▲ A crash test dummy is packed with sensors, including force and strain sensors in its neck that measure whiplash—how far and quickly the neck moves back and forth on impact.

Deep-sea OIL RIGS

Oil is a crucial substance used as a fuel both in power plants and as gasoline in motor vehicles. It is also a vital raw material in many industries, including the plastics industry. Oil is measured in barrels, with one barrel equal to 42 gal (158.9 l). Every year, the global population uses 30,000 million barrels of oil. The demand is enormous and grows every day, which has led to drilling for oil in water both close to coastlines and much further out to sea. These offshore platforms produce about one fifth of the world's oil.

▼ The Petronius platform in the Gulf of Mexico stands 246 ft (75 m) above the sea surface, but there's a further 1,754 ft (535 m) below the water to the seabed.

Towering high

The tallest part of an oil rig is usually its derrick. This is a strong metal frame that forms a tall tower. The derrick supports the weight of the drill string and the drill bit, which consists of a number of wheels with strong, sharp teeth that rip through the rock to reach the oil. A mixture of water, clay, and chemicals, called mud, is piped down to cool the drill bit as it drills.

Fiery flares

As oil is recovered from beneath the seabed, it is pumped into the rig's many storage tanks. Some rigs have a direct pipeline connection to the shore. Pockets of natural gas are often found when drilling for oil. Some of this gas is used on the rig, and burned to provide heating and hot water for the crew members living there. The remaining gas can either be piped away to be used as fuel or burned off at the flare boom—a long metal arm that sticks out to one side of the platform.

◀ Natural gas found when drilling for oil is burned off from flare booms, such as this one in the Persian Gulf.

Made of steel, the drilling derrick rises high above the rest of the platform.

The helipad allows people and urgent supplies to be ferried to and from the rig.

The flare boom, jutting out over the ocean, allows pockets of natural gas encountered while drilling to be burned off.

The platform is designed to drill for and pump 50,000 barrels—280 cu ft (8,000 cu m) of oil per day.

The steel frame, called the jacket, supports the platform.

Giant platforms

There are many different types of platform. Some are semisubmersible platforms, and have giant legs filled with air, giving them the buoyancy to float. This sort of rig is towed into the correct drilling position before its air-filled legs are flooded with water to make them sink. Large, heavy anchors are dropped to the seabed to help keep the rig in position. Other oil platforms are permanent structures, with giant concrete bases or tall, narrow towers of concrete and steel. The foundations are dug deep into the seabed.

Disaster!

Fire tenders pump water to try to dowse the flames as fire rages at the Deepwater Horizon oil rig in the Gulf of Mexico in 2010. After the rig collapsed, the well leaked vast amounts of oil into the Gulf, which devastated ocean and coastal life.

JET POWER

Jets transport millions of passengers on airliners and fly high in the skies as military aircraft. They are powered by extreme engines, which suck in cold air, ignite it with fuel, and eject the hot gases out of the rear to create enormous amounts of thrust.

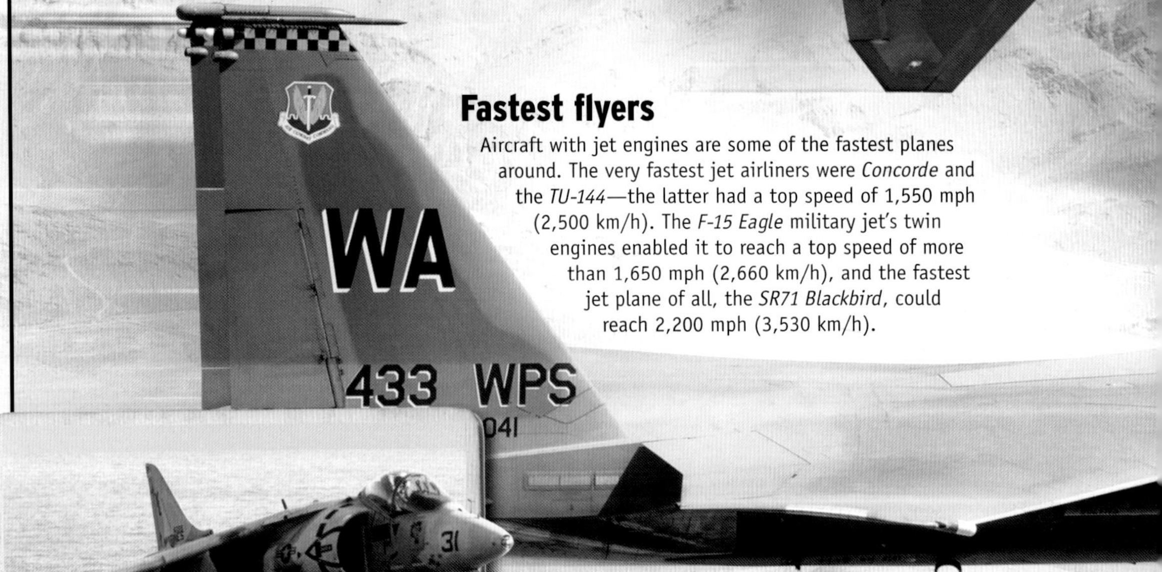

Fastest flyers

Aircraft with jet engines are some of the fastest planes around. The very fastest jet airliners were *Concorde* and the *TU-144*—the latter had a top speed of 1,550 mph (2,500 km/h). The *F-15 Eagle* military jet's twin engines enabled it to reach a top speed of more than 1,650 mph (2,660 km/h), and the fastest jet plane of all, the *SR71 Blackbird*, could reach 2,200 mph (3,530 km/h).

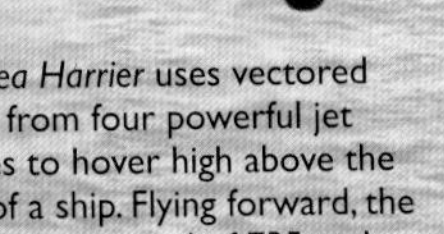

▲ A *Sea Harrier* uses vectored thrust from four powerful jet nozzles to hover high above the deck of a ship. Flying forward, the jet has a top speed of 735 mph (1,182 km/h).

Straight up

Some aircraft can redirect the flow of hot gases from their jet engines to make them more maneuverable in flight. This is called Vector In Forward Flight or VIFF and is found on the *F35B Lightning* and the *F22 Raptor*. Combat jets can use VIFF to change direction suddenly, crucial in air-to-air combat. Other aircraft use vectored thrust to achieve VTOL (vertical takeoff and landing), sending a 20,755-lb (9,415-kg) *AV8B Harrier* straight up into the air where it can even hover like a helicopter.

AT ITS TOP SPEED, THE F22 RAPTOR COULD FLY FROM NEW YORK CITY TO MIAMI IN LESS THAN 40 MINUTES!

▼ An *F22 Raptor* (top) turns away from an *F15 Eagle* jet. Both aircraft are powered by twin jet engines and have a top speed of more than 1,500 mph (2,410 km/h).

AFTER PULLING THE FIRING HANDLE, IT TAKES NO MORE THAN THREE SECONDS FOR THE MAIN PARACHUTE TO OPEN.

A quick exit

The pilot of a jet can exit his troubled aircraft using an ejection seat. Firstly, the cockpit canopy blasts away before sets of rockets thrust the seat up and out, at least 300 ft (90 m) from the aircraft. At the same time, winglike stabilizer fins fold out to help keep the pilot and seat stable. As the seat blasts away, a small explosive charge detonates in the seat's headrest, forcing open a parachute called a drogue. This slows the seat down and pulls out a much larger main parachute. Once this opens, the seat falls away and the pilot descends safely. Ejection seats have so far saved more than 10,000 lives.

◀ A military jet pilot rockets free of his plane strapped safely into his ejection seat.

POWER UP

Cold air sucked into a jet engine is squeezed to increase its pressure before entering the combustion chamber. Here, it is mixed with fuel and burned, reaching a temperature of about 1,650°F (900°C). This creates rapidly expanding gases, which exit the jet engine through the exhaust nozzle at the rear. The speeding gases create an opposite force, thrusting the aircraft forward.

SPEED Stars

With each advancement in engineering and technology, the speed aces of the day race to design, build, and test-drive new machines that they hope will smash records—and maybe bring them fame and a place in history.

1947: Railton Mobil Special
Bonneville Salt Flats, Utah, U.S.

Powered by two supercharged aircraft engines, Railton was the first land vehicle to break the speed of 400 mph (640 km/h).

1938: Thunderbolt
Bonneville Salt Flats, Utah, U.S.

George Eyston's huge car, Thunderbolt, weighed 7 tons (6,350 kg)—twice that of any of its competitors. It still managed to reach a speed of 357.5 mph (575.3 km/h).

1928: White Triplex
Daytona Beach, Florida, U.S.

Powered by three aircraft engines and driven by Ray Keech, White Triplex reached a top speed of 207.5 mph (334 km/h) on Florida's Daytona Beach.

Malcolm Campbell's son Donald followed in his father's risky footsteps, setting a new record of 403.8 mph (648.7 km/h).
1964: Bluebird CN7
Lake Eyre, Australia
19
20
1970: Blue Flame
Bonneville Salt Flats, Utah, U.S.
Blue Flame sets a new record, averaging a scorching 630.4 mph (1,014.5 km/h) on Bonneville Salt Flats.
THE BLUE FLAME
600
700
800
900
1000
1100
1000
1200
1400
1600
1800
18A
20
1997: Thrust SSC
Black Rock Desert, Nevada, U.S.
The first land vehicle to go faster than the speed of sound was driven by fighter pilot Andy Green. It clocked an average speed of 763 mph (1,228 km/h).
COLOR SAFETY
serco
2012: Bloodhound SSC,
Hakskeenpan, South Africa
This new car will be powered by a rocket bolted to a Eurofighter-Typhoon jet engine. The team behind it hopes to reach a speed of 1,000 mph (1,610 km/h).

▼ A *Bombardier 415* dumps 1,620 gal (6,140 l) of water from its hold onto a raging forest fire.

To the RESCUE

When an emergency call is taken or an emergency signal given out, technology is at work from the start. Communications centers and call centers use satellite links, radio, and even Internet connections to alert staff and other services such as the police or mountain rescue. This allows the services to plan and coordinate their actions quickly.

Water bombs

Some fires across dry scrubland or forests can rage out of control, putting towns and villages at risk and destroying valuable habitats and farmland. Water bombing is the use of aircraft and helicopters to drop large quantities of water on forest fires from above. Some fly between the fire and an airfield to be refilled with water. Other planes such as the *Bombardier 415* scoop up water into their large bodies by flying low over water.

◀ A water bomber flies so low that it skims the surface of the sea, filling its hold with water in less than 15 seconds. It can then fly back to the fire.

Breaking the ice

Icebreakers use powerful engines and their weight to plow through ice to help keep shipping lanes open, or to reach a boat or ship stuck in the ice. An icebreaker's hull is specially built and strengthened to withstand the enormous pressures of crunching through ice.

▼ The *L'Astrolabe* ship breaks through some ice on its way to the Antarctic coast. The ship carries a crew of 12 and up to 50 passengers.

SEEING THROUGH SMOKE

One of the biggest hazards and obstructions for firefighters is thick, heavy smoke. It's hard to see through and dangerous to be in for any length of time. Firefighters often use small, handheld thermal imagers, which detect infrared waves and build up a heat picture of an area. A human emits different infrared waves to an inanimate object, so the body's outline will stand out clearly from the background on the screen.

▼ Using a thermal imager, a person lying on the floor can be seen through smoke. The warmest parts of the body, the head and hands, glow brightly.

◀ A U.S. coastguard winchman descends from a hovering *Sikorsky HH-60* helicopter to pick up a survivor at sea. The helicopter can operate on patrols or rescue missions for up to 6.5 hours at a time.

Rapid response

Getting to the site of an emergency as quickly as possible is often a crucial factor in saving lives. Many emergency and rescue services are equipped with small, fast, maneuverable vehicles. Motorized snowmobiles can move quickly across icy land, speedy powerboats zoom across water, and rugged 4x4 offroad vehicles tackle uneven land. Helicopters can access places that are difficult for other forms of transport to reach.

One-way Missions

Space is a harsh, unforgiving place. There's no air or water, and temperatures can range from an average of -455°F (-255°C) to thousands of degrees when close to the fiery furnace of the Sun. Human beings are just not equipped to survive in space without vast amounts of support equipment and a method of getting back to Earth safely. Space probes, in contrast, are smaller, more compact machines that can withstand the extremes of space and can be sent deep into the Solar System on one-way missions, never to return.

LAUNCHED IN 1977, VOYAGER 1 HAS 65,000 WORKING PARTS AND HAS TRAVELED MORE THAN 10.6 BILLION MI (17 BILLION KM) SO FAR.

After a ten-year mission, the *Philae* probe (part of *Rosetta*) will land on a comet. Data from its analysis will be sent back to Earth via radiowaves.

FLY-BYS

Many space probes are designed to fly close by a planet, moon, or comet, so their scientific instruments can take various measurements. Some probes perform more than one fly-by within a single mission. The European Space Agency's *Rosetta* flew by Mars in 2007 and asteroids in 2008 and 2010 on its way to its main mission—to investigate a comet called Churyumov–Gerasimenko, which it will reach in 2014.

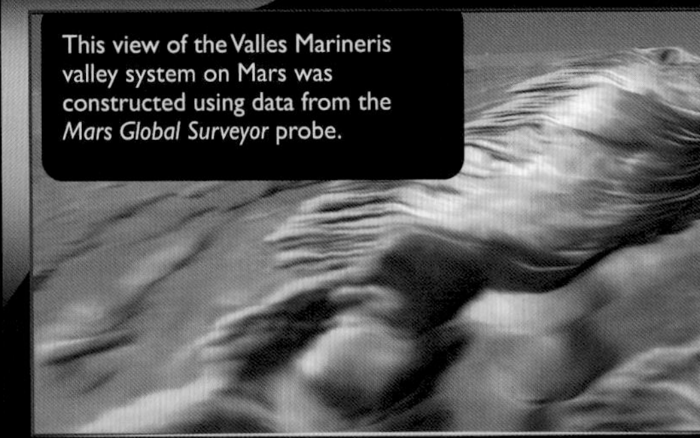

This view of the Valles Marineris valley system on Mars was constructed using data from the *Mars Global Surveyor* probe.

TWO-PART PROBES

Space probes are expensive, so scientists try to pack as many tasks into the mission as possible. The *Cassini-Huygens* probe made a journey of 2.2 billion mi (3.5 billion km) to Saturn, which took seven years. *Cassini* then orbited Saturn while the smaller probe, Huygens, traveled through the atmosphere of Saturn's largest moon, Titan, taking 700 images before landing. *Huygens'* mission was over in hours but *Cassini's* continues to this day.

The *Huygens* space probe (left) separates from the *Cassini* space probe shortly before landing on the surface of Saturn's moon, Titan, in 2005.

ORBITERS AND LANDERS

Probes are often classed according to whether they go into orbit around a planet or land on its surface. Both types of probe have been sent to Earth's nearest planetary neighbor, Mars. The first U.S. lander probe on Mars was *Viking I*, which reached the planet in 1976. NASA's *Mars Global Surveyor* began orbiting Mars 21 years later and took a staggering 240,000 digital images of the planet's surface.

The Mars Exploration Rover, *Opportunity*, landed in 2004 and is still exploring in 2011 having traveled more than 20 mi (32 km) across the planet's surface.

Water FORCE

Electricity is generated in many different ways, from nuclear to coal power plants. Hydroelectric power (HEP) plants harness the power in falling water to turn turbines that generate electricity. The largest and most extreme HEP plant is the Three Gorges Dam in China.

Huge demand

With a population of more than 1.3 billion, China has more people than any other nation and demand for electricity for homes, factories, schools, and offices is soaring. To help fulfil demand, a gigantic dam was built on the powerful Yangtze River, the third longest river in the world at more than 3,900 mi (6,300 km) long.

▶ The dam spans the Yangtze River and is becoming a major tourist attraction in China. Ships can travel past the dam through a series of large locks.

▼ A crowd watches the demolition of buildings in the old city of Fengjie to clear space for the Three Gorges Dam project.

Clearing the way

Work on the Three Gorges Dam began in 1993 and proved to be a massive task. More than 40,000 people worked on its construction day and night. The dam and the reservoir of water it held back covered a vast area of land. More than 80,000 sticks of dynamite were used to blast away rock and clear land and 134 million cu yd (102 million cu m) of earth had to be moved. About 1.4 million people were moved to new homes as hundreds of villages were submerged by the reservoir, which is around 410 mi (660 km) long—the distance from London to Paris and back!

▼ Part of one of the dam's giant electricity generators is lowered into place. Each generator weighs about 13 million lb (6 million kg).

Big results

The dam is simply enormous. It stands 607 ft (185 m) tall and 1.43 mi (2.3 km) wide. It is five times larger than the giant Hoover Dam in the U.S. The dam contains 26 massive electricity generating turbines. In total, they are able to generate around 85 billion kWh of electricity a year. That is almost one tenth of China's electricity needs and equal to electricity produced by up to 15 nuclear power plants. Many of China's other power plants burn coal and the energy produced by the Three Gorges Dam saves 50 million tons (50 billion kg) of coal every year.

THE HIGHEST FLOW OF WATER THROUGH THE DAM IS 10.5 MILLION GAL (40 MILLION L) PER SECOND.

Amazing benefits

The main purpose of the dam is to allow water to flow through turbines to generate electricity. In addition, the dam helps to prevent the Yangtze from flooding its banks and sweeping away homes and entire villages, which has occurred more than 200 times in the last 2,000 years.

◀ Water surges through the dam wall, which is 131 ft (40 m) thick at the top and 377 ft (115 m) thick at the bottom.

Into the FUTURE

No one can be certain what machines and technology we will be using in the future. Less than 15 years ago, for example, there were no iPods, iPhones, or Nintendo Wii, while 30 years ago, there was no broadband, World Wide Web, or CDs. What is certain is that thousands of people are working on exciting new machines around the world, some of which will help the future to become even more extreme.

Really, really small

A nanometer is just over one billionth of a yard or meter. It is so small that a human hair is about 80,000 nanometers in diameter. Nanotechnology is the science of making machines to this incredibly small scale. Advances in nanotechnology may see microscopic machines everywhere—they could repair machines from inside, be woven into smart materials to produce a rollable, pocket computer, or create smart clothes that extend or reduce the fabric depending on the temperature.

▼ In the future, tiny nanorobots may be injected into the body and travel through blood vessels fighting disease directly.

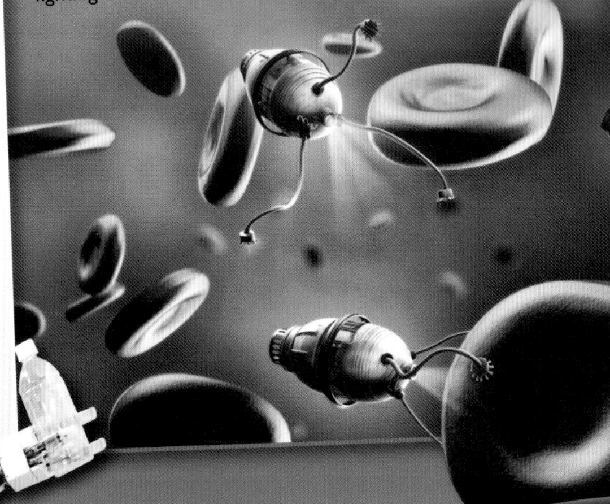

Smarter machines

Computers will continue to get faster, smarter, and smaller. Computing power will be packed into all sorts of machines, from household appliances to cars, which may be capable of self-parking or even self-driving. Robots will become more common and useful in everyday life. Some, with the ability to recognize individual faces and communicate, may become robotic babysitters, store security guards, and even robocops.

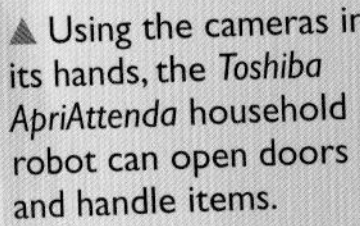

▲ Using the cameras in its hands, the *Toshiba ApriAttenda* household robot can open doors and handle items.

▶ General Motors *EN-V* car is a two-seater, two-wheeled electric vehicle that weighs just 900 lb (408 kg). Its sensors can detect obstacles in its path, such as pedestrians or other vehicles, and automatically stop.

Out of this world

In the future, unmanned space probes and robots will venture far into space with increasing frequency. More and more people may get the chance to experience space, staying in space hotels that orbit high above Earth. Humans may use technology to travel further, establishing bases on the Moon or even visiting Mars.

Body machines

More technology will be developed to help repair or improve the performance of the human body. Some of these parts will be controlled directly by a person's brain and nervous system. Sensors in the Cyberdyne Hybrid Assistive Limb (HAL) measure the angle of the knee, hip, and ankle joints, and detect whether the foot is on the floor. It helps people with damaged or weakened legs to walk properly again.

▲ Future space hotels may be luxurious orbiting space stations with passenger shuttles ferrying visitors to and from Earth.

▶ The *Cyberdyne HAL* robot leg can give the wearer up to ten times the strength of a healthy human leg.

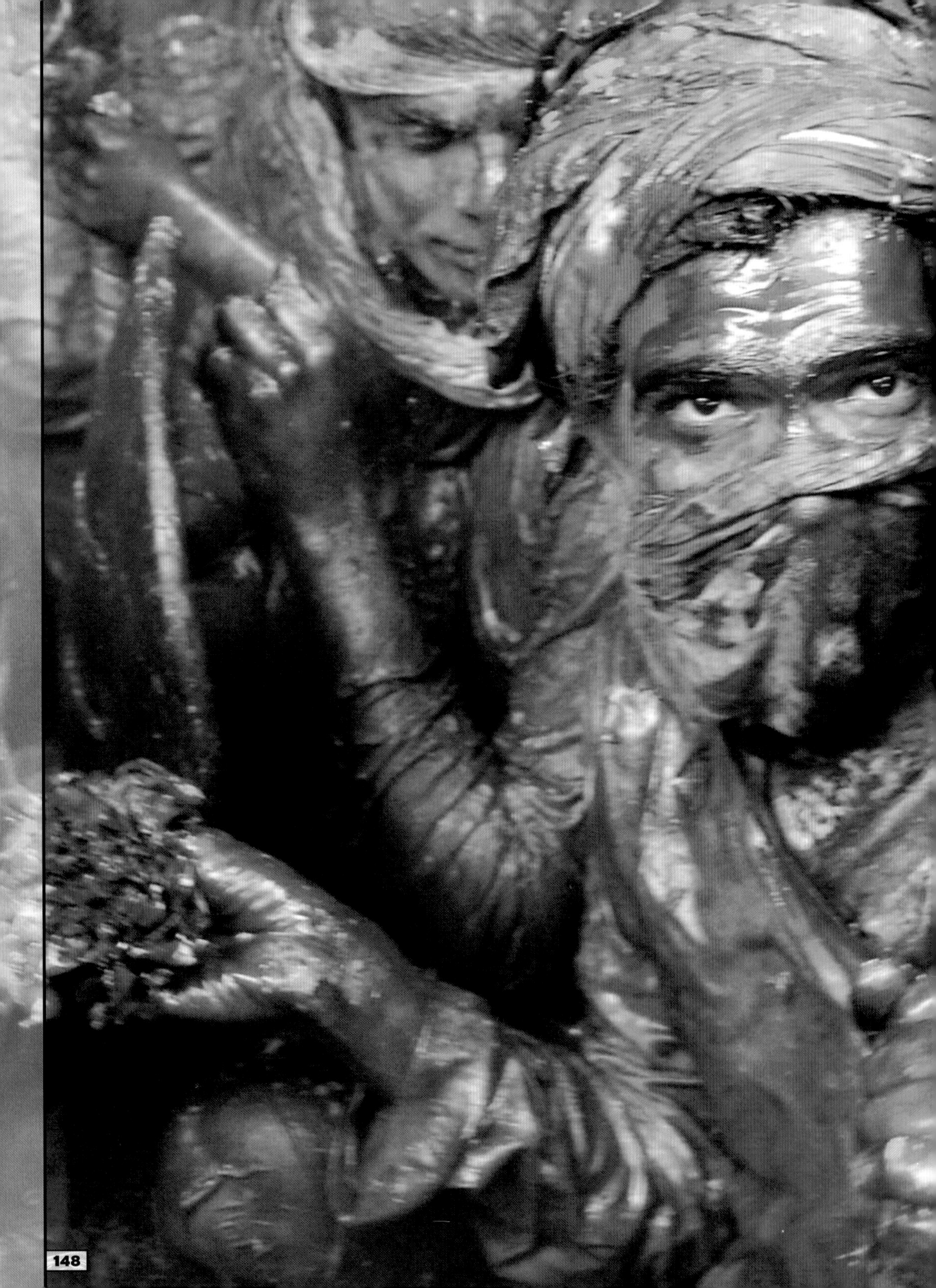

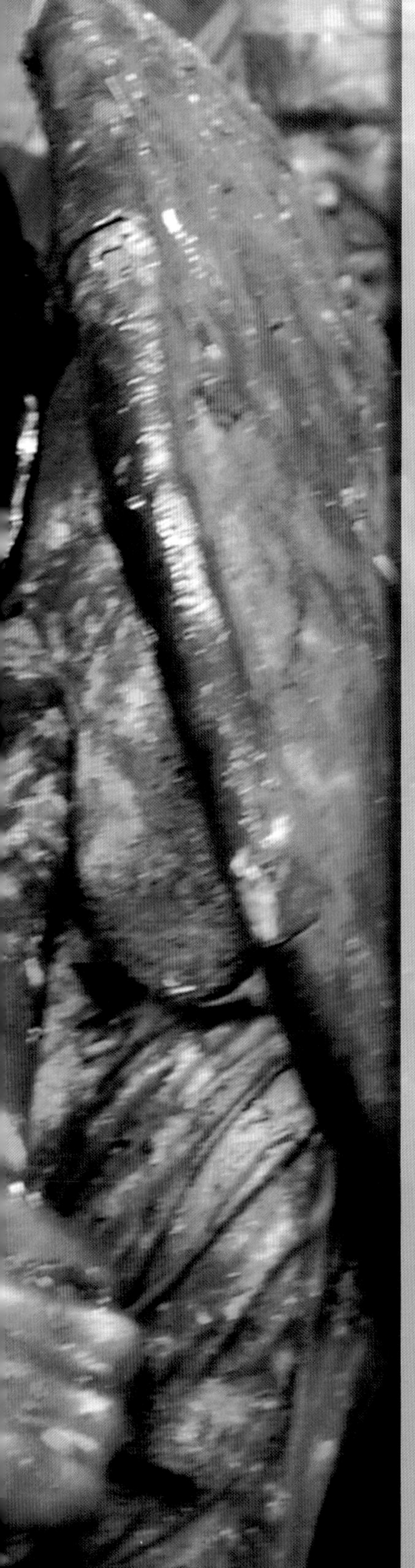

Super HUMANS

People are extraordinarily adaptable—constantly pushing the boundaries of what they can do and how they live.

◀ At Barsana, India, paint battles are all part of the fun before the Hindu spring festival of Holi.

The Amazing HUMAN BODY

The human body is built to survive. Babies are small and weak at birth, but as they grow they can expect to develop tough bones and powerful muscles. Humans can run at speed, jump high or jump long, swim underwater, carry heavy loads, and climb sheer rock faces. We are magnificent machines.

Adrenaline rush!

Bodies have an emergency mechanism that kicks in to deal with dangerous situations. A gland pumps a chemical messenger called adrenaline into the body. This increases oxygen in the blood and sends it to the muscles, which enables them to work harder. Fight or flight, the body is now ready to shift, really fast.

How fast can we go?

Like a bolt of lightning! In 2009, Jamaican athlete Usain Bolt ran the 100 m in 9.58 seconds and the 200 m in 19.19 seconds. Back in 1988 the late "Flo-Jo" (Florence Griffith-Joyner) ran the 100 m in 10.49 seconds and the 200 m in 21.34 seconds.

▼ *Bon anniversaire* Jeanne Calment! Or happy birthday to the oldest-ever woman, here celebrating her 122nd birthday.

▲ Maximum power! Usain Bolt sprints the 100 m in 2010. He holds World and Olympic records for the 100 m, 200 m, and 4 x 100 m relay.

How long can we live?

On average, humans can expect to live for 66.12 years. In Macau, China, life expectancy is as high as 84.36 years. Tragically, in Angola, Africa, it is only 38.2 years. The greatest age known to have been reached by a woman is 122 years and 164 days, by Jeanne Calment of France (1875–1997). The oldest-ever man was Shigechiyo Izumi of Japan (1865–1986), who reached 120 years and 237 days.

During an average lifetime you may: Walk 13,700 mi (22,000 km)... Produce 200 billion new red blood cells every day...

How strong can we get?

Olympic weightlifters take part in two events called the "snatch" (from squat to overhead) and the "clean and jerk" (from floor to shoulders, then an overhead push). Between 2002 and 2003, Iranian strongman Hossein Rezazadeh managed a 469-lb (213-kg) snatch, a 581-lb (263.5-kg) clean and jerk, and a total load of 1,041 lb (472 kg). Between 2008 and 2009, women's champion Jang Mi-ran of South Korea smashed the records with 309 lb (140 kg), 412 lb (187 kg), and a total of 719 lb (326 kg).

▼ Muscles bulge as Hossein Rezazadeh gets a grip. His nickname? The "Iranian Hercules."

▶ By the age of 22, Robert Wadlow measured 8ft 11.1 in (2.72 m).

THE HUMAN BODY HAS MORE THAN 620 MUSCLES. THE BIGGEST, THE GLUTEUS MAXIMUS, COVERS THE BUTTOCKS.

Tall and short

The tallest known human in history was an American called Robert Wadlow (1918–1940), nicknamed the "Giant of Illinois." The shortest man living in the world today is Khagendra Thapa Magar (b. 1992), from Nepal.

▶ Khagendra Thapa Magar is just 2 ft 2.5 in (0.6 m) tall.

THERE ARE 206 BONES IN THE ADULT HUMAN BODY. A BABY HAS MORE THAN 300, BUT SOME OF THESE SOON FUSE TOGETHER.

The Things WE CAN DO

The human body can survive in all sorts of environments, but it does have physical limits. At high altitudes mountaineers may require extra supplies of oxygen. Extreme cold may bring hypothermia and frostbite, while extreme heat can burn the skin and cause sunstroke. Even so, increasing numbers of people are pushing their bodies to the limit—with extreme sports and activities.

Ice climbing

Climbing a sheer rockface is a feat at any time, but climbing it when it is covered in thick ice is even more amazing. Ice climbers also tackle glaciers, icefalls, and frozen waterfalls using boot spikes (crampons), ropes, and ice axes to get a grip. All climbers need physical strength, stamina—and a keen sense of balance.

Super endurance

Every year, thousands of people take part in the Tough Guy competition in Perton, U.K. Participants face the ultimate stamina challenge, racing through water, mud, smoke, and ice in what is claimed to be the world's toughest test of strength and endurance.

▲ Ice climbers need to keep a cool head. This extreme sport depends upon technique and skill. Ice can be very strong and can safely support ropes and spikes—if they are used correctly.

◀ A would-be Tough Guy tackles a wall of flames. Many competitors don't finish the course.

An exhilarating tandem dive. At competition level, skydiving requires supreme body control.

A cliff diver leaps from La Quebrada clifftop, near Acapulco, Mexico. Sometimes people dive here by night, holding flaming torches.

Skydiving

After the jump from the aircraft you hurtle forward. For a mighty minute or so you go into glorious freefall as you drop. Then it's time for the parachute to open, and a gentle glide down to Earth. But a regular jump is not enough of a thrill for some—in 2006, 400 jumpers from 31 countries set a record for the largest formation freefall.

Taking the plunge

A 100-ft (30-m) dive into a narrow rocky cove near Acapulco in Mexico is a true test of nerves. These professional divers must avoid the cliff's deadly rocks and time their entry into the water—which is only 6–16 ft (2–5 m) deep—to perfection, while taking account of the waves.

Paralympic champions

The Paralympic Games are a major sporting competition for elite athletes with disabilities. Sports include swimming, judo, ice-sled hockey, tennis, shooting, and wheelchair basketball and rugby. They are just as competitive as the Olympic Games—around 4,000 athletes from nearly 150 countries participate.

Long jump triumph for Germany's Wojtek Czyz. At the Beijing Paralympics in 2008, he leaped 21.3 ft (6.5 m) to claim the gold medal.

People, People EVERYWHERE

It is called a population explosion—the rapid growth of the number of people living on our planet to more than **7 billion*** individuals. During the last **200 years** the world population has grown by about seven times, thanks to improvements in food production, water supply, healthcare, and medication. By **2050** the figure may have grown to about 12 billion—but we can only guess.

*7,039,924,240 and counting (world population estimate, September 2012).

The world's peoples live in **266** different nations, dependencies, and territories.

1 IN 10 people live on less than U.S. $10 (£6) per day.

27 PERCENT of the people in the world are under 14 years of age.

More than **5 BILLION** pizzas are eaten each year around the world.

About **1 IN 5** of the world's population is Chinese.

Over **60 PERCENT** of the world's population lives in the continent of Asia, while less than **ONE PERCENT** live in Oceania (including Australia).

How many languages are spoken in the world? Estimates vary, but about **6,800** might be a good guess.

The top 10 most densely populated lands include small territories, ministates, and islands with limited space. Top of these is the Chinese special region of **MACAU**, with 48,003 people per sq mi (18,534 per sq km).

On average, women live **3.78** years longer than men.

About **82 PERCENT** of adults in the world can read and write.

There are very slightly **MORE MEN** than women in the world.

Why do people talk so much? There are **5.3 BILLION** cellphones in the world, and **1.3 BILLION** landlines.

It has been estimated that for every single human on the planet there are **2 BILLION** insects.

267 babies are born every minute.

Traffic jam! There are about **128** motor vehicles for every 1000 humans in the world.

Every year, passengers make **3.2 BILLION** journeys on the Tokyo subway system in Japan.

About **15 MILLION** people worldwide are refugees, uprooted from their homes by disasters such as persecution, war, or famine.

Rice provides more than **20 PERCENT** of all the calories that humans consume around the world.

The loneliest independent nation is Mongolia. Its vast deserts and grasslands have only **4.4 PEOPLE PER SQ MI** (1.7 per sq km).

People over the age of **65** account for **7.6** percent of the world population.

The territory with the **LOWEST POPULATION GROWTH RATE** is the Northern Marianas Islands, in the Pacific Ocean, with a figure of **-7.8 PERCENT.**

1 IN 8 people in the world have no access to safe water supplies.

Humans only live on the **29.1** percent of Earth's surface that is dry land.

In the next minute, **133 passengers** will arrive or depart from London's Heathrow Airport in the U.K., one of the busiest airports in the world.

The population of **China** is estimated at **1,336,718,015**. Closing the gap is neighboring **India** with 1,189,172,906. India has a higher growth rate than China, which it is expected to overtake by 2040.

The world's continents have an overall population density of **119** per sq mi (46 per sq km).

Burundi in Africa and the **United Arab Emirates** in the Middle East both have the highest population growth rate, with an annual increase of **3.69** percent.

The Indian government's 2010 census is claimed to be the largest ever undertaken. It employed **2.5 MILLION** officials, cost $1.4 billion (£875 million), and created 13,000 tons of paperwork.

The most densely populated large country is Bangladesh, with **2,919** people per sq mi (1,126 per sq km).

The world's **most sparsely populated** territory is Arctic **Greenland**, with only **0.025** people per sq mi (0.067 per sq km).

The average age of a human being alive today is **28.4** years.

1 IN 8 people in the world are malnourished.

How many people have **ever lived** on Earth? It's very hard to say, but some experts have estimated a figure of about **115 BILLION**.

Icy **ANTARCTICA** is a continent with no permanent population. With the thousand or so international scientists based there, the population density is only about **0.00003** per sq mi (0.00007 per sq km).

SURVIVAL Around the World

Over hundreds of thousands of years, the human body has adapted to cope in all sorts of environments and climates. Modern city dwellers may no longer have to battle with the forces of nature every day, but many peoples around the world still struggle to survive in very hostile conditions.

THE SAAMI PEOPLE OF ARCTIC SWEDEN, NORWAY, FINLAND, AND RUSSIA USE A TENT CALLED A LAVVU AS A SHELTER WHEN HERDING REINDEER. IT WAS TRADITIONALLY MADE OF REINDEER HIDE SUPPORTED ON POLES.

▶ The Inuit from Ellesmere Island in Nunavut, Canada, wrap up warm to withstand the icy conditions of their homeland. Grabbing his harpoon, this Arctic hunter jumps from one ice floe to another in search of food.

▶ The Inuit can survive when hunting by building a shelter or *igdlu* from frozen blocks of snow.

The ice people

In the icy wilderness of northwest Greenland the temperature may drop to –40°F (–40°C) in winter, and during this season the Sun does not rise for 14 weeks. A nice summer day might reach 32°F (0°C)! This region is home to the most northerly native people in the world. They form a small community called the Inughuit, or Polar Eskimos. Only about 1,000 people speak their language, Inuktun. The Inughuit travel by dog sled and live by hunting walrus and fishing.

THE ABORIGINES OF AUSTRALIA'S DESERTS AND ARID SCRUBLAND HAVE LEARNED HOW TO OBTAIN WATER FROM TREE ROOTS, LEAVES, AND ROCK HOLLOWS.

Deep in the forest

The Yanomamo people of the Amazon rain forest in South America are experts in forest survival. They hunt animals with poisoned arrows, gather grubs, and grow plants. The population is declining because their lands in Brazil have been invaded by gold miners, who have brought in diseases to which the Yanomamo have no resistance.

◀ Dense rain forest may be a barrier to the outside world, but it provides food and shelter to the humans who live there.

▶ A view from a helicopter shows a Yanomamo village in perfect isolation, deep in the forest.

Desert survivors

In North Africa's Sahara Desert, temperatures may soar above 122°F (50°C). The only places where people can settle are around oases, or water holes. The Tuareg people are camel herders and traders. They are nomads who travel along ancient trade routes across the desert. Tuareg men traditionally wear black turbans and wrap their faces in dark blue scarves or veils.

▶ Desert survival depends on camels. They can carry a half-ton load for 25 mi (40 km) a day—and go for a week without water.

▼ Tuareg traders break for the night in the Algerian Sahara. Once the Sun goes down, the fierce heat of the day gives way to below freezing temperatures.

BIG WORDS & CRAZY NUMBERS

Talking, counting, and calculating are some of the key skills behind our success as human beings. They make it possible for us to teach and learn, to work out how to do things, and organize ourselves. The first forms of writing words and numbering appeared in Asia more than 5,000 years ago.

Alphabetti spaghetti

The 26-letter alphabet for the English language is quite a modest one. The world's longest alphabet is that of the Khmer language, used in Cambodia in Southeast Asia. It has 74 letters. The shortest is the Rotokas alphabet, used by about 4,000 people on the island of Bougainville in Papua New Guinea. It has just 11 letters.

◀ The teachings of Kong Fuzi, or Confucius (551–479 BC), were a key part of education in ancient China, and are still studied today.

Do you speak global?

Standard Chinese or "Mandarin" is spoken by about 845 million people as a first language. The number for Spanish is 329 million and for English is 328 million. Many millions speak English as a second language, and it is spoken in more countries than any other—112.

A language of symbols

The Chinese language does not use an alphabet, but symbols called characters. It traditionally has about 47,035 of them, but for everyday use between 3,000 and 4,000 is sufficient.

▼ A railway station sign for a town in Wales that bears the longest name of any place in Britain.

THE COUNTRY WITH THE HIGHEST NUMBER OF LANGUAGES IS PAPUA NEW GUINEA, WITH 820.

POLONIUS: What do you read, my lord?

HAMLET: Words, words, words.
Hamlet Act II, Scene II

Shakespeare

The genius William Shakespeare (1564–1616) is probably the best-known playwright of all time. His 38 plays contain 884,429 words, spoken by 1,221 characters.

ERATOSTHENES

How big is Earth?

The circumference of our planet at the Equator (the imaginary circle that runs around the center of Earth) is 24,901.8 mi (40,075.6 km). Ancient Greek mathematician Eratosthenes of Cyrene (276–195 BC) calculated it at 252,000 *stadia*, which is thought to have equaled 24,660 mi (39,690 km). If this is the case, Eratosthenes was only one percent off—not a bad effort, in the days before calculators and satellites!

"CLICK" SOUNDS FORM AN IMPORTANT PART OF SPOKEN LANGUAGE IN SOME AREAS OF SOUTHERN AFRICA.

THE LANGUAGE OF SILBO, FROM THE CANARY ISLANDS, USES PENETRATING WHISTLES THAT CAN BE HEARD OVER VERY LONG DISTANCES.

How many fingers?

Early methods of counting were based on people's fingers and toes, which is why most people today use a decimal counting system—one that is based on the number ten. The ancient Babylonians based their counting system on units of 60, which is why we still have 60 minutes in one hour and 360 degrees in a full circle.

$\pi = 3.14159$

Crunching numbers

The Greek letter *pi* is a handy little symbol. It is written as π and it helps you work out the area of a circle or its circumference. The value of $\pi = 3.1415926535...$ and so on, and so on. For how long? π has actually been calculated to more than a trillion decimal places!

In 2007, 16-year-old Australian student Peter Thamm recited pi to more than 10,000 decimal places. The current record-holder is Chinese student Lu Chao, who managed an incredible 67,890 decimal places.

Extreme CITIES

People usually build cities in an ideal spot with good supplies of food and water, deep harbors, good road and rail links, and a healthy climate. But sometimes cities have to be located in remote areas or difficult terrain, or where weather conditions are extreme.

On top of the world

La Paz is the highest capital in the world. It is the administrative center of Bolivia, sited amid the peaks of the Andes mountains. It has merged with the neighboring city of El Alto, so the total built-up area has altitudes of 9,800–13,600 ft (3,000–4,150 m) above sea level. Locals have adapted to living at high altitude, but visitors may suffer from severe headaches and sickness until they become acclimatized to low levels of oxygen.

Onward and upward—La Paz is still climbing up the mountainside.

La Paz boasts the world's highest velodrome, which has been used by cycling champions Arnaud Tournant of France and Sir Chris Hoy of Scotland to complete record-breaking one-kilometer time trials. The thin air is less resistant, but with less oxygen the body must work harder.

THE WORLD'S LOWEST CITY IS ALSO ONE OF THE OLDEST. JERICHO OR ARIHA IN PALESTINE IS 846 FT (258 M) BELOW SEA LEVEL, AND HAS STOOD THROUGH 11,000 YEARS OF HUMAN HISTORY.

Hot-hot-hot spots

The hottest temperature ever recorded on Earth was in 1922 in the city of Al 'Aziziyah in Libya, when the thermometer shot up to 135.9°F (57.7°C). Cities with exceptionally hot periods of the year include Kuwait City in Kuwait, and Ahvaz in Iran. Both have months where the average maximum temperature reaches 115°F (46°C).

Post Card

THIS SPACE FOR CORRESPONDENCE

The big fridge

Which is the coldest city on Earth? Yakutsk, in Siberia, is built on soil that remains permanently frozen, even in summer. In winter, temperatures can average –40°F (–40°C) and may drop below –50°F (–60°C), which is cold enough for people's glasses to freeze to their faces!

In most cities, a small leak in a water pipe means a small puddle. In Yakutsk, Siberia, it can mean one giant iceberg!

Monster metropolis

A global movement is taking place, as people all over the world move from the countryside into cities in search of work and a better life. Cities are massive consumers of power and water and produce mountains of waste and refuse.

OVER HALF OF THE WORLD'S POPULATION NOW LIVE IN CITIES.

Tokyo's Shinjuku district is a vast sprawl of offices and very busy people.

A DAY IN THE BIG APPLE

New York City is home to 2.7 percent of the U.S. population. Every day, New Yorkers...

- Use more than one billion gal (3.8 billion l) of water.
- Throw away enough garbage to fill the Empire State Building to the top floor.
- Make about five million trips on the subway.
- Are employed in 3.7 million jobs citywide.

Megacities and megaregions

Japan's capital Tokyo has grown so huge that it has merged with nearby cities such as Yokohama, Chiba, and Kawasaki. The joint urban area, or "conurbation," is home to about 35.7 million people.

On the south coast of China, conurbations have merged to create the most urban region on the planet, taking in cities such as Guangzhou, Shenzhen, and Hong Kong, with a population of about 120 million.

The most crowded city on Earth is Mumbai in India, with about 47,572 people per sq mi (29,560 per sq km).

No Place LIKE HOME

Many modern towns and cities look much the same wherever the location. But some people still live in traditional or unusual homes, where design is determined by climate and landscape, by available building materials, or by way of life.

CAVE DWELLINGS

Cappadocia, Turkey

In this area of exceptional natural wonders, the landscape is made up of volcanic rocks, which have been eroded into unusual pillars, columns, and caves. For thousands of years, local people have carved out homes, storerooms, and churches from the soft rock. The caves were often used as places of refuge when invading armies swept across the land. Today some have been made into hotels for tourists.

HOLE IN THE GROUND

Coober Pedy, Australia

To escape the heat of the Sun, the first opal miners often made their homes by converting disused mining shafts into living spaces. They were soon excavating new homes from the rock—they called them dugouts. Dugouts may include several bedrooms and spacious living rooms—all of them naturally air-conditioned!

LUXURY HOUSEBOAT

Kashmir, India

Houseboats are used in many parts of the world. Some of the most beautiful and decorative houseboats are moored around the lakes of Kashmir. Houseboats also line some of the canals of Amsterdam in the Netherlands, and provide homes for fishing families around Hong Kong's famous harbors.

TAKE TEA IN MY TENT

Eurasion steppes

The tent is the ideal living place for nomads—people on the move. The *yurt* or *ger* of the Mongols and Turkic peoples of the Eurasian steppes are domes of felt cloth supported by willow poles. They are cool in summer but warm in the bitterly cold winter, heated by stoves.

▶ These Mongolian tents look surprisingly cozy and inviting, despite the snowy grassland surrounding them.

Middle Eastern deserts

The tents used by nomadic herders in the Sahara and Arabian deserts are made of woven wool and hair from camels or goats. They are supported by poles and long guy ropes, and pitched low to provide a minimum of resistance to wind and sandstorms.

◀ This tent offers home comforts in the middle of the Moroccan Sahara.

FLOATING REED HOUSES

Southern Iraq

The Ma'dan or Marsh Arabs live in the wetlands of southern Iraq. Their traditional homes are built from reeds and sited on riverbanks or on artificial islands, made of mud and bundles of reeds. The people have suffered greatly from warfare and the draining of the marshes. Only now is the water beginning to flow once again through this landscape.

▼ For the Ma'dan, the wetlands provide natural resources, and act as a highway.

Enjoy *Your Meal*

An old saying goes: "One man's meat is another man's poison." We don't all enjoy the same kinds of food. Often the meals we were brought up on seem the safest and tastiest to us, while the dishes eaten by people in countries other than our own may seem strange, or even downright disgusting. But go on—be adventurous!

Frogs' Legs *France*

In parts of France, frogs' legs are eaten, fried in breadcrumbs. It's said that they taste a lot like chicken wings, and it's not just a French thing—they're also popular in the U.S. state of Louisiana and in China. And if you find yourself in Indonesia you might try *swikee*—a delicious frogs' legs soup.

Fugu *Japan*

Would you have the stomach to eat a fish dish that could kill you—even for a dare? One Japanese delicacy is fugu, or pufferfish, and some parts of this strange animal contain a deadly poison. Only specially trained chefs know how to prepare the meal so that it can be eaten safely. And accidents do happen...

Haggis *Scotland*

First you need a sheep. Chop up its lungs, heart, and liver and mix with oatmeal, suet, and onion. Then cook for three hours—once you've packed it all into a sheep's intestine. On January 25 each year, Scots honor their national poet, Robert Burns, by playing bagpipes and reciting a poem to the haggis before digging in.

Don't worry—you don't actually have to swallow sticks and mud! This soup is an expensive delicacy made from the edible saliva of cave swiftlet birds. The birds use the saliva to build their nests in the caves of Borneo, or in special nesting houses where it can be harvested.

China

Birds' Nest Soup

Also on the global menu...

Dog — Vietnam
The original hot dog? Dogs are eaten in many parts of east Asia.

Donkey salami — Italy
Most Italian salami is made of pork but donkey, horse, and goat are also used.

Sheep's eyes — Arabia
A whole roast sheep may be served at an Arabian feast, including—as a real treat—the eyeballs.

Iguana — South America
Stewed or roast iguana (a type of large lizard) is a traditional food in parts of Central America.

Locust — North Africa
Desert locusts are big grasshoppers. Perfectly bite-sized, they can be fried, roasted, boiled, and even sundried.

Alligator — USA
These huge reptiles have always been eaten in the southern states. Now scarce in the wild, they are farmed for their hides and meat.

Guinea pigs provide a really popular meal in Peru and in some other regions of the Andes mountains. These small, furry creatures can be raised in the home or bought at street markets, for frying or roasting. The meat is said to be low in fat and full of goodness.

Peru

Guinea pig

Witchetty grub

Yummy! These large larvae can be eaten raw or baked in hot ashes. The grubs are a traditional favorite of Australia's Aborigines. Other "bush tucker" (wild food) has become popular in restaurants—including kangaroo, emu, and goanna (lizard) meat.

Australia

Ultimate JOBS

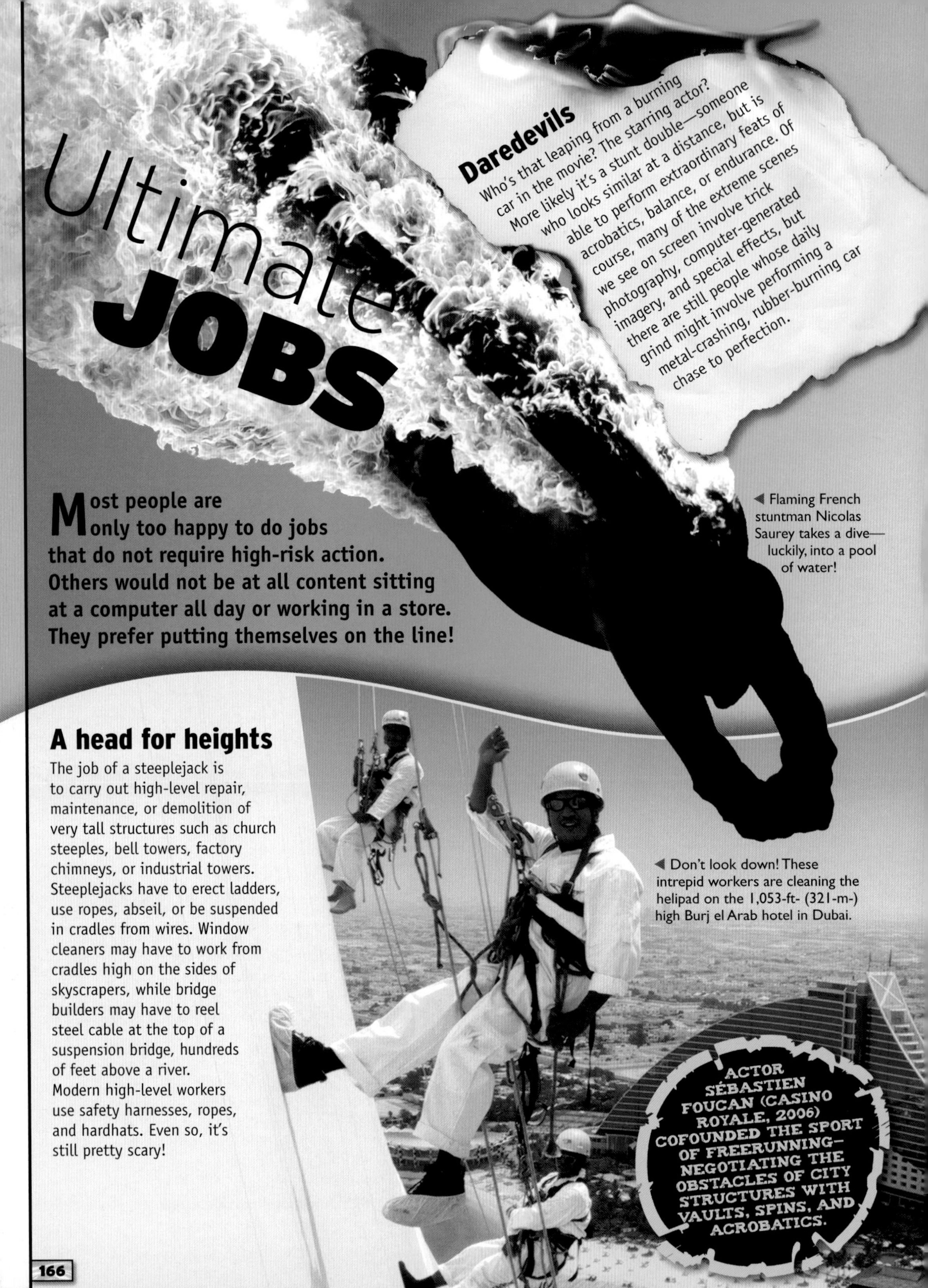

Daredevils

Who's that leaping from a burning car in the movie? The starring actor? More likely it's a stunt double—someone who looks similar at a distance, but is able to perform extraordinary feats of acrobatics, balance, or endurance. Of course, many of the extreme scenes we see on screen involve trick photography, computer-generated imagery, and special effects, but there are still people whose daily grind might involve performing a metal-crashing, rubber-burning car chase to perfection.

◀ Flaming French stuntman Nicolas Saurey takes a dive—luckily, into a pool of water!

Most people are only too happy to do jobs that do not require high-risk action. Others would not be at all content sitting at a computer all day or working in a store. They prefer putting themselves on the line!

A head for heights

The job of a steeplejack is to carry out high-level repair, maintenance, or demolition of very tall structures such as church steeples, bell towers, factory chimneys, or industrial towers. Steeplejacks have to erect ladders, use ropes, abseil, or be suspended in cradles from wires. Window cleaners may have to work from cradles high on the sides of skyscrapers, while bridge builders may have to reel steel cable at the top of a suspension bridge, hundreds of feet above a river. Modern high-level workers use safety harnesses, ropes, and hardhats. Even so, it's still pretty scary!

◀ Don't look down! These intrepid workers are cleaning the helipad on the 1,053-ft- (321-m-) high Burj el Arab hotel in Dubai.

ACTOR SÉBASTIEN FOUCAN (CASINO ROYALE, 2006) COFOUNDED THE SPORT OF FREERUNNING—NEGOTIATING THE OBSTACLES OF CITY STRUCTURES WITH VAULTS, SPINS, AND ACROBATICS.

All hands on deck

One of the most dangerous professions in the U.S. is crab fishing. Working for long hours on a trawler in freezing seas, with giant waves, gales, a slippery deck, nets, winches, rocks, and reefs can be a high-risk way to earn a living.

◀ Bringing in the catch is a feat of endurance for these fishermen.

Diving to great depths

Divers need to venture into very deep water for all sorts of reasons, including scientific research, archeology, geology, and industrial monitoring. One big problem is water pressure, which can damage the human body and cause a sickness called the "bends." An atmospheric diving suit or ADS allows a diver to go down to extreme depths—a maximum of 2,300 ft (700 m)—in safety. It is like a suit of armor, made of aluminum or special plastic.

▲ Wearing a "newtsuit" (a type of ADS) allows this rescue diver to descend to depths greater than 820 ft (250 m).

▶ Astronauts are weightless as they work far above Earth—and the view is spectacular!

Space walkers

An astronaut's job is literally out of this world. When leaving the spacecraft for extravehicular activity (EVA), he or she may be floating in space perhaps 220 mi (350 km) above our planet, often trying at the same time to fix a broken piece of equipment or carry out an experiment. The astronaut may be tethered to the spacecraft with an oxygen line, or be self-sufficient with a personal mobile maneuvering unit (MMU).

Awesome ARCHITECTURE

Humans have come a long way since they built the first simple huts from twigs and grass. Today we can design fantastic structures, made of a huge range of materials from steel and glass to concrete and plastic. Modern buildings can dazzle and deceive the eye, soar into the sky—or do the most amazingly clever things!

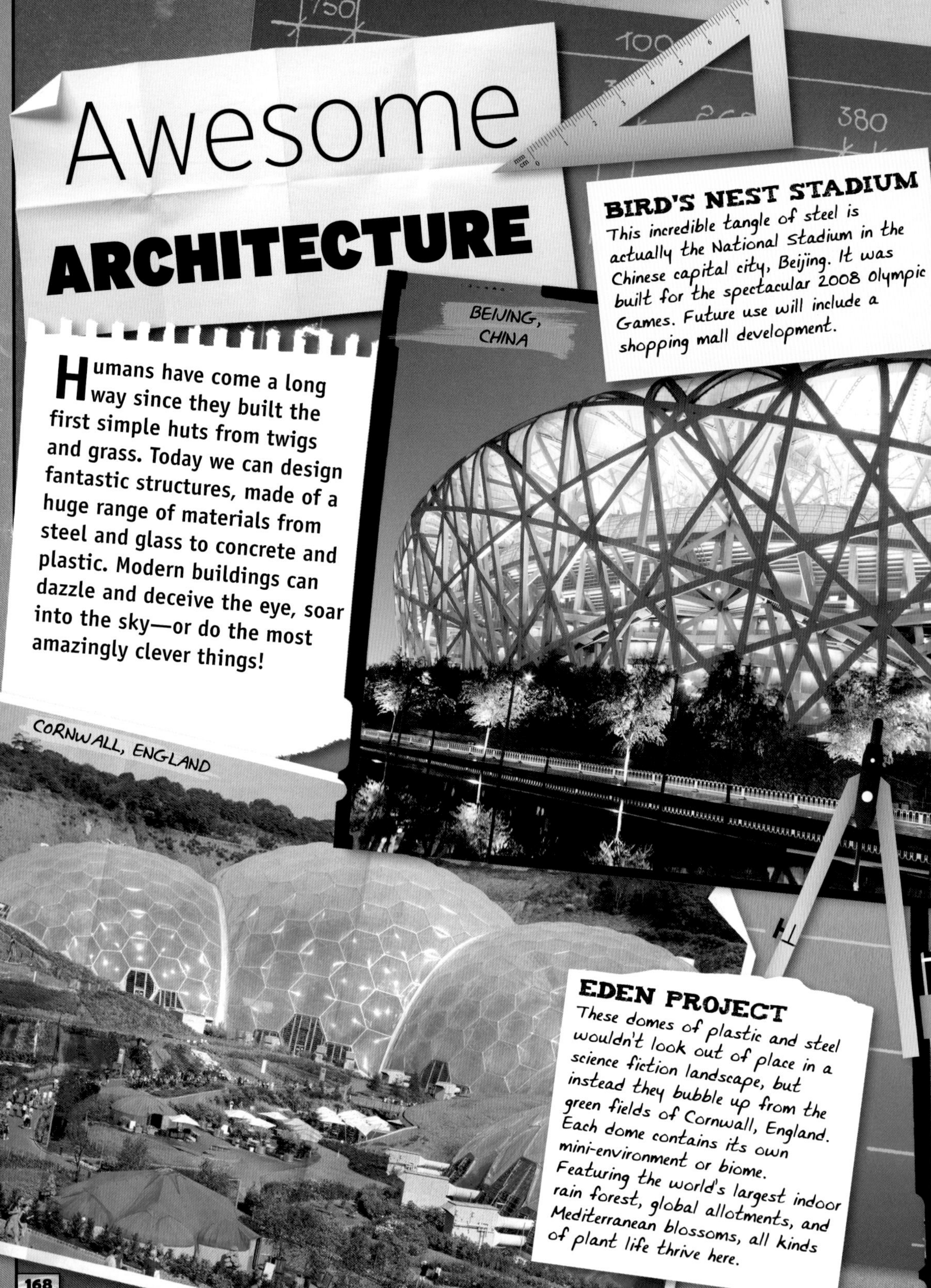

BIRD'S NEST STADIUM

This incredible tangle of steel is actually the National Stadium in the Chinese capital city, Beijing. It was built for the spectacular 2008 Olympic Games. Future use will include a shopping mall development.

EDEN PROJECT

These domes of plastic and steel wouldn't look out of place in a science fiction landscape, but instead they bubble up from the green fields of Cornwall, England. Each dome contains its own mini-environment or biome. Featuring the world's largest indoor rain forest, global allotments, and Mediterranean blossoms, all kinds of plant life thrive here.

SOLAR FURNACE

The giant mirrors at Odeillo, France, reflect the rays of the Sun onto a larger, curved mirror (shown here). The focused reflections create a single point where the temperature can reach up to 6,330°F (3,500°C), which can then be used for industrial purposes such as generating electricity and melting steel.

CUBE HOUSES

It looks a bit like massive children's playing blocks have tumbled across the square. Completed in 1984, these buildings are in fact a mini village of three-story houses in Rotterdam in the Netherlands, which were designed by Dutch architect Piet Blom to tilt at an angle of 45 degrees.

Brilliant BRAIN WAVES

Throughout history people have made great discoveries and come up with fantastic inventions to transform the way we live. Where would we be today without the wheel, or writing (both invented in ancient Iraq 5,000–6,000 years ago)? Or indeed more trivial inventions such as chewing gum (used in Stone Age Finland about 5,000 years ago)? Inventors are still working away today, to come up with new ideas for the 21st century.

Leonardo da Vinci

The greatest inventor of all time

Italian artist Leonardo da Vinci (1452–1519) had some of the best ideas for inventions long before their time, including helicopters, hang gliders, crank mechanisms, weapons, portable bridges, and a musical instrument called the viola organista, which was the first bowed keyboard instrument ever devised.

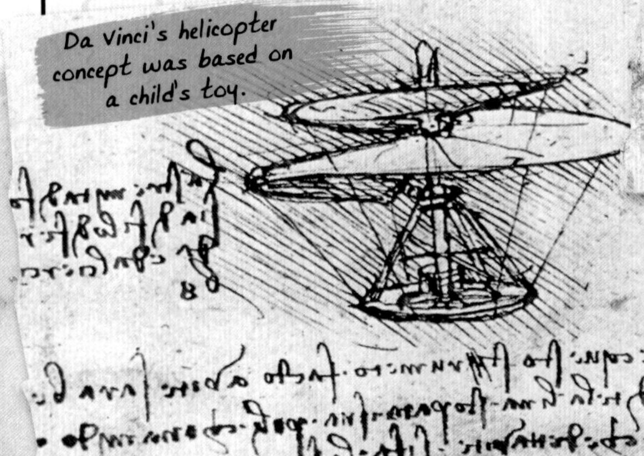

Da Vinci's helicopter concept was based on a child's toy.

Da Vinci's 1478 design for a self-propelled car.

5 PRETTY USELESS (IF NOT DOWNRIGHT WACKY) INVENTIONS

* Clockwork weights to drop on your head and wake you up (1882)
* Eagle-powered balloon (1887)
* Automatic hat-raiser (1896)
* Obstacle courses for goldfish (2009)
* Electric ear dryer (2009)

Deadly discovery

Invented in China about 1,200 years ago, gunpowder is arguably the most deadly invention ever. In World War I (1914–1918) alone, 9.7 million soldiers were killed worldwide, and 8.9 million civilians—many the victims of shells, rifle and machine gun fire, and bombs.

Terror strikes a World War I battlefield... gunpowder was a brilliant brain wave with terrible consequences.

Lifesaving science

Antibiotics are one of the most useful inventions of all time. These modern drugs have saved many millions of lives around the world. The credit is due to many scientists of the 19th and 20th centuries, including Louis Pasteur, Robert Koch, John Tyndall, Paul Ehrlich, Alexander Fleming, Gerhard Domagk, René Dubos, Howard Florey, and Ernst Chain.

ALEXANDER FLEMING DISCOVERED (BY ACCIDENT) THAT PENICILLIUM MOLD, FOUND ON STALE BREAD, COULD FIGHT DEADLY BACTERIA. THE ANTIBIOTIC WONDER DRUG PENICILLIN WAS BEING PRODUCED IN THE U.S. BY 1943.

Discovered: the secret of life

Genetics is one of the most important modern sciences. During the 1860s, Austrian botanist Gregor Mendel worked out the laws of inheritance—how living things pass on their characteristics down the generations. In 1869 it was discovered that cells contain a hereditary material called deoxyribonucleic acid—or "DNA." Scientists who tried to determine the structure of this chemical included Rosalind Franklin and Maurice Wilson, and in 1953 the code was finally cracked by James Watson and Francis Crick, providing a springboard for 21st-century science and medicine.

Gregor Mendel

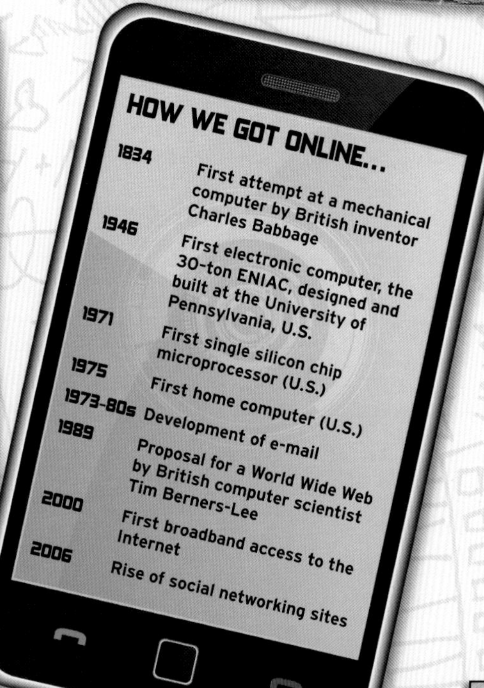

HOW WE GOT ONLINE...

- **1834** First attempt at a mechanical computer by British inventor Charles Babbage
- **1946** First electronic computer, the 30-ton ENIAC, designed and built at the University of Pennsylvania, U.S.
- **1971** First single silicon chip microprocessor (U.S.)
- **1975** First home computer (U.S.)
- **1973-80s** Development of e-mail
- **1989** Proposal for a World Wide Web by British computer scientist Tim Berners-Lee
- **2000** First broadband access to the Internet
- **2006** Rise of social networking sites

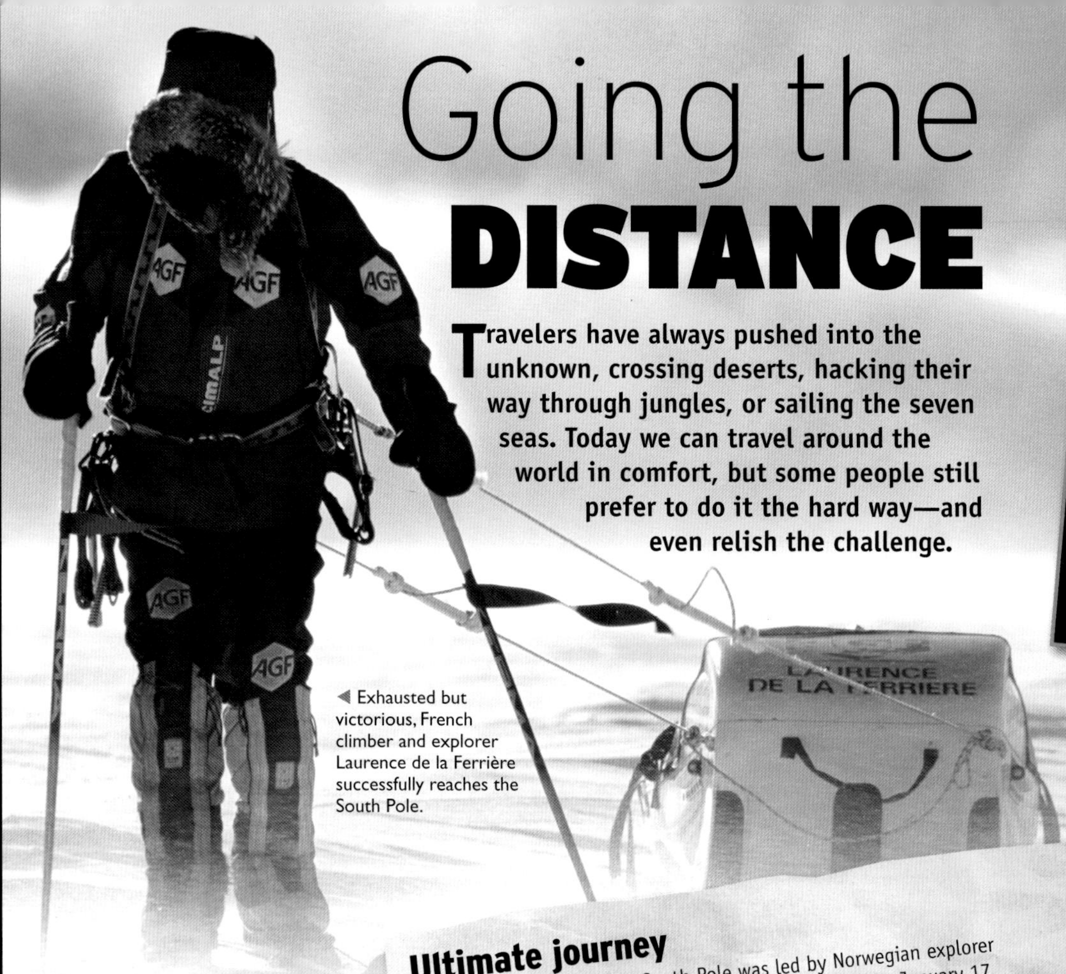

Going the DISTANCE

Travelers have always pushed into the unknown, crossing deserts, hacking their way through jungles, or sailing the seven seas. Today we can travel around the world in comfort, but some people still prefer to do it the hard way—and even relish the challenge.

◀ Exhausted but victorious, French climber and explorer Laurence de la Ferrière successfully reaches the South Pole.

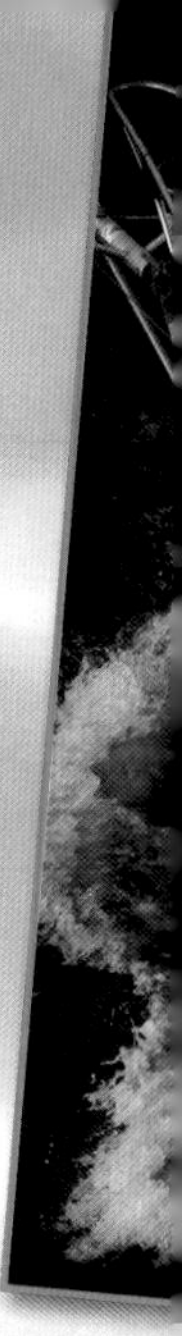

Into the deep freeze

Frenchwoman Laurence de la Ferrière has climbed Himalayan peaks, explored the ice floes of the Bering Strait, made a solo crossing of Greenland, traversed the whole range of the Alps, and made a two-stage solo crossing of Antarctica (1996–1997 and 1999–2000).

Ultimate journey

The first expedition to the South Pole was led by Norwegian explorer Roald Amundsen, and arrived on December 14, 1911. On January 17, 1912, a British team led by Robert Falcon Scott also reached the Pole—"Great God!" Scott wrote in his diary, "This is an awful place." On the return journey, Scott and his whole team perished in appalling conditions.

Members of Captain Scott's ill-fated expedition to the South Pole.

THE LOWEST TEMPERATURE EVER RECORDED AT THE SOUTH POLE IS A DECIDEDLY CHILLY -117°F (-82.8°C)!

▼ Jessica Watson takes the helm of her yacht, *Pink Lady*. She was declared Young Australian of the Year for 2011.

Up, up, and away

Steve Fossett (1944–2007) was an aviator, sailor, skier, and climber. In 2002 he became the first man to fly solo around the world in a balloon, without stopping. His flight from Australia covered 20,626 mi (33,195 km).

Going solo

In 2009–2010, Australian yachtswoman Jessica Watson sailed solo around the world. Although her route from Sydney across the Pacific, Atlantic, and Indian oceans was not the official one, it was an incredible achievement. At the time she was just 16 years old.

◀ Fossett's balloon, *Solo Spirit*, leaves the east coast of Australia behind and heads out over the open ocean.

Downriver

Does anyone fancy going for a stroll? There probably wouldn't be many volunteers if the stroll in question takes 860 days and is about 4,000 mi (about 6,400 km) long. This was the achievement of English explorer Ed Stafford. He followed the course of the mighty Amazon River from its source to the ocean, completing his trek in 2010.

◀ Ed Stafford and his companion "Cho" Sanchez Rivera trekked through swamps and dense forest—home to many potentially lethal creatures including jaguars, piranha, and killer bees.

Millions of Pilgrims

Some of the world's largest gatherings of people, biggest buildings, and most spectacular events are associated with religious belief and worship. The majority of the people in the world follow faiths, which may vary from traditional spirit beliefs to large, organized religions. More than one billion people around the world do not follow a religion or are nonbelievers.

THE GOLDEN TEMPLE OF THE SIKHS, IN AMRITSAR, INDIA, IS A SITE OF GREAT BEAUTY.

◀ Shwedagon attracts Buddhist pilgrims from all over Burma.

▲ Seville's great altarpiece shows 45 scenes from the life of Christ.

Golden glory

Some of the world's most spectacular religious buildings are built to sparkle! The altarpiece of the Christian Seville Cathedral in Spain, one of the biggest in the world, is covered in gold, and was the life's work of a single craftsman—Flemish sculptor Pieter Dancart.

The Harmandir Sahib, or Golden Temple, was built between 1585 and 1604 at Amritsar in India. It is the center of the Sikh faith and its gold roof and walls are reflected in the still waters of an artificial lake.

The Buddhist Shwedagon pagoda in Yangon, Burma, is plated in gold donated by the faithful. The crown at the top contains an incredible 5,448 diamonds and 2,317 rubies.

Christian Trappist monks speak only rarely, as they believe speech can be a distraction from thought and prayer.

Jain monks may wear masks out of reverence for all forms of life, in case they accidentally swallow a fly or inhale a microbe.

THE BIGGEST STATUE OF THE BUDDHA IS AT LESHAN IN CHINA AND IS 233 FT (71 M) HIGH. IT WAS CARVED FROM THE CLIFF FACE BETWEEN AD 713 AND 803.

Many, many people...

The world's biggest annual pilgrimage is the Hajj, the journey to Mecca in Saudi Arabia by more than two million Muslims every year. Pilgrimage is one of the basic "pillars" or duties of the Islamic faith, and the mosque at Mecca is the largest in the world.

The world's biggest religious gatherings are a series of Hindu pilgrimages held in northern India over cycles of four, six, 12, and 144 years. The biggest ever of these was a Maha Kumbh Mela at Allahabad in northern India in 2001, which may have attracted as many as 60 million people.

THE DRAMATIC LIGHTS OF ESALA PERAHERA, CELEBRATED BY SRI LANKAN BUDDHISTS.

All lit up

One of the most spectacular religious processions is the Esala Perahera, organized by Buddhist monks in Kandy, Sri Lanka. It honors a sacred relic, the Buddha's tooth. Elephants take part dressed in spectacular cloth that is decorated with electric lightbulbs, and there are flags, musicians, drummers, glittering costumes, cracking whips, flaming torches, and peacock dancers.

▼ Muslim pilgrims at Mecca must walk seven times around the Kaaba, a sacred structure covered in black silk.

In Turkey, mystics of the Sufi Mevlevi order perform a religious dance, which involves spinning round and round. They are known as "whirling dervishes."

On Jewish religious days such as Rosh Hashanah and Yom Kippur, a Tokea blows the sacred shofar—a ram's horn trumpet.

Lives on the LINE

The worst events often bring out the best in people. When there is an accident or emergency, ambulance crews, police, or firefighters are soon at the scene, helping out and saving lives. When there is a major natural or man-made disaster, people often show heroism in extremely difficult conditions, putting their own lives on the line to save others.

Lifeboat SOS!

No one chooses to go to sea during an extreme storm—unless there are lives to save. Towering waves, gale-force winds, blizzards, injured crew, loose cargo, and foundering ships may all be encountered on callouts. Helicopters may also be required to lower lines to stricken vessels in dangerous weather conditions or poor visibility.

In the U.K., search-and-rescue lifeboats are operated by volunteers of the Royal National Lifeboat Institution (RNLI). Since it was founded in 1824 this charity has saved more than 139,000 lives at sea. In 2009, RNLI crews were called out on 9,154 occasions and saved 8,186 people.

▲ An inshore lifeboat slams into the waves as a crew goes into action off the coast of Wales, U.K.

Fighting the blaze

Fires may break out naturally in hot, dry weather or when lightning strikes. Most fires are the result of human error—for example gas explosions or house fires. Firefighters are in the front line, directing water hoses, entering burning buildings, demolishing structures, or clearing vegetation to prevent fire spreading. Firefighters also attend other emergency incidents, such as chemical spillages, road and rail crashes, and air disasters.

◀ Fighting a wall of fire needs bravery, physical strength, and clear thinking in the midst of a crisis.

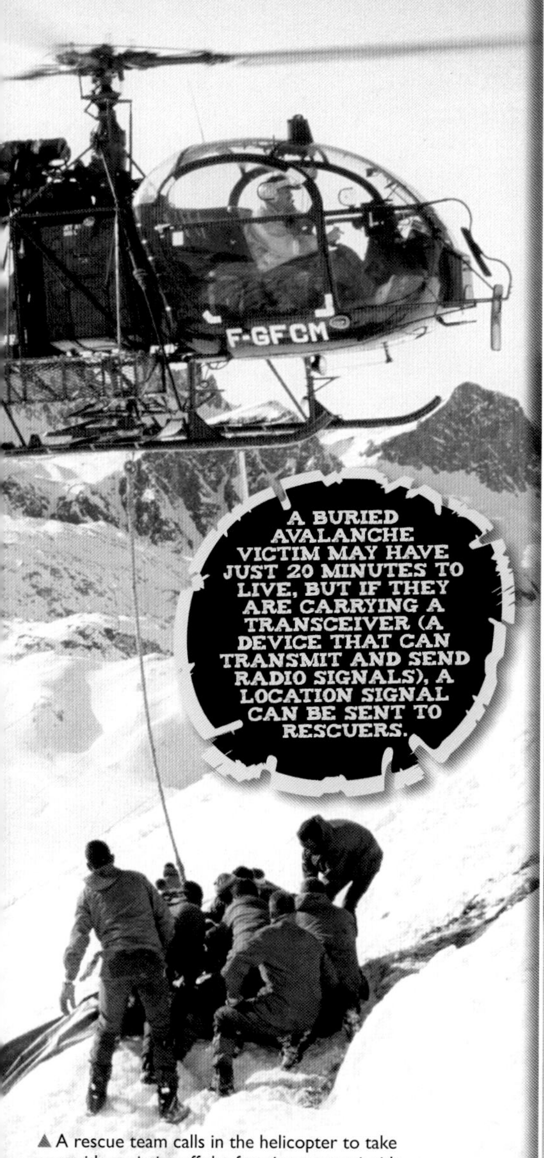

A BURIED AVALANCHE VICTIM MAY HAVE JUST 20 MINUTES TO LIVE, BUT IF THEY ARE CARRYING A TRANSCEIVER (A DEVICE THAT CAN TRANSMIT AND SEND RADIO SIGNALS), A LOCATION SIGNAL CAN BE SENT TO RESCUERS.

▲A rescue team calls in the helicopter to take an accident victim off the freezing mountainside, and away to the nearest hospital.

Precipice peril

Mountain search-and-rescue teams may be made up of full-time professionals, or volunteers. They often have to turn out in appalling conditions, and must know the terrain, and be experts at climbing, first aid, and communications. They may use dogs and probes to locate people buried in avalanches, and call in support from helicopter rescue services. Piloting helicopters in mountainous areas in poor conditions is a hazardous and highly skilled task.

UNDERGROUND SURVIVAL

On August 5, 2010, a tunnel at the San José gold and copper mine in Chile, caved in. For 69 days the world held its breath—33 miners were trapped about 2,300 ft (700 m) beneath the ground, some 3 mi (5 km) from the mine's entrance. How would they ever make it back to the surface?

▼The rescue capsule (called Phoenix 2) started to go down at 23:18 local time.

Mine rescue teams face some of the most daunting conditions of all—there may be floods, explosions, or cave-ins at any time. The Chilean rescuers had to come up with their own scheme...

The 33 miners reached a small refuge chamber. Every other day, each person ate one biscuit and two small spoonfuls of tuna, and drank a little milk.

On Day 17, a drill from the surface reached a point near the trapped miners, and they were able to attach a note to it, telling the world that all 33 of them were alive and safe.

Shafts were drilled down and widened. With the help of U.S. space agency NASA, the Chilean navy built steel rescue capsules.

On October 12, a rescue worker was lowered into the refuge chamber. Up came the first miner, Florencio Ávalos. Within 24 hours, all 33 miners were safely at the surface—and the world rejoiced.

300 ft
600 ft
Mine shaft
900 ft
Phoenix 2 rescue capsule
1,200 ft
Escape shaft
1,500 ft
1,800 ft
Location of mine shaft collapse
2,100 ft
Location of the refuge chamber where the miners waited to be rescued
2,400 ft

Looking GOOD

Humans have always put a lot of thought and effort into their appearance. Even when people wear similar clothes in cities around the world, there's still all sorts of variation, from wedding dresses, fashion statements, and performance gear, to military uniforms, traditional clothes, or religious dress.

Silver headdress

GUIZHOU PROVINCE, CHINA
Spectacular silver jewelry is worn on special occasions by the women of the Miao people.

Pearly king

LONDON, ENGLAND
Cockneys (people from the East End of London) used to decorate their clothes with pearl buttons. Today "pearly kings and queens" raise money for charity.

Masked reveler

SWABIA, GERMANY
In southern Germany and the Alps, the *Fastnacht* carnival is celebrated with weird masks and ribboned costumes.

Painted bride

KOSOVO/MACEDONIA
In the Shar mountain region, the brides of the Torbesh community have their faces painted for good luck.

Catwalk couture

PARIS, FRANCE
High fashion looks are paraded on the catwalk in stylish cities such as Paris, Milan, New York, and London.

Temple dancer

THAILAND
Beautiful costumes and headdresses are worn by Thailand's graceful dancers.

Stilt balancer

MALI
The funerals of the Dogon people feature masked and costumed dancers, some of them on tall stilts.

Feathered highlander

PAPUA NEW GUINEA
Fantastic feathers, costumes, and face paints are still worn at tribal gatherings in the mountains of Papua New Guinea.

Haka warrior

NEW ZEALAND
Hakas are traditional dances of the Maori people, still performed on ceremonial occasions. High-ranking Maoris used to have intricate facial tattoos.

The Art of PERFORMING

Shows and displays provide performers with an excuse to go that extra mile for the sake of their art. Many great creative types love working on a grand scale, or shocking the audience. And when it comes to pop music or the circus, spectacular and extraordinary sights are just what the public expects.

Making a splash

Between 2005 and 2007, Henry Purcell's opera *Dido and Aeneas* was staged by a Berlin-based dance company called Sasha Waltz & Guests. The 17 dancers performed the opening prologue underwater, in a tank filled with 9,000 gal (about 34,000 l) of water.

▲ *Dido and Aeneas*—the oldest known English opera still performed—was reinvented with innovative underwater choreography.

That's a wrap

Some of the most spectacular art installations of the last 50 years were made by the artists Christo and Jeanne-Claude. They wrapped up famous public buildings, bridges, and monuments. In 1971 they placed a 150,700 sq ft (14,000 sq m) orange curtain across a valley in the Rocky Mountains, and two years later built a 25-mi- (40-km-) long fence in California, U.S. In 1983 they surrounded 11 islands in the U.S. state of Florida with 6,499 sq ft (604 sq m) of pink plastic, employing 430 workers.

◀ In 1997–1998 Christo and Jeanne-Claude wrapped these trees in Switzerland in woven polyester fabric.

Live Aid had the biggest ever global audience, all in a good cause. It was organized by rock stars Bob Geldof and Midge Ure.

The giant gig

In 1985, Live Aid rock concerts were held at multiple venues around the world to raise funds to relieve the famine in Ethiopia. Thanks to satellite television, Live Aid was viewed by about two billion people in 60 countries, and raised around $50 million (£30 million).

The legendary skills of the Chinese State Circus.

Celebrated ceiling

The Sistine Chapel in Rome has a beautiful painted ceiling—the work of Italian artist Michelangelo. It covers 11,840 sq ft (1,100 sq m), with the nine central panels showing the stories of the Book of Genesis. The ceiling took around four years to complete (1508–1512), and over 4.3 million visitors a year continue to visit five centuries later.

Michelangelo's masterpiece contains more than 300 figures.

Circus spectaculars

Animals are now rarely used in circuses. Instead, incredible human feats are being taken to new limits. Popular acts in both the traditional and the modern circus (which places greater emphasis on artistry, music, storytelling, and theater) include juggling, mind-boggling contortion of the human body, daring work on the trapeze and high wire, sword swallowing, and fire-eating.

Fun, Fun, FUN!

▲ The *Palio*—a giddy gallop in the center of Siena, Italy.

Fairs and festivals offer people a chance to relax and have fun. Traditionally, carnival permits outrageous behavior that would not be accepted at any other time of the year. There may be costumed parades, fireworks on a lavish scale, funfair rides, music, dancing, singing, and feasting.

Palio!

Twice a year the Piazza del Campo, in the Italian town of Siena, is taken over by crowds and colorful flags that represent each of the city's 17 wards. The event is a fast and furious, no-holds-barred, bareback horse race for three laps of the square. It is an exciting, dangerous contest, which recalls public games such as jousting and bullfights in medieval Italy. The race is known as the *Palio*, after the banner awarded to the winner.

Samba city

The world's most famous carnival parade and samba dancing extravaganza is in Rio de Janeiro, Brazil. The festivities in the city date back to 1723 and the highlight is the parade of floats that head for the "sambadrome." Each float is packed with members of rival samba "schools," flanked by dancers, all wearing the most fantastic, glittering costumes. There are costumed balls, parties on the streets and beaches, and everywhere fantastic drumming to a samba rhythm can be heard.

▶ Rio's samba schools practice all year round to prepare for the flamboyant spectacle of Carnival.

▶ A "Viking longship" is set ablaze in Lerwick, Scotland. Up Helly Aa is claimed to be the biggest fire festival in Europe.

Up Helly Aa

This fire festival is celebrated in the darkness of winter in Shetland, off the coast of Scotland. The biggest celebration, in the town of Lerwick, is marked by a procession of 1,000 "guizers" (costumed revelers) carrying flaming torches, led by a Jarl (the Norse word for an earl). The torches are hurled into a boat resembling the old dragon-prowed longships of the Viking age, more than 1,000 years ago.

AT THE TOMATINA FESTIVAL IN BUÑOL, SPAIN, PARTICIPANTS HURL MILLIONS OF SQUASHED TOMATOES AT EACH OTHER.

Great towers of buns!

An amazing festival is held each year on the island of Cheung Chau, Hong Kong. There are religious rituals, and parades with lion dancing, dragon dancing, lanterns, drums, and gongs. Children in traditional costume are held up high in the air on poles. Towers of buns 65-ft (20-m) high are erected, and teams climb them to grab the buns for good luck.

◀ The big bun scramble, bringing good fortune for the coming year.

OoooOOOOOOOOOAAAhhh!

In many countries, national days or independence days are marked by fairs and public celebrations. The big day in the U.S. is July 4. Many cities stage awesome firework displays on this special day, lighting up the night sky. One of the biggest firework fests is held in Detroit, Michigan, which joins up with the Canada Day (July 1) celebrations going on just over the border in neighboring Windsor, Ontario, for an International Freedom Festival. About 3.5 million people come to see the sparks fly!

History REVEALED

Go back in time and uncover a host of extreme events, ideas, and people that changed the course of history.

◀ The movie *Troy* (2004) tells the story of the Trojan War—the ancient Greeks believed a great war, lasting for ten years, was fought in the 1200s BC between the Greeks and the Trojans.

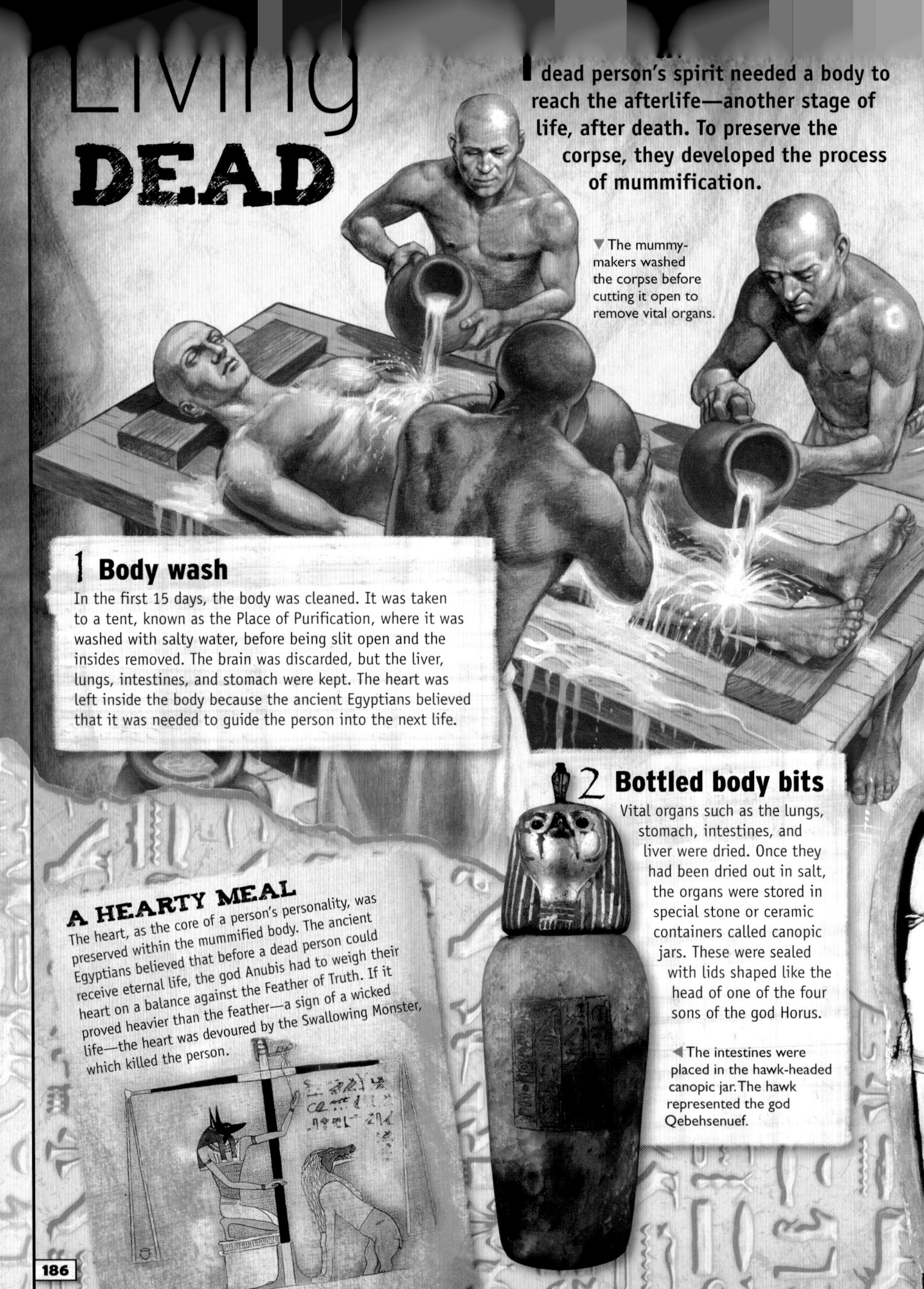

Living DEAD

dead person's spirit needed a body to reach the afterlife—another stage of life, after death. To preserve the corpse, they developed the process of mummification.

▼ The mummy-makers washed the corpse before cutting it open to remove vital organs.

1 Body wash

In the first 15 days, the body was cleaned. It was taken to a tent, known as the Place of Purification, where it was washed with salty water, before being slit open and the insides removed. The brain was discarded, but the liver, lungs, intestines, and stomach were kept. The heart was left inside the body because the ancient Egyptians believed that it was needed to guide the person into the next life.

2 Bottled body bits

Vital organs such as the lungs, stomach, intestines, and liver were dried. Once they had been dried out in salt, the organs were stored in special stone or ceramic containers called canopic jars. These were sealed with lids shaped like the head of one of the four sons of the god Horus.

◀ The intestines were placed in the hawk-headed canopic jar. The hawk represented the god Qebehsenuef.

A HEARTY MEAL

The heart, as the core of a person's personality, was preserved within the mummified body. The ancient Egyptians believed that before a dead person could receive eternal life, the god Anubis had to weigh their heart on a balance against the Feather of Truth. If it proved heavier than the feather—a sign of a wicked life—the heart was devoured by the Swallowing Monster, which killed the person.

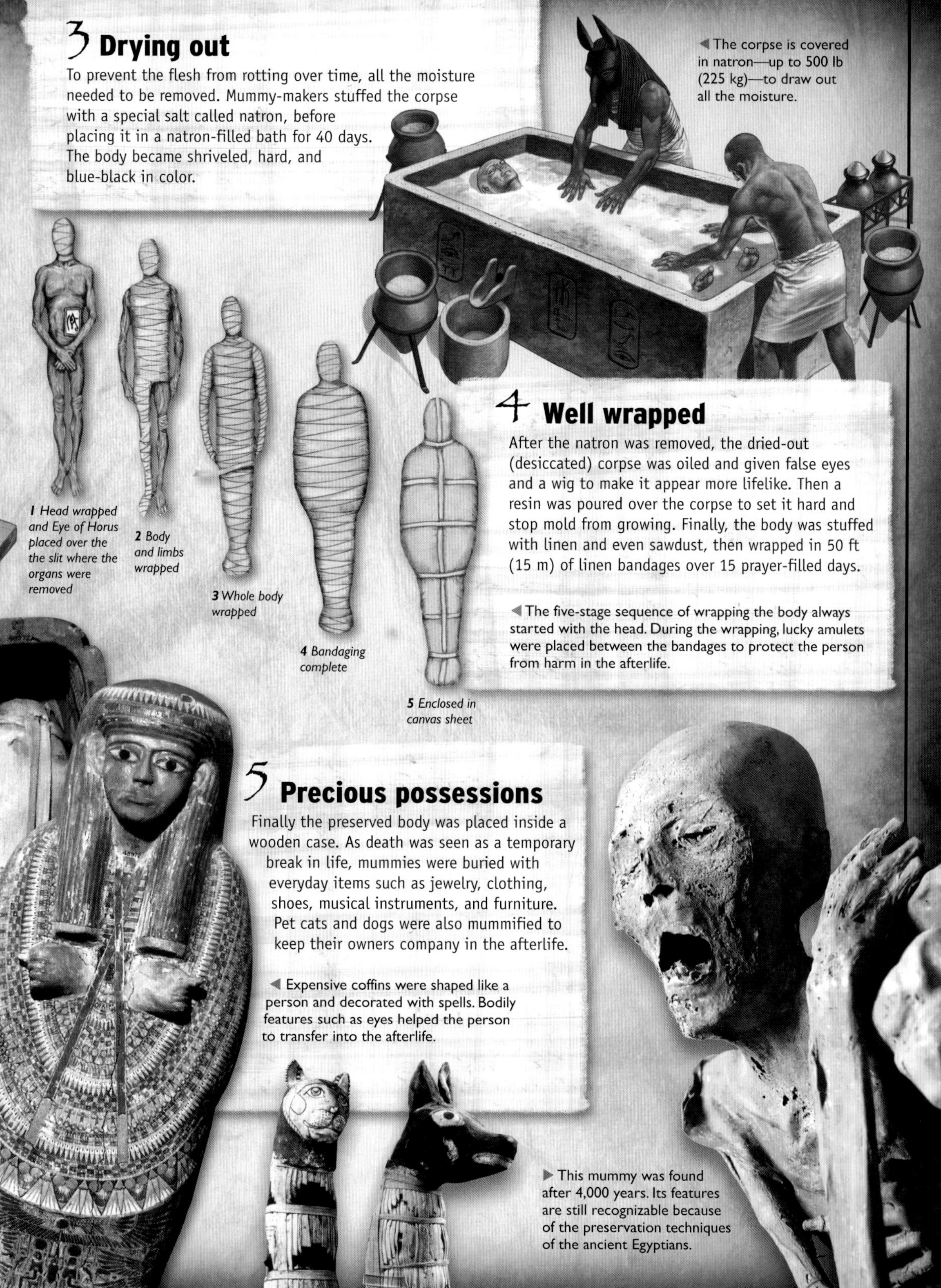

3 Drying out

To prevent the flesh from rotting over time, all the moisture needed to be removed. Mummy-makers stuffed the corpse with a special salt called natron, before placing it in a natron-filled bath for 40 days. The body became shriveled, hard, and blue-black in color.

◀ The corpse is covered in natron—up to 500 lb (225 kg)—to draw out all the moisture.

1 Head wrapped and Eye of Horus placed over the the slit where the organs were removed

2 Body and limbs wrapped

3 Whole body wrapped

4 Bandaging complete

5 Enclosed in canvas sheet

4 Well wrapped

After the natron was removed, the dried-out (desiccated) corpse was oiled and given false eyes and a wig to make it appear more lifelike. Then a resin was poured over the corpse to set it hard and stop mold from growing. Finally, the body was stuffed with linen and even sawdust, then wrapped in 50 ft (15 m) of linen bandages over 15 prayer-filled days.

◀ The five-stage sequence of wrapping the body always started with the head. During the wrapping, lucky amulets were placed between the bandages to protect the person from harm in the afterlife.

5 Precious possessions

Finally the preserved body was placed inside a wooden case. As death was seen as a temporary break in life, mummies were buried with everyday items such as jewelry, clothing, shoes, musical instruments, and furniture. Pet cats and dogs were also mummified to keep their owners company in the afterlife.

◀ Expensive coffins were shaped like a person and decorated with spells. Bodily features such as eyes helped the person to transfer into the afterlife.

▶ This mummy was found after 4,000 years. Its features are still recognizable because of the preservation techniques of the ancient Egyptians.

Battle BEASTS

During early warfare, commanders used a variety of animals to gain an edge over their enemy. The most common was the horse—it carried cavalry, pulled chariots, and transported heavy loads. The camel, though slower, served well in desert campaigns. By far the most spectacular warrior animal was the mighty elephant, a living tank that trampled and terrorized its foes across Asia, North Africa, and Southern Europe.

▼ In 218 BC, the Carthaginian general Hannibal launched a surprise attack on his Roman enemies by leading an army, backed by war-trained elephants, across the Alps and into Italy. Hannibal won three great victories before he was forced to retire.

Anti-elephant

Ears flapping, trunk raised, tusks lancing... the awesome sight of a war elephant on the charge was enough to turn the legs of the bravest warrior to jelly. However, tactics were devised to halt the 30-mph (50-km/h) onslaught. The Romans learned to step aside at the last minute, Alexander the Great's men slashed at the beasts' hamstrings with axes, the Mongols catapulted rocks at them, and in more modern times the beasts were brought down by cannon fire.

Charge!

While several peoples of Central Asia were renowned for being able to shoot arrows accurately while on horseback, it was only with the invention of the stirrup in the 4th century AD that cavalry came into their own. Their grandest form was the mounted medieval knight. Although no longer armored, cavalry remained a vital element of warfare well into the 20th century.

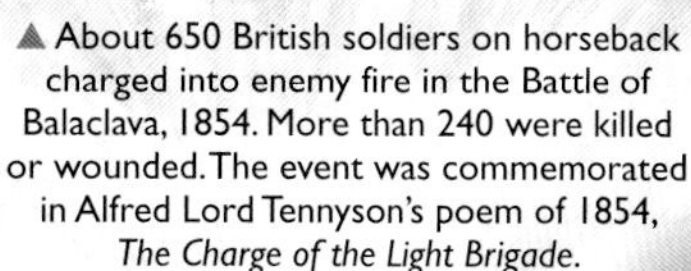

▲ About 650 British soldiers on horseback charged into enemy fire in the Battle of Balaclava, 1854. More than 240 were killed or wounded. The event was commemorated in Alfred Lord Tennyson's poem of 1854, *The Charge of the Light Brigade*.

▲ During World War I (1914–1918), dogs were not only used to deliver messages, but also to transport machine guns.

▲ G. I. Joe, part of the United States Army Pigeon Service, is decorated for valiant service in World War II (1939–1945). He delivered a message about an imminent bombing, perhaps saving more than 1,000 lives.

Woof and wing

Humans are slow and vulnerable message carriers. Before it was possible to send messages by radio, there was no better way of quickly delivering long-range information than tying it to the leg of a carrier pigeon; and no one could beat a messenger dog when it came to bounding over treacherous terrain.

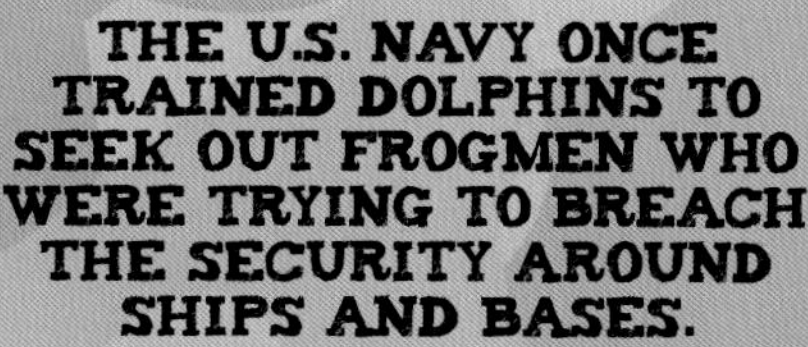

THE U.S. NAVY ONCE TRAINED DOLPHINS TO SEEK OUT FROGMEN WHO WERE TRYING TO BREACH THE SECURITY AROUND SHIPS AND BASES.

Camel corps

The Imperial Camel Corps (1916 -1918) was manned by British, Indian, Australian, and New Zealand riders and served with distinction in the Middle East during World War I (1914–1918). The camel's ability to go for five days without water made it ideal for desert operations.

Extreme SIEGE

A medieval castle was an uncompromising symbol of the owner's power, might, and majesty, and if it fell, their importance and prestige tumbled with it. The masterbuilder's task, therefore, was to use every possible form of defense, from crenellations to moats, to make it as impregnable as possible. Outside, attackers devised whatever means they could to break through the stronghold.

EXTREME TACTICS

BY CATAPULTING A DISEASE-RIDDEN BODY OVER THE WALLS, ASSAILANTS PUT THE DEFENDERS IN IMMEDIATE PERIL.

DEFENDERS OF A CASTLE COULD SNEAK UP ON THE ENEMY THROUGH A HIDDEN DOORWAY CALLED A SALLY PORT. THE DEFENDING SOLDIERS OF HADLEIGH CASTLE IN ESSEX, U.K., ARE SAID TO HAVE BOMBARDED THEIR ASSAILANTS WITH FRESH FISH THAT THEY HAD SMUGGLED IN.

IN 1306, SCOTLAND'S KILDRUMMY CASTLE FELL TO EDWARD, PRINCE OF WALES, WHEN OSBOURNE, THE TRAITOROUS BLACKSMITH, SET FIRE TO THE CASTLE GRAIN STORE.

IN 1204, FRENCH SOLDIERS TOOK CHÂTEAU GAILLARD FROM ENGLAND'S KING JOHN BY CLIMBING UP THE TOILET CHUTE.

Fame and FORTUNE

Human curiosity is the driving force behind many of history's greatest quests, discoveries, and adventures. People have explored to increase scientific knowledge, spread religious beliefs, gain riches and power, or just out of plain interest. However, many explorers are simply motivated by wealth and fame.

A NEW WORLD

In 1492, **Christopher Columbus** (1451–1506) set sail from Spain in an attempt to find a new route to Asia, to buy spices. When he found land, Columbus thought he'd reached Japan. In fact, he'd found a new continent—the Americas. Upon his return to Spain, the new continent became known as "the New World." In return for his many voyages of discovery, Columbus desired "great rewards" for both himself and his family.

HIDDEN HOARD?

Edward Teach (c. 1680–1718), also known as **Blackbeard**, was a ruthless pirate renowned for his deliberately frightening appearance—he even wore slow-burning fuses under his hat. He ambushed and plundered ships in the Caribbean Sea and Atlantic Ocean until he was killed by the Royal Navy. Treasure seekers have since hunted high and low in the hope of finding Teach's legendary buried treasure.

CUT SHORT

In 1519, Portuguese admiral **Ferdinand Magellan** (1480–1521) set out to travel westward around the world to the Spice Islands, sailing around South America and crossing the Pacific Ocean on the way. The landmark journey made Magellan famous, but he never lived to enjoy it—he was killed by Filipino warriors before his fleet reached its destination.

GOLD DIGGER

Most educated Europeans in the 19th century had read Homer's *Iliad* and believed that Troy—one of the cities featured in the poem—was just a legend. From 1871–1873, businessman and amateur archeologist **Heinrich Schliemann** (1822–1890) uncovered the site of Troy at Hissarlik, Turkey. No fewer than nine different cities had been built and destroyed at this spot over the ages. Schliemann also uncovered a hoard of gold jewelry in the process.

EPIC JOURNEY

In *Il Milione*, an autobiographical account about the extraordinary travels of **Marco Polo** (c. 1254–1324), Polo stated that he had not mentioned one half of what he had seen because no one would believe him. In total, he traveled more than 25,000 mi (40,000 km) around the world and discovered many amazing inventions and innovations.

ONE LAST TRY

Howard Carter (1874–1939) was sure that the intact tomb of an ancient pharaoh lay somewhere in Egypt's Valley of the Kings. In 1922, after five years of exploration, Carter's patron, Lord Carnarvon, agreed to fund just one more season of excavation. It was enough—at the end of the year, Carter uncovered the most celebrated archeological find of all time—the tomb of Pharaoh Tutankhamun, untouched since 1327 BC.

PIRATE OR PATRIOT?

Sir Francis Drake (1540–1596) sailed round the world from 1577–1580, attacking Spanish treasure-laden vessels and pillaging their invaluable cargoes. On his return, Drake was hailed a hero and knighted by Queen Elizabeth I for his service to England. In Spain, however, Drake was deemed a murderous pirate.

Wonders OF THE WORLD

We know about the Seven Wonders of the Ancient World from ancient Greek tourist guides. Historians are in disagreement over which monuments were on the list and even how many actually existed—we may never know for sure because only the Great Pyramid is still standing.

GREAT PYRAMID OF GIZA

WHAT: A giant stone tomb

WHERE: Near Cairo, Egypt

WHEN: Built during the reign of King Khufu (c. 2575–2465 BC)

SIZE: Base 755 sq ft (230 sq m); 480 ft (145 m) high

DESCRIPTION: Orientated on the four points of the compass and containing about 2.3 million limestone blocks, the pyramid was the tomb of King Khufu and his queen. The shape may have been chosen because it points to the sky—the domain of the sun god Ra.

HANGING GARDENS OF BABYLON

WHAT: Remarkable terraced gardens

WHERE: In Babylon, the capital city of ancient Mesopotamia (now southern Iraq)

WHEN: During the reign of either Queen Sammuramat (810–783 BC) or King Nebuchadnezzar II (c. 605–561 BC)

SIZE: Unknown

DESCRIPTION: Described as being irrigated by an elaborate system of pumps and channels that brought water from the River Euphrates, the gardens were said to be a leisure feature of the royal palace. One legend says Nebuchadnezzar built them to remind his queen, Amytis, of the green forests of her Persian homeland.

WHAT: A vast gold and ivory statue

WHERE: Olympia, in the Peloponnese, Greece

WHEN: Constructed by the sculptor Phidias around 430 BC

SIZE: 40 ft (12 m) high

DESCRIPTION: As the Olympic Games had deep religious significance, a temple to the king of the gods adorned the sporting complex. The statue of Zeus was shown seated, giving the impression that if he stood, he would burst through the roof.

TEMPLE OF ARTEMIS AT EPHESUS

DESCRIPTION: Constructed of gleaming white marble, the Temple of Artemis was packed with works of art. Artemis (also known as Diana) was an ancient goddess of the moon. The temple was destroyed in AD 268, rebuilt, and finally razed in AD 401.

WHAT: A gigantic marble-columned temple

WHERE: Ephesus was in modern-day Turkey

WHEN: Built by King Croesus of Lydia c. 550 BC

SIZE: 350 ft (110 m) long, 180 ft (55 m) wide

MAUSOLEUM OF MAUSOLUS AT HALICARNASSUS

DESCRIPTION: The gleaming tomb consisted of a plain rectangular base, topped with a colonnade, a pyramid roof, and a statue of Mausolus and Artemisia in a chariot pulled by four horses. It was built to demonstrate Artemisia's love for her Mausolus, and to glorify them both.

WHAT: A vast tomb shaped like a jewel box

WHERE: Overlooking the ancient city of Halicarnassus (now Bodrum), Turkey

WHEN: Built at the command of Queen Artemisia II of Caria, Mausolus' sister and widow, c. 353–350 BC

SIZE: Square base, with sides about 36 ft (11 m) long; 148 ft (45 m) tall

COLOSSUS OF RHODES

DESCRIPTION: The people of Rhodes erected this mighty bronze and iron statue of the sun god, Helios, to thank the deity for saving their city from enemy attack.

WHAT: A huge statue of a god beside the harbor entrance

WHERE: Mediterranean island of Rhodes, Greece

WHEN: Built 292–280 BC

SIZE: More than 107 ft (30 m) tall

PHAROS OF ALEXANDRIA

DESCRIPTION: The stone building rose in three tapering stages: square, octagonal, and cylindrical. The fire at the top was reflected in mirrors and visible 29 mi (47 km) away—it warned sailors of the treacherous banks around the Nile.

WHAT: The archetypal lighthouse

WHERE: Island of Pharos, Alexandria, Egypt

WHEN: Built 280–247 BC

SIZE: 350 ft (110 m) tall

Heroes are seen as role models that inspire virtue and nobility, guiding the behavior of fellow citizens. In the past, many societies idolized warriors for their strength and courage. Today, however, we tend to admire those who promote peace and well-being.

Marcus Aurelius (AD 121–180)
Rome's beloved, peace-loving philosopher and emperor, Aurelius' work *Meditations* has inspired thousands, including Prussia's Frederick the Great, on how to best act in times of conflict.

Confucius (Kong Fuzi, in Chinese) **(551–479 BC)**
A successful Chinese civil servant, Confucius became a traveling philosopher, passing on moral values to guide all peoples and all states.

HEROES & Villains

Cruel, unpredictable, power-hungry, and selfish, history's villains are famous for their wicked deeds and extreme behavior, usually letting little stand in their way to achieve their goals.

Attila the Hun (c. AD 406–453)
The founder of the Hunnic Empire across Eastern Europe, Attila the Hun was known by his enemies as the "Scourge of God" for his ruthless campaigns of conquest—for both land and wealth.

Caligula (AD 12–41)
Murderous, incestuous, impulsive, extravagant, vain, vindictive, and probably insane—accounts of this Roman emperor paint a foul picture. He is even said to have proclaimed himself to be a god.

Abraham Lincoln (1809–1865)
The 16th president of the United States, Lincoln led his nation through the American Civil War (1861–1865) and ended the country's slavery. He was assassinated in 1865 while attending a play with his wife.

Florence Nightingale (1820–1910)
Renowned for her work during the Crimean War (1853–1856), English nurse Nightingale cared for wounded soldiers, known to them as "the lady with the lamp" because she often made her rounds at night. She campaigned for nursing to be accepted as a profession for women.

Nelson Mandela (b. 1918)
In 1948, South Africa implemented a policy of apartheid (forced racial segregation). Mandela was a leader of the resistance movement, and became an international symbol of the fight for tolerance and equality. He was imprisoned for 27 years, and on his release became a respected statesman.

Genghis Khan (c. 1162–1227)
Born a simple tribal leader in northeast Asia, Khan united the nomadic tribes of Mongolia. The self-styled "Universal Ruler" carved out one of the largest empires the world has ever seen—by tireless campaigning and the heartless slaughter of local populations.

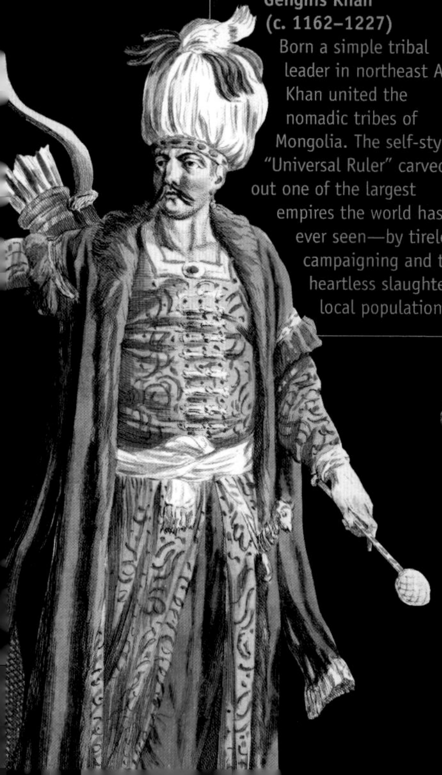

Ivan the Terrible (1530–1584)
Russia's first tsar, Ivan IV, became a corrupt and unstable tyrant who massacred thousands and even slew his own son in a fit of rage.

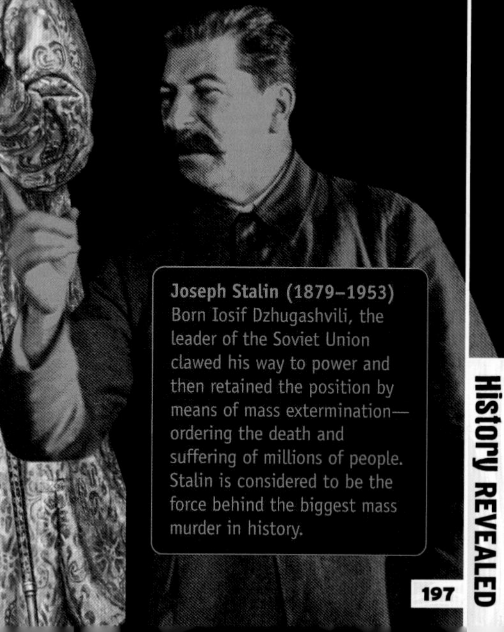

Joseph Stalin (1879–1953)
Born Iosif Dzhugashvili, the leader of the Soviet Union clawed his way to power and then retained the position by means of mass extermination—ordering the death and suffering of millions of people. Stalin is considered to be the force behind the biggest mass murder in history.

Great WARRIORS

Battles were won with the mind as much as muscle. First impressions counted, so warriors who looked intimidating and strong were often victorious. From medieval knights in shining armor to Viking marauders, history's finest fighting men were often extremely successful.

HOPLITE

Category: Citizen infantry
Place of operation: Ancient Greece
Dates: 8th–4th centuries BC
Headgear: Helmet with cheekplates
Body armor: Breastplate and greaves (leg armor), bronze cuirass or linen corselet
Weapons: 8-ft (3-m) spear and short sword
Shield: Round in shape, and made of wood and bronze
Discipline: Good
Notable success: Smashing Persian invasion at Marathon, 490 BC

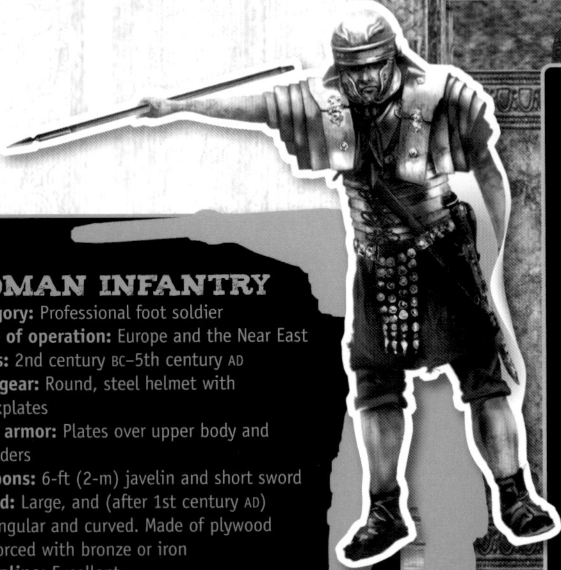

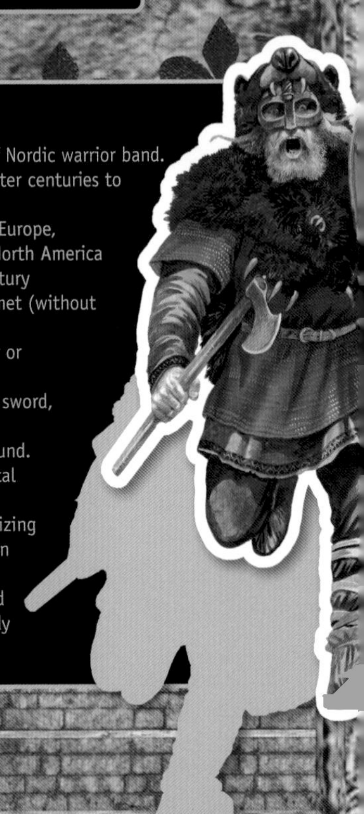

VIKING

Category: Member of Nordic warrior band. Joined together in later centuries to form large armies
Place of operation: Europe, North Atlantic, and North America
Dates: 8th–11th century
Headgear: Steel helmet (without horns)
Body armor: Leather or chainmail tunic
Weapons: Spear, ax, sword, and dagger
Shield: Small and round. Made of wood or metal
Discipline: Poor
Notable success: Seizing the province of Rouen from the Kingdom of France in AD 911, and renaming it Normandy

ROMAN INFANTRY

Category: Professional foot soldier
Place of operation: Europe and the Near East
Dates: 2nd century BC–5th century AD
Headgear: Round, steel helmet with cheekplates
Body armor: Plates over upper body and shoulders
Weapons: 6-ft (2-m) javelin and short sword
Shield: Large, and (after 1st century AD) rectangular and curved. Made of plywood reinforced with bronze or iron
Discipline: Excellent
Notable success: Conquest of Britain, 1st century AD

MEDIEVAL KNIGHT

Category: Gentleman warrior
Place of operation: Europe and Middle East
Dates: 11th–15th century
Headgear: Varies according to the period—among the most well known was a style of helmet that totally enclosed the head, called the great helm
Body armor: In later years, full plate armor (made from plates of metal) worn over chainmail
Weapons: 13-ft (4-m) lance, heavy sword, ax, and dagger
Shield: All shapes, made of wood and steel
Discipline: Poor
Notable success: In the Battle of Arsuf in 1191, Richard the Lionheart defeated Saladin

AZTEC SOLDIER

Category: Citizen army spearheaded by professional nobility
Place of operation: Central America
Dates: 14th–16th century
Headgear: Quilted cotton helmet, often highly decorated
Body armor: Quilted cotton suit covering most of the body
Weapons: Wooden javelins and clubs, bows and arrows, knives made of a razor-sharp stone called obsidian
Shield: Wooden and feather-fringed
Discipline: Average
Notable success: Victory over Azcapotzalco in 1428

ZULU WARRIOR

Category: Tribal infantryman
Place of operation: Southern Africa
Dates: 18th and 19th centuries
Headgear: Circlet of animal pelt
Body armor: None
Weapons: Spears—the *isijula* for throwing and the *iklwa* for stabbing—and club
Shield: Leaf shaped, and made of animal hide
Discipline: High
Notable success: Defeat of British at Isandlwana in 1879

SAMURAI

Category: Military nobility
Place of operation: Japan
Dates: 12th–19th centuries
Head gear: Metal helmet splayed to protect neck; sometimes with face mask
Body armour: Elaborate combination of metal, bamboo, and quilted cloth covering the entire body
Weapons: *Katana* sword, club, bow, spear, knife, and firearms
Shield: Where carried, round in shape. Made of wood and metal
Discipline: Good
Notable success: Japanese invasion of Korea, 1592–1593

LOST LEADERS

Throughout history, the lives of many key figures—popular and unpopular—have been brought to an untimely close. Assassinations are targeted killings, usually motivated by political differences, but may also be driven by religious beliefs, military opposition, or monetary gain.

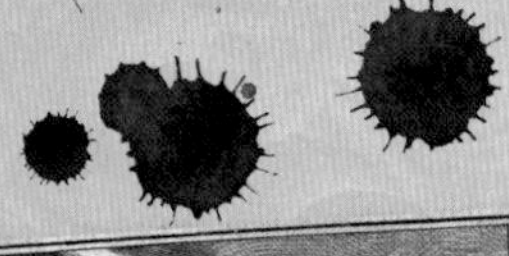

French King Henry IV

Fanaticism knows no bounds, as France's popular King Henry IV (1553–1610) discovered in 1610. Born a Protestant, he converted to Catholicism and, to heal his country's religious divisions, granted toleration to those of his former faith. All this was too much for François Ravaillac, who stabbed the king to death when the royal carriage was stopped in busy traffic on the way to the queen's coronation.

Roman general Julius Caesar

The career of one of Rome's greatest generals and reformers, Julius Caesar (100–44 BC), came to an abrupt end on March 15, 44 BC, when he was stabbed to death in the Senate House. The assassins' motive? To save the Roman republic from a would-be king.

ENGLISH KING WILLIAM II

William II (c. 1056–1100) was not one of England's more popular kings. Tongues began to wag, therefore, when he went hunting in the New Forest and did not return. His body, pierced by an arrow, was found the next morning—and his brother Henry immediately seized the throne. Was the king's death an accident, or assassination?

Russian Tsar Alexander II

For all his reforming zeal, notably setting free his country's serfs in 1861, Russian Tsar Alexander II (1818–1881) did not go far enough for the People's Will, an extreme terrorist organization. Whether the people willed it or not, the gang's assassins killed the tsar in a bomb attack as he rode in his carriage through the streets of St. Petersburg.

Austro-Hungarian Archduke Franz Ferdinand

On June 28, 1914, the Serbian nationalist Gavrilo Princip fired two fatal shots in Sarajevo, Bosnia, that started World War I (1914–1918). His victim was the Austro-Hungarian prince, Archduke Franz Ferdinand. Austria soon attacked Serbia. Russia came to the aid of its Serbian ally, and Germany did the same with Austria. France, Russia's ally, was drawn in next... and within weeks a whole continent, then the whole world, was at war.

JFK moments before the shooting took place.

U.S. President John F. Kennedy

As U.S. President John F. Kennedy was driving through Dallas, Texas, U.S., on November 22, 1963, at precisely 12:30 p.m. four shots were fired. The president, hit in the body and head, died shortly afterward. A suspect, Lee Harvey Oswald, was arrested but shot dead before he was brought to trial. So one of modern history's great mysteries began—who killed JFK and why?

Israeli President Yitzhak Rabin

Israel and its Arab neighbors have long been at each other's throats. So when Yitzhak Rabin (1922–1995) signed the Oslo Accords with the Palestinians in 1993, he was awarded the Nobel Prize for Peace. Two years later, he was assassinated by Israeli Yigal Amir who opposed the agreement.

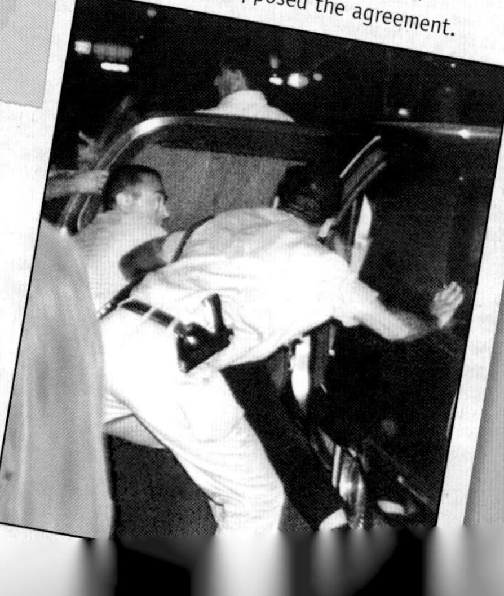

Security agents push Rabin into a car after he was shot in Tel Aviv after addressing a peace rally.

Wipe OUT!

It came from the east, spreading like a wave of death across Europe. In just four years (1347–1351), half of the continent's population was wiped out. Rich and poor, men and women... no one was immune from the bubonic plague, also known as the Great Plague or the "Black Death." Although population levels recovered surprisingly swiftly, the continent would never be the same again.

Spread of death

The Black Death, first brought to Europe by rats aboard vessels sailing from the Eastern Mediterranean, persisted for more than 400 years. Its name came from its most obvious symptoms—pus-oozing, black swellings, called buboes, under the arms, on the neck, and in the groin. Those infected had a one-in-five chance of survival—the majority were dead within a week.

Dirty rats

Most scientists believe the plague was spread by fleas that lived on black rats. In an age when basic hygiene was almost nonexistent, rat fleas flourished in bedding and clothing. It took just one flea bite to infect a person. Modern medics, however, have suggested that the disease was actually caused by a bacterium called *Yersinia pestis*.

▼ This grim depiction shows how people were dying in the street, leaving piles of diseased bodies.

Doctor, doctor

At a time when some doctors believed the plague could be spread by just looking at someone, so-called "cures" were bizarre. They included swallowing emeralds, pearls, or gold, placing dried human excrement on the buboes, and drinking a mixture of apple syrup, lemon, rose water, and peppermint.

▶ Doctors wore "plague-proof clothing." The "beak" acted like a gas mask, stopping them from inhaling air that may carry the plague when treating victims.

ONE MEDIEVAL REMEDY FOR THE PLAGUE WAS TO DRINK A GLASS OF YOUR OWN URINE TWICE A DAY.

…-YEAR-OLD JOAN, THE DAUGHTER OF ENGLAND'S KING EDWARD III, DIED OF THE PLAGUE ON THE WAY TO HER WEDDING WITH A SPANISH PRINCE.

Mass graves

The bodies of plague victims had to be disposed of as quickly as possible, otherwise the bodies would rot and spread further disease. With so many deaths, individual funerals were impossible. Corpses were simply collected in carts and dumped in mass graves.

▶ Hundreds of dead bodies were buried in pits.

Heaven's judgment

In a fiercely religious age, the plague was seen as God's judgment on a wicked world. Prevention and cure came not from science, but from prayer, confession, and penance.

Flagellation (beating or whipping the body) was believed to atone for the sins that had brought the plague.

▼ More than 1,000 bodies were discovered in Black Death graves near the Tower of London, England, in 1987.

On and on...

Evidence of the dreadful Black Death has come from the excavation of mass graves. Outbreaks of this terrifying epidemic have also occured in modern times—as recently as 1994 there was an outbreak in Seurat, India.

Supreme SACRIFICE

The early gods were a grim bunch. Erratic and demanding, a number of them could be appeased only with the ultimate sacrifice—human life. No one did this in a more spectacularly gory fashion than the Aztec people of what is now southern Mexico.

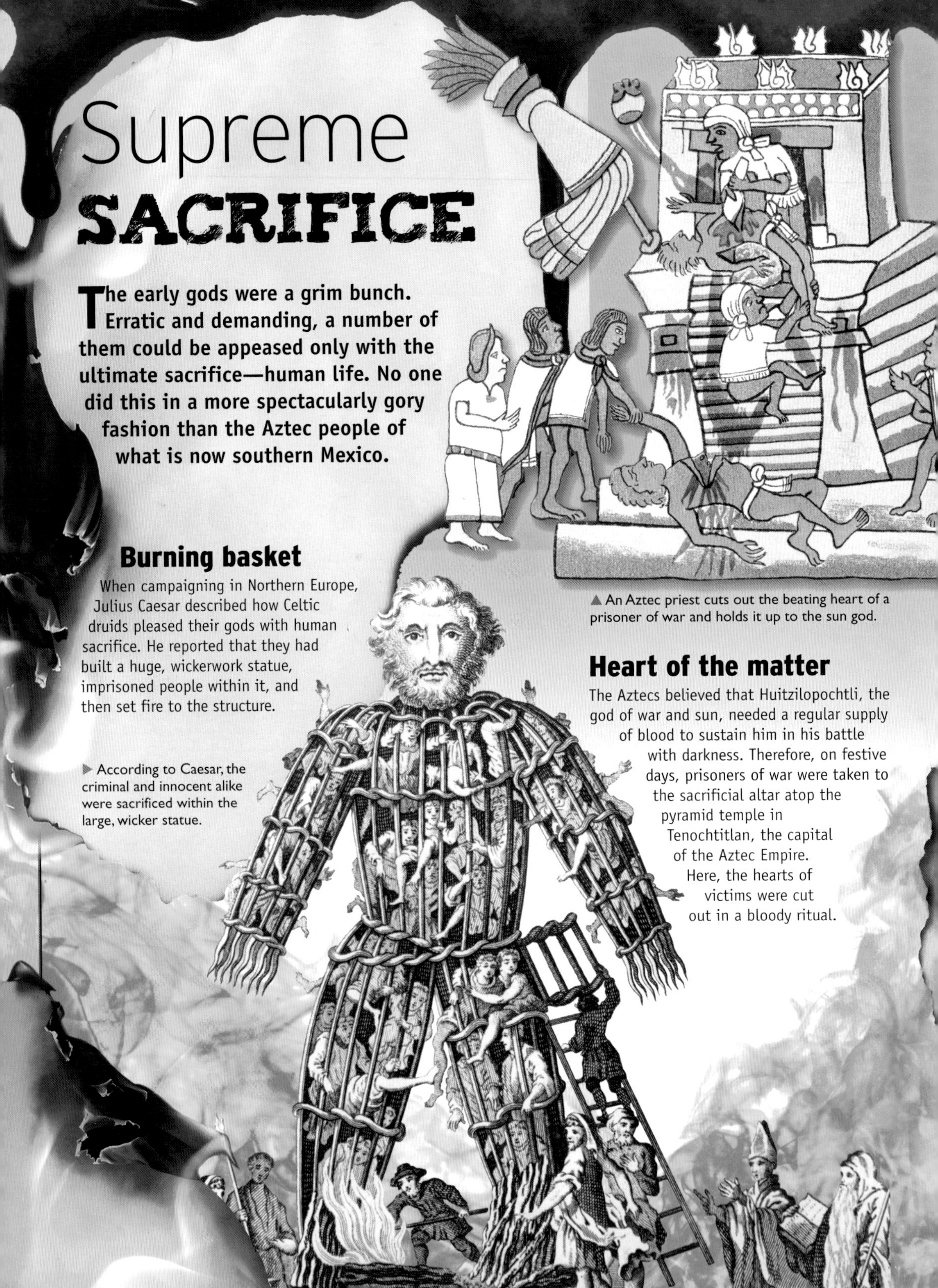

▲ An Aztec priest cuts out the beating heart of a prisoner of war and holds it up to the sun god.

Burning basket

When campaigning in Northern Europe, Julius Caesar described how Celtic druids pleased their gods with human sacrifice. He reported that they had built a huge, wickerwork statue, imprisoned people within it, and then set fire to the structure.

▶ According to Caesar, the criminal and innocent alike were sacrificed within the large, wicker statue.

Heart of the matter

The Aztecs believed that Huitzilopochtli, the god of war and sun, needed a regular supply of blood to sustain him in his battle with darkness. Therefore, on festive days, prisoners of war were taken to the sacrificial altar atop the pyramid temple in Tenochtitlan, the capital of the Aztec Empire. Here, the hearts of victims were cut out in a bloody ritual.

Sati is the ancient Hindu custom of burning a bereaved wife on the funeral pyre of her dead husband.

Pyre power

The Hindu ritual, Sati, demanded that a wife be burned to death, voluntarily or otherwise, on the funeral pyre of her dead husband. It was believed that the custom arose to stop young wives poisoning elderly and unwanted husbands.

Pleasing Thor

According to the medieval German chronicler Adam of Bremen, the ancient temple at Uppsala, Sweden, witnessed some pretty grim events. The worship of Thor and other Norse gods and goddesses involved ritual human sacrifice.

The Nordic King Domalde prepares to sacrifice himself for the good of his people.

GREEK MYTHS TELL HOW EVERY SEVEN YEARS THE ATHENIANS SENT 14 CHILDREN TO BE EATEN BY THE MINOTAUR, A TERRIFYING MONSTER.

A Japanese kamikaze plane attempts to smash into a U.S. warship.

Divine wind

The term "kamikaze," meaning "divine wind," was originally used to describe the tropical typhoons that broke up Chinese invasion fleets heading for Japan in the late 13th century. In World War II, the term was adopted by Japanese suicide pilots who deliberately smashed their planes into U.S. warships—about 2,800 kamikaze attacks sank or crippled hundreds of ships.

FANCY **DRESS**

As soon as our ancestors started wearing clothing more than 100,000 years ago, they wanted to look good. Most garments were attractive and designed to accentuate the wearer's best features. But at the extremes, people's fashion obsessions became peculiar—for example, women piling their hair 12 in (30 cm) high. Some fashion trends were even cruel, such as the Chinese practice of binding girls' feet so they could fit into shoes many sizes too small for them.

◀▼ The toga was both a garment and a badge of citizenship.

Roman robe

The toga of ancient Rome was much more than a simple 20-ft- (6-m-) long robe of fine wool, draped around the body and slung over the shoulder. It also showed the wearer's place in society—by law, the garment could be worn only by male citizens of Rome.

◀ Proud of a shapely leg, 16th-century men wore tights to show theirs off.

Elizabethan costume

Shakespeare's theater company's most valuable possession was its wardrobe of costumes. Not surprisingly, it cost more than most Elizabethans earned in a year to dress a gentleman in a lined, embroidered doublet (jacket) with detachable sleeves, neck ruff, padded tights over the upper thigh and silk stockings below, and elegant shoes.

Geisha girls

Since the 18th century, highly trained Japanese Geisha have been used for entertainment. With a chalk-white face, scarlet lips, hair decorated with flowers, an elegant kimono, a brilliant obi (sash), and platform shoes, a Geisha captivated her guests with elaborate dance and music.

◀ Geishas still work today, attending parties and gatherings.

Aristocratic excess

Late 18th-century European dress is a fabulous example of fashion at its most extreme. A lady's gown ballooned like a bell from her tiny waist, and the puffed sleeves were trimmed with ruffles. The hairdo, many times the size of the wearer's head, looked like a bird had made its nest atop the entire extraordinary collection.

▶ Costumes in the 18th century were low at the front and high on the head.

▼ The marked faces of New Zealand's Maori warriors made them look ferocious.

Bone-cut beauty

The Maori people of New Zealand boasted a long tradition of Tã moko, marking the body permanently with incisions and natural dyes. Carved with bone chisels, the markings were used to indicate power and authority. They appeared most commonly on the face, thighs, and buttocks.

Eagle signals

When in battle, an opponent knew immediately whether to fight or flee from a Native American Sioux, Crow, Blackfeet, Cheyenne, or Plains Cree warrior. Each eagle feather in the striking warbonnet of a warrior represented an act of outstanding bravery. Lots of feathers? Get out of the way—fast!

◀ The feathers in the warbonnet of Sitting Bull, the war chief of the Sioux, continued down his back.

Remarkable rears

Late 19th-century fashion designers created bustle dresses that expanded so much at the rear, they had to be supported by steel cages.

◀ The bustle dress exaggerated a woman's rear to make her appear more attractive.

RAT-atouille

Humans are omnivorous—we eat both plants and meat. During the reign of England's James I (1603–1625), starving soldiers resorted to sharing the diet of their cows—grass. At the other extreme, Henry VIII (1491–1547) sat down to vast feasts of hare, venison, veal, chicken, plums, and pomegranate seeds... and that was just the first course!

DURING THE CIVIL WAR THAT FOLLOWED THE RUSSIAN REVOLUTION OF 1917, STARVING PEASANTS WERE PHOTOGRAPHED SELLING HUMAN FLESH FOR PEOPLE TO EAT.

GREEDY ROMANS SOMETIMES MADE THEMSELVES SICK IN ORDER TO BE ABLE TO EAT MORE.

Hand to mouth

For most of history, people used knives to cut meat and spoons to scoop up liquid, but they generally used their fingers to transfer food to their mouths. Fine if your hands are clean...

Extreme generosity

In 1900, the French government employed 3,600 cooks and waiters to prepare a feast for the country's mayors that featured, among other things, more than 2 tons of pheasant and 50,000 bottles of wine. *Bon appétit!*

LITTLE LUXURY

Ancient Romans were partial to a mid-morning snack, and one of their favorite nibbles was a crunchy edible dormouse.

A feast of beasts

Chronicles say that around 484 BC, King Darius of Persia had 1,000 animals slaughtered for a special feast. The menu was said to have included smoked camel, ox, zebra, and ostrich.

Big bird

Until the 17th century, swan was a popular dish among the wealthiest in society. The bird was roasted for a long time and served "like beef."

Raise a glass?

Before the late 16th century, most Europeans drank their tipple from pewter, pottery, or leather. Drinking vessels made from leather were lined with resin to make them watertight.

Boozy breakfast

In medieval times, water and milk frequently carried diseases. To avoid illness, those who could afford to drank beer and wine at all times of the day and night.

Fitting the CRIME

Legal systems claim that a person's punishment should fit their crime. Yet from hanging for stealing a sheep to crushing bones for lifting a loaf, the past is littered with examples of extreme punishments given out for apparently trivial crimes.

Off with his head

One of the most shocking punishments took place during the French Revolution's Reign of Terror (1793–1794). Once the revolutionary leader Maximilien Robespierre had defined the crime—being an enemy of the people, and the punishment—death, thousands of men and women were guillotined for the crime of simply being who they were. An aristocrat, for instance, was by definition an enemy of the people.

GET OUT!

The ancient Athenians devised a fail-safe way of dealing with those who were regarded as a political nuisance. A meeting of citizens was called, at which all present wrote on a potsherd (a fragment of pottery, called an *ostrakon*) the name of anyone they wished to remove. Anyone receiving a large number of votes was ostracized—banished from the state for ten years.

▼ The name of an unpopular Athenian citizen is scratched onto a piece of pottery.

▶ In the late 18th century, the iron maiden was used as a form of torture. The victim was shut inside the cabinet and pierced with sharp objects.

In 1793, Marie Antoinette was executed by guillotine for treason.

TOOLS OF TORTURE

Torture has long been a means of extracting information from a person—usually using brutal methods. There was no question of punishments fitting the crime for slaves in ancient Rome. In the pre-Christian era, slaves accused of a crime, even a minor one, were automatically tortured—it was seen as the only way of getting the truth out of them. Harsher still, in imperial times, when a slave was found guilty of murder, it was quite common for all other slaves belonging to the same master to be crucified.

CHOP CHOP

English puritan William Prynne (1600–1669) believed the theater to be unlawful and immoral, and set out his ideas in the 1,000-page book *Histriomastix* (1632). Shortly after the book appeared, Queen Henrietta Maria appeared in a private court drama. In light of this, parts of *Histriomastix* were interpreted as an attack on the queen. Prynne was fined, imprisoned, and punished by having his ears sliced.

Prynne was put in the pillory—a wooden frame—to have the tips of his ears chopped off.

IN ANCIENT CHINA, THE PUNISHMENT FOR KILLING A PARENT, EVEN ACCIDENTALLY, WAS EXECUTION. BUT A FATHER WHO BEAT HIS SON TO DEATH WOULD USUALLY RECEIVE NO MORE THAN A FINE.

▼ Many women were burned at the stake from the 15th to 18th century, after being found guilty of witchcraft.

▼ In medieval times, the neck and hands of offenders would be locked between two wooden planks—the pillory—in a public place, so they could be humiliated.

▶ The "Chair of Torture" was covered in spikes along the back, seat, and arms. The spikes would penetrate the flesh, causing slow blood loss, and eventual death.

The last witch

In 1782, Anna Göldi of the Swiss town of Glarus was executed by decapitation. She had confessed under torture to having seen the Devil in the form of a black dog, and that it had helped her put needles into the food of her master's daughters. She was the last person to be executed for witchcraft in Europe.

Cure OR KILL

Until the scientific revolution of the late 17th century, most medicine was a mix of superstition, religion, folklore, myth, trickery, and guesswork. "Cures" included rubbing the affected part of the body with a live toad (a treatment for the plague), drinking a cup of tea made from ground-up insects (antirabies medicine), and dressing a wound with a scribe's excrement and milk. Many so-called treatments did more harm than good, and those who stayed out of the hands of doctors often had the best chance of survival!

MEDIEVAL MEDICINE WAS BASED ON THE IDEA THAT THE BODY CONTAINED FOUR "HUMORS"—BLACK BILE, YELLOW BILE, PHLEGM, AND BLOOD. AN EXCESS OF BLACK BILE, FOR EXAMPLE, WAS THOUGHT TO PRODUCE MELANCHOLY.

FEELING THE HEAT

A person suffering from toothache in medieval Europe may be instructed to hold a lit candle close to the affected area. Apparently this would cause the worms that were eating away the inside of the tooth to drop out into a waiting cup.

Burning away the badness: curing toothache with a lit candle.

▼ Cure by hot cups in a German bathhouse.

TOXIN TREATMENT

The traditional treatment of placing hot cups on the skin has been used since the time of the ancient Egyptians. This "cure" is intended to draw unwanted fluids from the body as the air inside the cups cools and contracts. The procedure creates circular marks on the skin and has no proven benefits.

Cups are still used today in alternative medicine.

PENNY DREADFUL

Not until modern times was mental illness properly recognized or treated. Until the 19th century, London's Bethlem Royal Hospital (once known as Bedlam) was a kind of freak show where visitors paid a penny to gawp at unfortunate "mad" inmates held in chains.

◀ The well-dressed women in this scene from *A Rake's Progress* by 18th-century English artist William Hogarth are visiting Bedlam (London's hospital for the mentally ill) as entertainment.

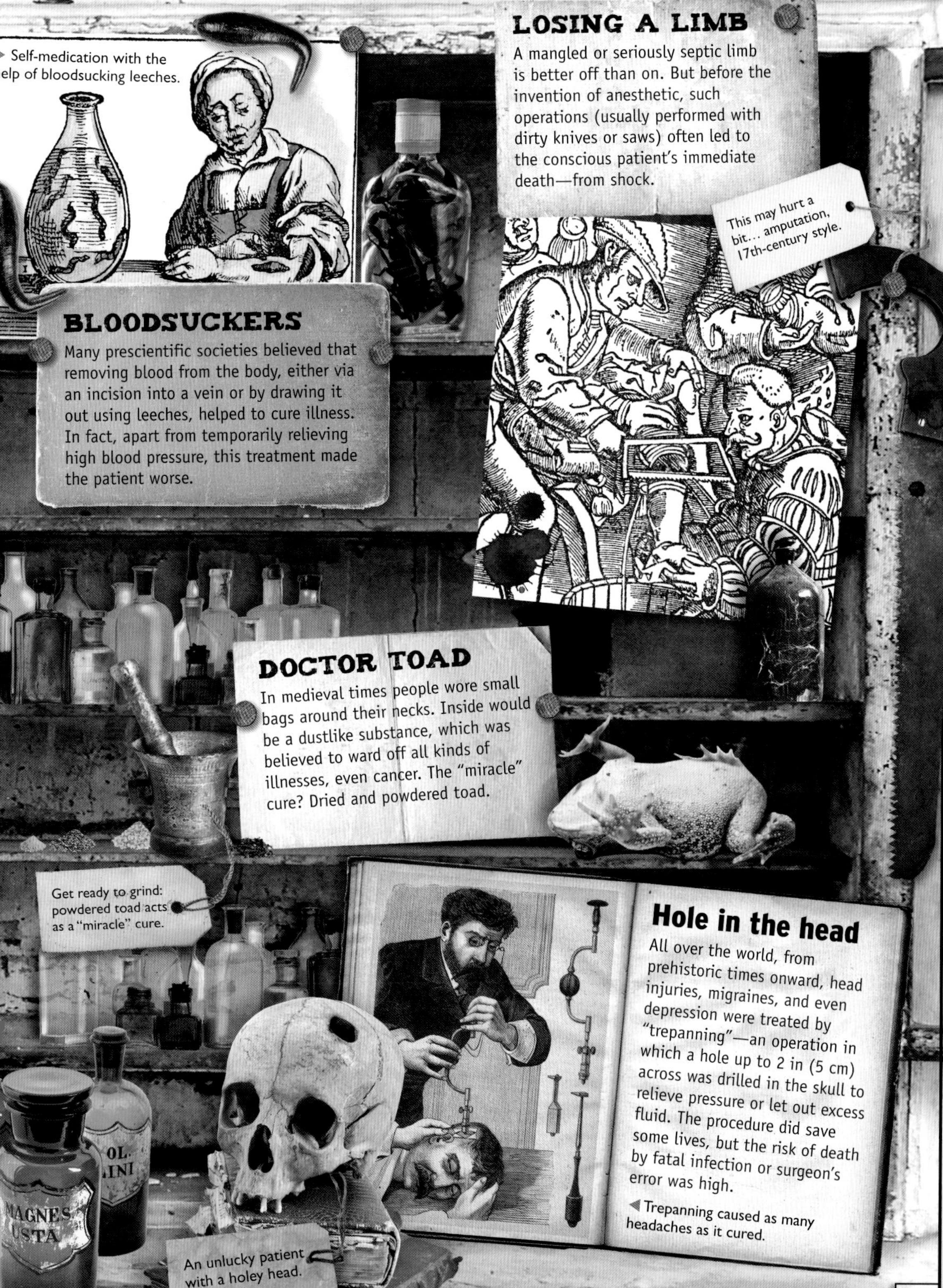

Self-medication with the help of bloodsucking leeches.

LOSING A LIMB

A mangled or seriously septic limb is better off than on. But before the invention of anesthetic, such operations (usually performed with dirty knives or saws) often led to the conscious patient's immediate death—from shock.

This may hurt a bit... amputation, 17th-century style.

BLOODSUCKERS

Many prescientific societies believed that removing blood from the body, either via an incision into a vein or by drawing it out using leeches, helped to cure illness. In fact, apart from temporarily relieving high blood pressure, this treatment made the patient worse.

DOCTOR TOAD

In medieval times people wore small bags around their necks. Inside would be a dustlike substance, which was believed to ward off all kinds of illnesses, even cancer. The "miracle" cure? Dried and powdered toad.

Get ready to grind: powdered toad acts as a "miracle" cure.

Hole in the head

All over the world, from prehistoric times onward, head injuries, migraines, and even depression were treated by "trepanning"—an operation in which a hole up to 2 in (5 cm) across was drilled in the skull to relieve pressure or let out excess fluid. The procedure did save some lives, but the risk of death by fatal infection or surgeon's error was high.

Trepanning caused as many headaches as it cured.

An unlucky patient with a holey head.

There have always been rich and poor people, but when the Industrial Revolution began in the mid-18th century—first in Britain, then spreading to Europe, North America, and eventually the rest of the world—this gulf became more obvious. Workers who swarmed into cities lived in makeshift, squalid housing, while across the ocean, transported Africans endured even worse conditions as unpaid slaves. All the while, thousands of mill and mine owners, bankers, shippers, and builders were growing rich beyond their wildest dreams.

All in one room

Until the 20th century, it was quite common for European working-class families to have no more than a single room to live in. The situation was especially bad in the rapidly expanding industrial cities.

▲ It was common for large families to live, sleep, and eat in just one room.

SLUMDOGS and MILLIONAIRES

Royal riches

Queen Victoria received £385,000 a year from the British government just for being queen. That's equivalent to £21 million, or $34 million in today's money. When she died in 1901, she left a fortune of over £2 million (about £24 million, or $50 million today).

THE DUKE OF PORTLAND HAD A 1.5-MI (2.4-KM) UNDERGROUND TUNNEL BUILT SO HE COULD TRAVEL FROM HIS HOME (WELBECK ABBEY, U.K.) TO THE RAILWAY STATION AT WORKSOP WITHOUT BEING SEEN.

No expense spared—the coronation of Queen Victoria (1838) cost £70,000.

Paupers' palaces

Too poor to support yourself? Off to the workhouse! These bleak establishments housed the poor and their children, providing low-grade shelter and food in return for soul-destroying labor. With prisonlike rules and punishments, workhouses were kept deliberately unpleasant to deter scroungers.

▼ Paupers sit down to a meager meal in the Marylebone workhouse in London, U.K.

▼ Factory workers lived in rows of small houses, with no inside bathrooms or running water. The air was dirty, filled with smoke from the nearby factories.

Dirty work

Many factories were built during the Industrial Revolution, and both adults and children had to work long hours in unhealthy conditions. Until 1850, only the factory owners benefited from the wealth generated by industry, with the workers living in dirty, crowded, busy towns, called slums, that sprang up around the factories.

Dazzling display

In 1849, Queen Victoria's husband, Prince Albert, conceived a plan for a global exhibition to take place in London. The exhibition opened on May 1, 1851, with more than 14,000 people gathered in the newly built Crystal Palace to show off their gadgets to millions of dazzled visitors. By the time the exhibition closed, one quarter of the British population had visited Crystal Palace.

London's Crystal Palace (1851) was a symbol of the Industrial Revolution that made some Britons fabulously wealthy.

WAR AND PEACE

Humans, said the poet Alexander Pope, are "The glory, jest, and riddle of the world"—and never more so than in matters of war and peace. After the horrors of World War I (1914–1918), monuments to peace went up all over Europe; yet barely 20 years later the continent was tearing itself apart once again. Although many of history's most celebrated figures were promoters of peace, we also have a fascination with the heroic (and sometimes barbaric) deeds of warriors and military leaders.

Prince of peace

Horrified by the 100,000 casualties resulting from the Kalinga War (c. 265 BC), the great Indian emperor Ashoka (304–232 BC) converted to Buddhism and inaugurated one of the most peaceful, fair, and tolerant reigns history has ever witnessed. Education, health, justice, welfare—every branch of government felt the touch of his nonviolent outlook. After Ashoka's death, he was remembered as Samraat Chakravartin—the Emperor of Emperors.

A reputation for destruction

Hollywood has made a pretty good job of portraying the Roman Empire as a place of war and gratuitous violence, but this picture is unfair. For over 200 years (AD 27–180) the empire fought few major wars and spread a relatively civilized blanket of law and order across the Mediterranean world, over which it held sway.

▼ Many people's views of the Roman Empire are informed by movies such as *Gladiator* (2000), which emphasize its violence rather than its imposition of law and order.

Land grab

In 1066, William of Normandy seized the English crown and so began a conflict that finally ended in 1558, when Calais, England's last continental possession, fell to the French. Essentially, the struggle was dynastic—fueled by kings trying to expand their territories by force rather than ethical issues. This unworthy conflict reached its climax in the Hundred Years' War (which actually lasted for 116 years, 1337–1453).

◀ French, Spanish, and English forces battle for power at Nájera, in 1367.

Stacks of skulls

The central Asian conqueror Tamerlane (1336–1405) specialized in acts of extreme barbarity. While carving out an empire around Persia and the Caspian Sea, his forces may have killed 100,000 innocent citizens in a single day. On a more personal note, he took pleasure in firing human heads from cannon, and built huge pyramids from the skulls of his victims.

▶ Ruthless conqueror Tamerlane was also known as "Amir Timur" or (inaccurately) "Timur the Great."

Ultimate weapon

On August 6, 1945, the atom bomb nicknamed "Little Boy" obliterated the Japanese city of Hiroshima, and humankind saw that it now had the power to destroy itself and the planet on which it lived. U.S. President Harry S. Truman had thought long and hard about using the bomb, eventually deciding that dropping it would, in the long run, save lives. We all live with the consequences of that decision.

▲ Hiroshima, 1945: the utter devastation provides a stark warning to humanity.

Crazy ACTS

When Mr. Bumble declared in Charles Dickens' *Oliver Twist*, "The law is an ass!" he was not so far off the mark. History is littered with ill-considered laws, and while some were merely foolish, others were downright nasty. An English law banning entry into Parliament in full armor might have made sense in 1313, but was still on the statute book in 2011. A law passed in 1908 in the U.S. state of Oklahoma banned marriage between a "person of African descent" and "any person not of African descent."

Lean and mean

Debates about obesity often present it as a modern issue. However, an English law of 1336, designed to prevent the population from becoming fat and unfit, made it illegal to eat more than two courses at a single meal.

The "Rich Kitchen" by Jan van der Heyden, 1563.

Crazy cabs

The rules and regulations for taxicabs are very specific. In London, U.K., it is illegal to hail a taxicab if you are suffering from the plague. Furthermore, it is forbidden for a taxicab to carry corpses or rabid dogs.

Single or married?

In Florida, U.S., an unmarried woman may face jail if she parachutes on a Sunday. In Vermont, U.S., a husband must give written permission for his wife to be allowed to wear false teeth.

Dressing up

Lawmakers love to interfere in daily life, especially when it comes to dress. The Italian capital Rome banned low-cut dresses during the 16th century, and in Massachusetts, U.S., a law of 1651 outlawed the wearing of gold or silver buttons, lace, and other finery by anyone not worth at least £200.

Mulberry madness

China ferociously guarded its hold over the immensely profitable silk industry, and punished anyone who let slip the top-secret processes involved. One law stated that any person who revealed how the cocoons of the larvae of the mulberry silkworm were harvested and turned into thread would be put to death by torture.

Loony law

A law allegedly passed by an absentminded U.S. state of Florida legislature in the 1960s made it illegal to carry firearms "except for the purpose of shooting vermin or policemen in the course of their duty." The wording was amended before a law officer was harmed.

The power of names

Although he was an undemocratic dictator, the people of France had huge admiration for Emperor Napoleon I (1769–1821)—so much so that they made it illegal to name a pig after him. The move inspired English writer George Orwell to use the name for the tyrannous pig in his book *Animal Farm* (1945).

▼ Black passengers on a South African train give the thumbs up from a carriage that was previously reserved for white people only.

Racist rot

Having legislated to define everyone by their race, in 1950 the South African government passed a law (the Group Areas Act) stipulating where members of each racial group were allowed to live. Needless to say, the white sections of society, who had made the law, were allocated the best areas.

INDEX

Entries in **bold** refer to main subject entries; entries in *italics* refer to illustrations.

ACKNOWLEDGMENTS

The publishers would like to thank the following sources for the use of their photographs:

KEY
Dreamstime=D
Fotolia=F
Frank Lane Picture Agency=FLPA
Getty Images=GI
istockphoto.com=iS
Minden Pictures=MP
The Moviestore Collection Ltd=MSC
NASA Goddard Space Flight Center=NASA-GSFC
NASA Jet Propulsion Laboratory=NASA-JPL
NASA Johnson Space Center—Earth Sciences and Image Analysis=NASA-JSC-ES&IA
NASA Marshall Space Flight Center=NASA-MSFC
naturepl.com/Nature Picture Library=NPL
Photolibrary=P
Rex Features=RF
Robert Harding World Imagery=RHWI
Science Photo Library=SPL
Shutterstock=S

t=top, a=above, b=bottom/below, c=center, l=left, r=right, f=far, m=main, bg=background

COVER: FRONT Mike Parry/Minden Pictures/FLPA, 2happy/S, Jubal Harshaw/S, Michael Stokes/S, Eugene Berman/S; BACK Eugene Berman/S

ACTIVE EARTH: 4–5 Adam Jones/SPL **6–7**(m) NASA Earth Observatory/SPL, (l) Tony Craddock/SPL, (tr) NASA-JSC-ES&IA, (frame) Shawn Hine/S, (br) Gordon Garradd/SPL **8–9**(bg) Jose AS Reyes/S, (m) mangiurea **8**(l) Andrea Danti, (br) George Steinmetz/SPL **9**(tl) Vitaly Korovin, (tr) Michael Peuckert/P, (br) Arctic-Images/Corbis **10–11**(m) Grant Dixon/MP/FLPA **10**(c) Doug Allan/NPL, (frame) imagestock/iS, **11**(cr) Galen Rowell/Corbis, (br) Valentyn Volkov/S **12–13**(c) Vulkanette/S, (cb) Doug Perrine **12**(bl) Peter Oxford/NPL/RF **13**(tr) Alexander Gatsenko/S **14** Carlyn Iverson/SPL **15**(t) Michael Krabs/Imagebroker/FLPA, (cr) Nadezda/S, (b) Dr. Richard Roscoe, Visuals Unlimited/SPL **16–17**(bg) KPA/Zuma/RF **16**(cl) Gary Hinks/SPL, (br) Sipa Press/RF **17**(tr) UC Regents, Natl. Information Service For Earthquake Engineering/SPL, (cl) Corbis, (br) dpa/Corbis **18–19**(water bg) Dudarev Mikhail/S, (bl) Aaron Amat/S, (tl) Frank Siteman/Science Faction, (cl) Jacques Jangoux/Peter Arnold Images/P, (cr) Kevin Schafer/MP/FLPA, (tr) Kevin Schafer/MP/FLPA, (br) Planetobserver/SPL **20**(bg) Jack Dykinga/NPL, (c) Scott Prokop/S, (b) Konstantin Sutyagin/GI **21**(bg) ImageState, (sign tr) Steve Collender/S and dusan964/S, (m) Albo/F, (sign b) Lou Oates/S, (b) Grant Dixon/MP/FLPA **22–3**(m) Bernhard Edmaier/SPL, (bl) Marcos Brindicci/Reuters/Corbis, (paper tr) pdtnc/F, (br) Colin Monteath/P **24–5**(m) Steven Kazlowski/Science Faction/Corbis **24**(c) KeystoneUSA-ZUMA/RF, (paper cl) Alexey Khromushin/F, (sign br) marekuliasz/S **25**(sign tl) Steve Collender/S, (sign tr) maxkovalev/S, (cl) Ashley Cooper/Corbis, (cr) Carsten Peter/Speleoresearch & Films/GI, (sign bl) Lou Oates/S, (br) Tony Waltham/RHWI/Corbis **26–7**(bg) Mirek Hejnicki/S, sspopov/S, SeDmi/S, kilukilu/S and leolintang/S; (objects on conveyor belt, l–r, t–b) Serhiy Shullye/S, Outsider/S, E.R.Degginger/SPL, Picsfive/S, Denis Selivanov/S, Keith Wilson/S, Konovalikov Andrey/S, Alexander Kalina/S, Bragin Alexey/S, Jean-Claude Revy, ISM/SPL, Kamil Krzaczynski/epa/Corbis, Juri/S, dslaven/S, Krasowit/S, Jens Mayer/S, stocksnapp/S, Maria Brzostowska/F, Steve Vidler/P, Jason Reed/Reuters/Corbis; (tr) Jon T. Fritz/MCT **28**(tr frame) diak/S, (tr) NPL, (gold plate) Alaettin YildIrim/S, (cr) Argus/S, (bl) Jeffrey L. Rotman **29**(tr) Victor Habbick Visions/SPL, (cl) NPL/RF, (laptop bl) Edhar/S, (bl) Dr Ken Macdonald/SPL, (br) Jamie Cross/S **30–1**(bg) Planetobserver/SPL **30**(t–b, l–r) John Wollwerth/S, Mike Hollingshead/Science Faction/Corbis, Jim Reed/Jim Reed Photography - Severe &/Corbis, dswebb/iStock **31**(t–b, l–r) Caitlin Mirra/S, jam4travel/S, Carsten Peter/GI, Irwin Thompson/Dallas Morning News/Corbis **32**(m) Gene Rhoden/P, (c) 2010 Gallo Images/GI, (bl) AFP/GI, (br) Jim Reed/FLPA **33**(tl) Olivier Vandeginste/SPL, (tr) mtkang/S, (c) Ivan Cholakov Gostock-dot-net/S, (b) AFP/GI **34–5**(m) Scott Warren/P **34**(bl) Joel Blit/S, (br) Steve Collender/S **35**(bl) Picimpact/Corbis, (c) Brandelet/S **36–7**(tm) Ward Kennan/P, (t, l–r) Dan Burton/NPL, AlaskaStock/P, Planetary Visions Ltd/SPL, (bm) Juniors Bildarchiv/P, (b, l–r) George Steinmetz/Corbis, Frans Lanting/Corbis, Planetary Visions Ltd/SPL **38**(bg) Sasha Buzko, (tl) Tischenko Irina/S, (cl) Anan Kaewkhammul/S, (cr) Mikhail/S, (frame, bl) imagestock, (bl) Kordcom Kordcom/P **39**(tl) Michael Freeman/Corbis, (frame c) Cre8tive Images/S, (c) T Carrafa/Newspix/RF, (r) Anan Kaewkhammul/S

AWESOME ANIMALS: 40–1 Christian Ziegler/MP/FLPA **42**(t) Jurgen & Christine Sohns/FLPA, (b) Hugh Lansdown/FLPA **43**(t) Stephen Dalton/NPL, (c) Stephen Dalton/NHPA, (b) Gisela Delpho/P **44**(m) Jurgen & Christine Sohns/FLPA, (bl) Kim Taylor/NPL **45**(t) Stephen Dalton/NPL, (b) Hue Chee Kong/S **46–7**(bg) Alex Kuzovlev, (m) Reinhard Dirscherl/P **46**(t) Natutik/S **47**(t) Michael & Patricia Fogden/MP/FLPA, (br) Malcolm Schuyl/FLPA **48–9**(bg) S, (bullet holes) Krisdog/D, (nails) dusan964/S, (wanted posters) Chyrko Olena/S, (keys) Simon Bratt/S **48**(tl) Konstantin Sutyagin/S, (tr) Fred Bavendam/MP/FLPA, (bl) Frank Stober/Imagebroker/FLPA, (br) ZSSD/MP/FLPA, (br, bg) Kirsty Pargeter/F **49**(tl) Austin J Stevens/P, (tr) Norbert Wu/MP/FLPA, (bl) Mitsuaki Iwago/MP/FLPA, (bl, bg) Triff/S, (br, handcuffs) Zsolt Horvath/S, (br, badge) Peter Polak/S **50–1**(m) Piotr Naskrecki/MP/FLPA, (frame) Undergroundarts.co.uk/S **50**(l) Piotr Naskrecki/MP/FLPA, (b) Mark Payne-Gill/NPL, (b, frame) Robert Adrian Hillman/S **51**(t) S & D & K Maslowski/FLPA, (b) Ron Austing/FLPA **52–3**(bg) Gudrun Muenz/S, (labels) Picsfive/S, (balloons) Michael C. Gray/S, (streamers) hans.slegers **52**(tl) Ariadne Van Zandbergen/FLPA, (cl) Milena_/S, (c) Manfred Kage/P, (c, frame) Natalie-art/S, (br) Sherjaca/Shutterstock **53**(tl) Eduardo Rivero/S, (tl, frame) vector-RGB/S, (tr) laschi/S, (cl) Pete Oxford/NPL, (cl, bg) LeonART/S, (cr) Eky Studio/S, (cr, frame) Nira/S, (b) Paul Kay/P, (b, party hat) Stacy Barnett/S **54**(m) Sea Pics, (b) Bruce Davidson/NPL **55**(t) javarman/S, (cl) Ron O'Connor/NPL, (b) Paul Nicklen/GI **56–7**(colored paper) Alexey Khromushin/F, (frame) Picsfive/S, (pins) Oleksii Natykach/S, composite image: (hind legs) Steffen Foerster Photography/S, (tail) NREY/S, (body) Eric Isselée/S, (front legs) Eric Isselée/S, (neck) prapass/S, (ears) Johan Swanepoel/S 56(t) Dhoxax/S, (c) Mark Beckwith/S, (b) Mogens Trolle/S, (paper) Milos Luzanin/S **57**(tl) michael Sheehan/S, (tr) BlueOrange Studio/S, (cl) Kjersti Joergensen/S, (cr) Ludmila Yilmaz/S, (bl) Jurgen & Christine Sohns/FLPA, (br) Steffen Foerster Photography/S **58–9**(tl) Aflo/NPL, (tc) pixelman/S, (tr) Villiers Steyn/S, (bl) Stephen Bonk/S, (br) Neil Bowman/FLPA **60–1**(bg) Lightspring/S, (c) Roger Powell/NPL, (panels) tkemot, (stars) Tomasz Wojdyla **60**(tl) Geoff Simpson/NPL, (bl) Andy Rouse/NPL, (br) Tui De Roy/P **61**(tl) Eric Isselée/S, (tr) Dietmar Nill/NPL, (cr) Doug Allan/NPL, (br) Ed Reschke/P **62–3**(bg, wood) Brian Weed/S, (bg, book) thumb/S, (doodles) Petr Vaclavek/S, (c) Tyler Boyes/S, (bc) Danny Smythe/S **62**(l) vilax/S, (tr) Angelo Gandolfi/NPL, (b) Suzi Eszterhas/MP/FLPA **63**(tl) Constantinos Petrinos/NPL, (tr) Marie Read/NPL, (bl) Premaphotos/NPL, (br) Doug Perrine/NPL, (acorns) dionisvera/S **64–5**(m) Tan Hung Meng/S, (leaves) maxstockphoto/S **64** Colin Marshall/FLPA, **65**(t) S Charlie Brown/FLPA, (b) Bruce Davidson/NPL **66–7**(bg) Lasse Kristensen/S **66**(tr) Katherine Feng/MP/FLPA, (c) Cathy Keifer/iS (b) ImageBroker/FLPA, (bl) Cathy Keifer/F **67**(t) Mitsuaki Iwago/MP/FLPA, (c) Donna Heatfield/S, (b) Visuals Unlimited/NPL **68**(m) Neale Cousland/S, (l) Vinicius Tupinamba/S **69**(tl) Johan Swanepoel/S, (tr) mike lane/Alamy, (cl) Joseph DiGrazia/S, (cl, frame) Iwona Grodzka/S, (b) Kurt Madersbacher/P **70–1**(medal) Fotocrisis/S **70**(m) Gerry Ellis/MP/FLPA, (b) Flip De Nooyer/FN/MP/FLPA 71(t) Johan Swanepoel/S, (b) Mike Parry/MP/FLPA **72–3**(bg) Pete Oxford/NPL, (yellow leaf) Iurii Konoval/S, (green leaf) maxstockphoto/S **72**(tr) Staffan Widstrand/NPL, (bl) Thomas Marent/MP/FLPA **73**(t) Heidi & Hans-Juergen Koch/MP/FLPA, (c) Solvin Zankl/NPL, (b) Gerry Ellis/MP/FLPA, (frames) PhotoHappiness/S **74–5**(tc) Richard Fitzer/S, (tc, sign) Loskutnikov/S, (bc) Flip Nicklin/MP/FLPA, (r) Anan Kaewkhammul/S, (boards) aborisov/S

INCREDIBLE SCIENCE: 76–7 David Scharf/SPL **78**(tl) Pedro Nogueira/S, (tr) NASA-JPL, (bl) Lane V. Erickson/S, (b, l–r) Top Photo Group/RF **79**(tl) Pedro Nogueira/S, (bl) James Balog/ Aurora Photos/Corbis, (r, t–b) oku/S, David Arts/S, Dmitri Melnik/S, Sergey Kamshylin/S, Andrey Burmakin/S, (frame) Phase4Photography/S **80–1**(m) NASA/GI, (b) Joseph C Dovala/P **80**(l) Edward Kinsman/SPL, (c) Abel Tumik/S, (b, panel) Matthias Pahl/S, (b, chain) Henry Nowick/S, (r) Phase4Photography/S **81**(l) E.R.Degginger/SPL, (r, t–b) Melli/S, Vakhrushev Pavel/S, Arsgera/S, ArtmannWitte/S **82–3**(bg) lolloj/S **82**(m) GI, (t) Eye of Science/SPL, (bl) Nicemonkey/S, (br) Lawrence Berkeley National Laboratory/SPL **83**(tl) NASA/SPL, (tr) RF, (bm) Innespace Productions/SEABREACHER, (bl) Dmitri Mihhailov/S, (br) Gwoeii/S **84–5**(bg) dinadesign/S, (frame) ivn3da/S, (c) adziohiciek/S, (ice cubes) Alex Staroseltsev/S **84**(tr) NASA/Science Faction/Corbis, (bl) Vitaly Raduntsev/S, (br) SPL **85**(tl) Patrick Landmann/SPL, (tr) Ria Novosti/SPL, (tr, frame) Hintau Aliaksei, (bl) Diego Barucco/S, (br) Yva Momatiuk & John Eastcott/GI **86–7**(bg) Zinatova Olga/S, (c) Gordan/S, (b) Sergey Mironov/S, (t) NASA-JPL **86**(l) Edward Kinsman/SPL, (r) Jean-Luc & Françoise Ziegler/P **87**(t) NASA-GSFC, (bl) NASA-JPL, (br) NASA/WMAP Science Team/SPL **88–9**(bg, wood) Ford Photography/S, (bg, book) Valentin Agapov/S, (doodles) Bukhavets Mikhail/S, (masking tape) Studio DMM Photography, Designs & Art/S, (frames) Phase4Photography/S **88**(t) NASA-MSFC, (b) NASA-JPL **89**(tr) Viktar Malyshchyts/S, (r) happydancing/S **90–1**(m) Tony Craddock/SPL **90**(b) J.C. Revy, ISM/SPL **91** Volker Springel/Max Planck Institute for Astrophysics/SPL **92–3**(bg) Kheng Guan Toh/S, (atoms) Johan Swanepoel/S, (molecules) Serdar Duran/S **92**(l) Steve Gschmeissner/SPL, (tr) David McCarthy/SPL, (br) Susumu Nishinaga/SPL **93**(t) Dr Gary Gaugler/SPL, (cl) Dr Linda Stannard, UCT/SPL, (cr) Omikron/SPL, (b) Jan Kaliciak/S **94**(t) Eye of science/SPL, (c) Ower and Syred/SPL, (b) SPL **95**(tl) Jan Hinsch/SPL, (tr) Susumu Nishinaga/SPL, (bl) Steve Gschmeissner/SPL, (br) Astrid & Hanns-Frieder Michler/SPL **96**(bg) argus/S, (m) Thierry Berrod, Mona Lisa Production/SPL, (b) Bristish Museum/ Munoz-Yague/SPL **97**(m) Stephen & Donna O'Meara/SPL, (tl) Jochen Tack/P, (tr) Augusto Cabral/S, (bl) Smit/S **98–9**(m) Anakaopress/Look at sciences/SPL **98**(b) optimarc/S **99**(t) Stephen Alvarez/GI, (c) Carsten Peter/GI, (b) Jeff Rotman/NPL **100–1**(t) shelbysupercars.com, (b) David J. Cross/Photolibrary **100** GI **101** NASA/SPL **102**(bg, pink) Panos Karapanagiotis/S, (bg, writing) Inga Nielsen/S, (tl) National Library of Medicine/SPL, (tr) Dmitrijs Bindemanis/S, (cl) Library of Congress/digital version by Science Faction, (bl) Bettmann/Corbis, (br) Dominik Michálek/S **103**(tl) Jacqueline Abromeit, (tr) RF, (cl) Bettmann/Corbis, (bl) Graeme Dawes/S, (bc) NASA-MSFC, (br) Reuters/Corbis **104–5**(m) Russell Kightley/SPL **104** NASA/ESA/STSCI/J.Kenney & E.Yale, Yale University/SPL **105** Chandra X-ray Observatory/NASA/SPL **106–7**(bg) David Parker/SPL, (clockwise starting bl) Christophe Vander Eecken/Reporters/SPL, Adam Hart-Davis/SPL, Tim Wright/Corbis, optimarc/S, Sylverarts/S, Emilio Naranjo/epa/Corbis **108–9**(border) gorica/S **108**(tl) INSAGO/S, (cl) R-studio/S, (bl) GI **109**(tl) Christophe Boisvieux/Corbis, (bl) Time & Life Pictures/GI, (r) Omikron/SPL **110–1** Jose Antonio Peñas/SPL

ULTIMATE MACHINES: 112–3 Juerg Schreiter/S **114–5**(b) KPA/Zuma/RF **114**(m) Corbis, (bl) AridOcean/S, (panel) Anan Kaewkhammul/S **115**(tl) Space Frontiers/Stringer/GI, (tr) studio online/S **116–7**(bg) Neo Edmund/S **116**(metal) caesart/S, (m) South West News Service/RF, (r) Eky Studio/S, (bl) Peter Menzel/SPL, (br) akiyoko/S **117**(t) National Geographic/GI, (b) Issei Kato/Reuters/Corbis **118–9**(t) David Griffin/Icon SMI/Corbis **118**(bl) Robert Young/S, (flag) Stephen Aaron Rees/S, (b) David Allio/Icon SMI/Corbis **119**(tr) kobi nevo/S, (bl) Brian Bahr/Stringer/GI **120–1**(bg) Dariush M./S, (m) Icon Images/RF, (border) Gordan/S, (b) Tischenko Irina/S **121**(br) Kesu/S **122–3**(bg) Peter J. Kovacs/S **122**(tl) apostol/S, (tr) Henry Groskinsky/Time & Life Pictures/GI, (b) Terence Dewaele/AFP/GI **123**(t) Norbert Wu/GI, (c) Jon Freeman/RF, (b) Georges de Keerle/Sygma/ Corbis **124–5**(m) racefotos2008/S **125**(tr) Carl de Souza/AFP/GI, (tracks) hugolacasse/S, (bl) hoboton/S, (br) AFP/GI, (spikes) Rolf Kosecki/Corbis **126–7**(bg) 4designersart/S **126**(t) Mai/Mai/Time Life Pictures/GI, (b) George Steinmetz/Corbis **127**(t) Jim Watson/ AFP/GI, (bl) Ethan Miller/GI, (br) Ed Oudenaarden/epa/Corbis **128–9**(m) Jonathan Hordle/RF, (ticket panels) George Pappas/S, (pipe panels) Zlatko Guzmic/S **128**(l) GI **129**(r) Debbie Egan-Chin/NY Daily News Archive via GI, (inset) Joe McNally/GI **130–1**(m) Michael Stokes/S **130**(tl) Presniakov Oleksandr/S, (bl) Jose Gil/S, (br) 808isgreat/S **131**(tr) Sipa Press/RF, (bl) Mighty Sequoia Studio/S, (negative) Hintau Aliaksei/S, (br) RTimages/S **132–3**(b, bg) archetype/S, (t, bg) R-studio/S, (m) Yuriko Nakao/Reuters/Corbis, (border) gorica/S **132**(b) Michael Caronna/Bloomberg via GI, (b, frame) Maria Toutoudaki/iS **133**(t) Dmitry Nikolajchuk/S, (b) Bill Pugliano/GI **134–5**(border) S, (m) Jessica Rinaldi/Reuters/ Corbis, (labels) S **134**(bg) Anteromite/S, (t) Leo Francini/S, (c) Jakub Krechowicz/S, (b) Mark Carrel/S **135**(tr) USCG/SPL, (br) pashabo/S **136–7**(m) Master Sgt. Kevin J. Gruenwald/RF **137**(bl) Corbis, (bl, bg) Ana de Sousa/S **138**(t) The Labor Shed/S, (panels) James Nemec/S, (bl, frame) frescomovie/S **138–9**(bg) Sasha Buzko/S, (c) MarketOlya/S, (clockwise starting bl) Jakub Krechowicz/S, Bettmann/Corbis, GI, Time & Life Pictures/GI, SSPL/GI, Zdenko Hirschler/RF, Curventa/RF **140**(t) Kai Forsterling/epa/Corbis, (bl) Yves Forestier/Sygma/Corbis **141**(cl) Justin Sullivan/GI, (cr) nikkytok/S, (b) U.S. Coast Guard – digital ve/Science Faction/Corbis **142–3**(bg) Hywit Dimyadi/S, (b) yuyangc/S, (tl) Erik Viktor/SPL, (bl) Linali/S, (c) NASA/SPL, (tr) NASA/SPL, (br) NASA/SPL **144–5**(bg) Molodec/S, (m) Du Huaju/Xinhua Press/Corbis, (panels) Stefan Delle/S **144**(t) Reuters/ Corbis, (bl) RF, (br, paper) pdtnc/F, (br, sign) Raia/S **145**(t) Reuters/Corbis, (c) Vitaly Korovin/S **146–7** (bg, metal) R-studio/S, (bg, ipad) Viktor Gmyria/S, (panels) S **146**(t) Andrea Danti/S, (bl) AFP/GI, (br) Bloomberg via GI 147(l) Detlev Van Ravenswaay/SPL, (l, frame) Dic Liew/S, (r) News Pictures/MCP/RF

SUPER HUMANS: 148–9 Stringer/india/Reuters/Corbis **150–1**(m) Sebastian Derungs/AFP/ GI **150**(t) Hal_P/S, (bl) Parrot Pascal/Corbis Sygma/Corbis, (candles br) DVARG/S, (cake br) Susan McKenzie/S **151**(l) GI, (b) AFP/GI, (c) John T Takai/S, (r) Bettmann/Corbis **152–3**(m) Daniel H Bailey/P **152**(bl) Darren Staples/Reuters/Corbis **153**(tl) Digital Vision/GI, (tr) AFP/GI, (b) Wang Song/Xinhua Press/Corbis **154**(t) Monkey Business Images/S, (c) Hung Chung Chih/S, (cb) jovannig/S, (bl) Laitr Keiows/S, (br) Alangh/D **155**(t) jan kranendonk/S, (c) Kaido Karner/S, (b) Nikola Spasenoski/S **154–5**(globe l, t–b) Steve Estvanik/S, Alvin Ganesh/S, Dmitry Nikolaev/F, PavelSvoboda/S, (globe c, t-b) Nikola Spasenoski/S, BartlomiejMagierowski/S, Elenathewise/F, (globe r, t–b) Pichugin Dmitry/S, Steve Estvanik/S **156**(m and inset) Bryan and Cherry Alexander/NPL, (b) hoboton/S **157**(tm) Mark Edwards/P, (tm, inset) Wave RF/P, (tl) Anna Kaminska/S, (bm) Martin Harvey/Corbis, (bm, inset) Babak Tafreshi/SPL **158**(t, bg) Michael D Brown/S, (b, bg) Len Green/S, (tl) dimitris_k/S, (tr) Gunnar Pippel/S, (cl) nuttakit/S, (c) Bettmann/Corbis, (br) S, (bl) Roman Sigaev/S **159**(bg) DiverS-photo/S, (tl) The Art Gallery Collection/Alamy, (tl, b) Marilyn Volan/S, (symbol c) Petr Vaclavek/S, (cr) Ambrophoto/S, (bl) Toponium/S, (br) Newspix/RF **160–1**(bg) Steve Estvanik/S, (book) Valentin Agapov/S **161**(t) gualtiero boffi/S, (c) George Steinmetz/Corbis, (c, bg) bartzuza/S, (bl) GI for Red Bull/GI, (br) Alexey Khromushin/F **161**(t) Arcticphoto/Alamy, (c) Karen Kasmauski/Corbis, (b) Bloomberg via GI **162**(l) Günter Flegar/P, (tr) AFP/GI, (br) Corbis **163**(tl) Seleznev Oleg/S, (tr) KPA/Zuma/RF, (bl) Nik Wheeler/Corbis, (br) Sipa Press/RF **164–5**(bg) nubephoto/S **164**(l) SINOPIX/RF, (tr) Riou/Corbis, (br) Tim Hill/P **165**(t) Envision/Corbis, (c) Mariana Bazo/Reuters/Corbis, (b) Ted Mead/P **166**(t) Mike Keating/Newspix/RF, (b) Barcroft Media via GI **167**(t) Alaska Stock Images/P, (cl) Alexis Rosenfeld/SPL, (bubble bg) fuyu liu/S, (b) NASA/SPL, (metal frame) Shawn Hine/S **168–9**(bg) Molodec/S, (measurement instrument set) Leremy/S, (c) Natchapon L./S **168**(bl) Superstock Inc/P **169**(t) Factoria Singular/P, (b) Javier Larrea/P **170–1**(bg) Andrey Burmakin/S, (science doodles) Lorelyn Medina/S, (b) Max Baumann/S **170**(blue bg) Alexey Khromushin/F, (l) S, (tr) Jakub Krechowicz/S, (br) Sheila Terry/SPL **171**(t) Bettmann/Corbis, (bl) Time & Life Pictures/GI, (br) hfng/S **172–3**(m) John Van Hasselt/Sygma/Corbis **172**(b) Bettmann/ Corbis **173**(tl) Sam Rosewarne/Newspix/RF, (tr) Reuters/Corbis, (b) Keith Ducatel **174**(bg) Pallaske Pallaske/P, (t) R-studio/S, (t, b) Kompaniets Taras/S, (c) Luciano Mortula/S, (c, frame) kak2s/S, (b) Sukree Sukplang/X90021/Reuters/Corbis **175**(m) JTB Photo/P, (t) Per-Andre Hoffmann/P, (frame) SuriyaPhoto/S **176–7**(m) François Pugnet/Kipa/Corbis **176**(t) RF, (c) Marco Beierer/S, (b) Kazela/S **177**(t) Ian Salas/epa/Corbis **178**(l) Valdrin Xhemaj/epa/Corbis, (tc) 2010 GI, (bc) Christian Kober/P, (r) imagebroker RF/P **179**(tl) Sipa Press/RF, (tr) Charles & Josette Lenars/Corbis, (c) Zdorov Kirill Vladimirovich/S, (bl) Bildagentur RM/P, (br) GI **180–1**(m) Alastair Muir/RF **180**(b) Bildarchiv Monheim GmbH/ Alamy, (parcel) Oliver Hoffmann/S **181**(tl) GI, (cl) markrhiggins/S, (bl) Richcat/S, (r) Ray Tang/RF **182**(t) AFP/GI, (b) Zhang Chuanqi/XinHua/Xinhua Press/Corbis **183**(t) Jeff J Mitchell/Reuters/Corbis, (bl) Victor Fraile/Reuters/Corbis, (br) PILart/S

HISTORY REVEALED: 184–5 Warner Bros. Pictures/Helena Productions/Latina Pictures/ Radiant Productions/Plan B Entertainment/MSC **186–7**(bg)Jenny Solomon/F, (bg, bl) Binkski/S **186**(bl) 2003 Charles Walker/TopFoto, (br) Sandro Vannini/Corbis **187**(bl) The Granger Collection/TopFoto, (bc) The Granger Collection/TopFoto, (br) Studio 37/S **188–9**(frame) Ladyann/S **188**(m) Time & Life Pictures/GI, (tl) grivet/S, (tr) kanate/S **189**(c) 2001 Topham/PA/TopFoto, (cl) Roger-Viollet/TopFoto, (bl) GI **192–3**(bg) Hywit Dimyadi/S, (game board) Katherine Welles/S, (map) ilolab/S, (counters) Lars Kastilan/S, (dice) Bombaert Patrick/S, (panels) Stephen Aaron Rees/S **192**(heading paper) Jakub Krechowicz/S, (tr) Charles Walker/TopFoto, (cl) Bettmann/Corbis, (bl) National Geographic/GI **193**(tl) Bettmann/Corbis, (tr) GI, (bl) GI, (br) Popperfoto/GI **194–5**(bg) pashabo/S, (postcard) ronstik/S, (stamps) vesves/S, (colored pins) oriori/S **194**(tr) Patryk Kosmider/S, (bl) 2005 TopFoto, (br) Historical Picture Archive/Corbis **195**(tl) Michael Nicholson/Corbis, (tr) Print Collector/HIP/TopFoto, (bl) The Granger Collection/TopFoto, (br) De Agostini/GI **196–7**(t, l–r) ClassicStock/TopFoto, Luisa Ricciarini/TopFoto, Corbis, ullsteinbild/TopFoto, 2002 Topham/UPP/TopFoto, (b, l–r) GI, Bettmann/Corbis, Stapleton/ HIP/TopFoto, RIA Novosti/TopFoto, Topham Picturepoint/TopFoto **198–9**(bg) Cindi L/S **198**(t) O.V.D./S **199**(tr) National Geographic/GI **200–1**(bg) Eky Studio/S, (book) charles taylor/S, (blood) robybret/S, (panels) Christopher Hudson/iS **198**(l) Bettmann/Corbis, (tr) The Granger Collection/TopFoto, (br) Print Collector/HIP/TopFoto **201**(tl) The Granger Collection/TopFoto, (tr) Ullstein Bild/TopFoto, (bl) TopFoto, (br) AFP/GI **202**(cl) Maslov Dmitry/S, (cr) Bettmann/Corbis, (bl) Bettmann/Corbis, (br) Anna Hoychuk/S **203**(tl) KUCO/S, (tr) Charles Walker/TopFoto, (bl) World History Archive/TopFoto, (br) Topham/ AP/TopFoto **204–5**(blood) Steve Collender/S, (fire) Sergey Mironov/S **204**(tr) SuperStock/GI, (b) GI **205**(t, bg) JeremyRichards/S, (t) Historical Picture Archive/Corbis, (bl) TopFoto **206–7**(bg) zhanna ocheret/S, (book) Evgenia Sh./S **206**(tl) optimarc/S, (cl) GI, (cr) Mary Evans Picture Library/Alamy, (bl) Studio DMM Photography, Designs & Art/S, (br) ullsteinbild/TopFoto **207**(tl) The Granger Collection/ TopFoto, (tr) GI, (tr, fan) Margo Harrison/S, (bl) PoodlesRock/Corbis, (br) GI **208–9**(bg) val lawless/S, (bg, stains) Picsfive/S, (c) Bochkarev Photography/S **208**(header panel) Sibear/S, (tr, sock) Antonov Roman/S, (tr, bowl) Ron Zmiri/S, (blue napkins) Arogant/S, (white napkins) Lim Yong Hian/S, (folded napkins) Tobik/S, (knife and spoon) Natalia Klenova/S, (wooden spoon) Nekrasov Andrey/S **209**(tl, plate) Kulish Viktoriia/S, (tl, mouse) marina ljubanovic/S, (tl, sugar mouse) Lucie Lang/S, (tr, ostrich) Timo Jaakonaho/RF, (tr, camel) mmattner/S, (tr, kebab) S, (c) Martina I. Meyer/S, (cr, glass) jesterlsv/S, (cr, tankard) Peter Lorimer/S, (cr, mug) Lipowski Milan/S, (bl) Sergey Shcherbakoff/S, (bc) Lagui/S, (br) discpicture/S **210–1**(bg) L.Watcharapol/S **210**(tl) Vitaly Korovin/S, (tl, chain text) Steve Collender/S, (tr) Chyrko Olena/S, (l) Picsfive/S, (cr) Gianni Dagli Orti/Corbis, (bl) The Gallery Collection/Corbis, (br) pandapaw/S, (br, panel) Vitaly Korovin/S **211**(tl) David Burrows/S, (tl, window) Lusoimages/S, (tc) GI, (tc, panel) Matthias Pahl/S, (tr, noose) Iwona Grodzka/S, (tr, ear) Washington Post/GI, (cl) M.E. Mulder/S, (cr) Charles Walker/TopFoto, (bl) William Attard McCarthy/S, (br) ID1974/S **212–3**(bg) charles taylor/S, (nails) dusan964/S, (tags) val lawless/S **212**(tr, candle) Litvinenko Anastasia/S, (tr, teeth) Le Do/S, (cr, hot cups) Mary Evans Picture Library/Alamy, (cr, books) Brocreative/S, (bl) Roger-Viollet/RF, (bc) SPbPhoto/S, (br, bottle) Lakhesis/S, (br, cups) Coprid/S **213**(tl) The Granger Collection/TopFoto, (tl, leeches) Mircea Bezergheanu/S, (tc) Steve Lovegrove/S, (tr) Classic Image/Alamy, (r) terekhov igor/S, (cl, bottles) Milos Luzanin/S, (cl, mortar and pestle) Pshenichka/S, (cl, spices) Noraluca013/S, (cr) eduard ionescu/S, (bl) Noam Armonn/S, (br) Mary Evans Picture Library/Alamy, (br, bg) F **214–5**(t, bg) Rémi Cauzid/S, (b, bg) zhu difeng/S, (mud) Ultrashock/S, (tl, panel) photocell/S, (cl, panel) Excellent backgrounds Here/S, (t, l–r) GI, Fotomas/TopFoto, Museum of London/HIP/ TopFoto, (b, l–r) Hank Frentz/S, Popperfoto/GI, Corbis **214**(br, frame) kak2s/S **215**(b, frame) SuriyaPhoto/S **216–7**(bg) jayfish/S, (panels) Hintau Aliaksei/S **216**(header panel) Raia/S, (t) irin-k/S, (c) Ewa Walicka/S, (bl, sacks) Dee Golden, (bl, glasses) Saveliev Alexey Alexsandrovich/S, (bc) Dreamworks/Everett/RF **217**(tl) The Gallery Collection/Corbis, (tr, mud) Ultrashock/S, (tr, helmet) bocky/S, (cl) Mettus/S, (cr) TopFoto, (bc) Leigh Prather/S, (br) AP/Topham, (br, bg) Ana de Sousa/S **218–9**(panels) Dim Dimich/S, (scrolls) koya979/S **218**(header panel) inxti/S, (bg) Kompaniets Taras/S, (tr) The Granger Collection/TopFoto (bl) Andrey Burmakin/S **219**(tl) Sophy R./S, (tr) papa1266/S, (tc, silkworms) holbox/S, (tc, scroll) Roman Sigaev/S, (tc, gun) Kellis/S, (c) PaulPaladin/S, (cr) Bettmann/Corbis, (bl) composite image: StudioSmart/S, PhotoHouse/S, (br) Molodec/S

All other photographs are from:
Corel, digitalSTOCK, digitalvision, Dreamstime.com, Fotolia.com, iStockphoto.com, John Foxx, PhotoAlto, PhotoDisc, PhotoEssentials, PhotoPro, Stockbyte

Every effort has been made to acknowledge the source and copyright holder of each picture. The publishers apologise for any unintentional errors or omissions.